AN ERK'S-EYE VII

First published in 2003 by

WOODFIELD PUBLISHING
Bognor Regis, West Sussex, England
www.woodfieldpublishing.com

© Ted Mawdsley, 2003

The right of Ted Mawdsley
to be identified as Author of this work
has been asserted in accordance with
the Copyright, Designs and Patents Act 1988

ISBN 1-903953-38-3

An Erk's-Eye View of World War II

A former airman's experiences with 103 Squadron at RAF Elsham Wolds, Lincolnshire 1942-43

TED MAWDSLEY

Woodfield

The Elsham Wolds memorial.

*To those men and women with whom I served
in 103 Squadron at RAF Elsham Wolds.*

*To the memory of those who died then and old
comrades who have passed away in more recent times.*

*I dedicate the book also to my three lovely
grandaughters, Bethany, Victoria and Christina (and to
the fourth, Summer, whose arrival may well coincide
with the publication of this book) in the hope that by
reading this book one day they will know more about
their grandad. But above all, with the fervent wish that
the world in which they grow up will be one of peace and
goodwill between all peoples.*

Ted Mawdsley, Serviceman, 1940.

CONTENTS

Lancaster in the air and on the ground.

Foreword

by Squadron Leader J W B ("Jock") Murray[1]
former President of the RAF Elsham Wolds Association

A book of this kind is long overdue. As an air gunner in RAF Bomber Command during the Second World War I was always aware of the dedicated support we of the aircrews received from our ground-staff. There was, as the author of this book has written, a splendid rapport between those who flew in the bombers and the various mechanics who serviced the aircraft. It is one of the warm memories we share of those tense and demanding times.

I commend this book to all past, and present, members of the RAF; and to anyone who cares for history and who is interested to know what it was like to be on a heavy bomber base during that terrible war.

It is especially pleasing for me to write this foreword to the book as the author and I both served with 103 Squadron, and now share membership of, and affection for, our Association of old comrades.

---

[1] Sadly, Squadron Leader Murray died in April 2001. He was a valued friend and a popular president of the RAF Elsham Wolds Association. He will be sorely missed. (Author).

The View from the Ground

This book was written, at least to some extent, in response to a challenge made by the co-authors of the excellent series, *Lancaster at War*, Brian Goulding and Mike Garbett.

In one of the editions they drew attention to an omission from the volumes of literature appertaining to the exploits of the RAF during the Second World War.

If, for you aircrew there is an abundance of nostalgia or sadness, even bitterness or remorse each time you recall your war with wings, how do you suppose those who assisted and supported you, react when reminded of the part they played? Does a stores wallah or MT driver, sick quarters nurse or mess waitress even want to remember? Forgotten as they have been for too many years, do they now bother to tell anyone they, too, were there? Is it really as it appears.... that it is only the fitters and riggers and armourers who tended your kite who turn up at reunions, or make the odd pilgrimage to your old haunts? Do you wonder what became of your adjutant, your barber, your cooks, your clerks? Do they feel as you feel when confronted with a torment of crumbling concrete... of rusting corrugated sheeting... of total dissolution? Have they stood as you have stood.. and thought.... and heard.. remembered? Have they seen as you have seen a Lancaster lowering her wheels to land in silence, etched black against a back-cloth of sunset when huge spears of light fan down and saturate your mind, your whole being with burning sunlight? Have they wandered, as you have wandered, over the acres of emptiness, on days when howling winds failed to drown the murmur of voices coming from your billet, your mess, your section?

What does it take to stir a radar mech, an instrument basher? No Rigger has written his account of what life was like on a Lancaster station. As much as you regard it as important for aircrew to record their memoirs, do you consider it high time some of you who stayed with your feet firmly on the ground balanced things up?

... Must you all remain unnamed prisoners of history?

Acknowledgements

I am indebted to so many people who have encouraged me in the writing of this book and it is not possible to mention them all. But there are some to whom I must express my gratitude for not only being supportive, but also for 'being there' for me in various practical ways. Without their help the task – and the enjoyment – of writing *An Erk's Eye View* would have been much less amenable. My heartfelt thanks, then, to:

Ethel, my wife, for her infinite patience and belief; my two sons, David and Simon for their advice and 'know how' in areas where I am an ignoramus; Christine Foley who has somehow managed to decipher my atrocious handwriting, and has transcribed it onto the word processor; but has also shown a lively interest throughout and has guided me when I needed it most. And then there were, Albert Poulter and Roy Poulter; Harry Fawcett; John Boothe; Ann and Peter Gould; Joe Barrett; Debbie Murphy; Roy and Sheila Smith; Pip Beck; and David Fell, Ann Hynd and Phil Potts.

Ex-comrades at Elsham Wolds and 103 Squadron, Bas Lowe; Ron Grantham; "Jock" Murray; Frank Sharples; Don Charlwood and Shirley Westrupp.

Knowingly, and sometimes unknowingly, all of these good people have given me a welcome hand with my word-smithing.

Others, with whom I served at Elsham have since passed on or, regretfully, have eluded any attempts to find them. But, again, they are men who walk across the pages of my book and are part of the story: Frank Wain, Dougie Tyler, George Turner, "Bud" Senior and all those others.

~ ~ ~

In the course of putting this book together I have come across pieces of verse which have been so relevant and appropriate to the text that I was moved to quote them. In each case they appeared on duplicated printed sheets picked up for instance at random, at the RAF Elsham Wolds Association reunions, and I have not been able to trace the original sources. But in the absence of that information I nevertheless express my gratitude to: John Walsh for *War Days*; Noel

Coward for *Sit in the Dark and Listen*; and Henry Trace for *Lincolnshire Bomber Station*.

The article by Basil Cardew about Bert, the dedicated engine fitter featured in Chapter 8 appeared in the *"Daily Express"* in 1943 and I kept the cutting for many years. I trust the *"Express"* will not object to my use of it in the context of this book.

Among the many newspaper and periodicals I have perused over the years there was one quite outstanding in relation to *An Erk's Eye View* which was particularly helpful in jogging my memory on some points. This was the 'Bygone' series published in the *"Evening Telegraph"* with its main circulation in Lincolnshire. The articles covered the war-time history of No. 1 Group RAF Bomber Command. (The articles, or rather features, were closely related to three books: *Maximum Effort: the North Lincolnshire Bomber*; *Maximum Effort: a Group at War*; and *Maximum Effort: the untold story*.) But the reference to mine-laying in Chapter 9 is taken from the newspaper. Either way, I acknowledge the 'reminder' they provided for me.

Although throughout *An Erk's Eye View* I have, when quoting passages from other sources, referred to the authors and the publishers of those works, I would like to acknowledge, once again, the invaluable help they have all been to me:

BLACK SWAN by Sid Finn, published by Newton Publishers, Hartfield Road, Edenbridge, Kent.

JOURNEYS INTO NIGHT by Don Charlwood, published by Hudson Publishing, 6 Muir Street, Hawthorn, 3122, Victoria, Australia.

A WAAF IN BOMBER COMMAND by Pip Beck, published by Goodall Publications Ltd, London and St Albans.

FINEST HOUR by Tim Clayton and Phil Craig, published by Hodder and Stoughton, 338, Euston Road, London, NW1 3BH.

ONCE UPON A WARTIME III by Molly Burkett, published by Barny Books, Hough on the Hill, Grantham, Lincolnshire.

THE FEW AND THE MANY published by Production Consultants plc.

THE LANCASTER AT WAR series by Mike Garbett and Brian Goulding, published by Ian Allen, Riverdene Business Park, Molesey Road, Hersham, Surrey.

STRIKE HARD by John Hilling, published by Sutton Publishing Ltd, Phoenix Mill, Thrupp, Gloucester.

Author's Notes

Most wartime memoirs are written by much-decorated heroes or by those of high position who decided policy, or who implemented strategies.

This book is not one such and is a narrative composed by one of low military rank whose role in World War II was a modest one – *a spear carrier in a major production* – and who makes no claim to heroic deeds.

Nevertheless, within the pages of this book, the reader will find a constant *tribute to courage*, to the bravery of young men, so many of whom died before their lives had hardly begun. They were the air-crews of Bomber Command, but whilst they are given rightful recognition, the essence of this story, the central core of it, is an acknowledgement of the largely overlooked and unacclaimed service of those men and women who "kept 'em flying" – the RAF ground crews.

The vital role played by the RAF in the defeat of Nazi Germany is surely unquestioned – but the operations carried out by *all* Commands of the Air Force could have been mounted and sustained only with the dedicated contribution – in all kinds of conditions – of those who performed myriad supporting functions on the ground.

The author knew these people and worked with and among them, never ceasing to be amazed at their tenacity and resourcefulness. And that is why the writing of this book has been such a pleasure.

On the frontispiece of the book I have stated that I am, within these pages, responding to the "challenge" issued by Mike Garbett and Brian Goulding in one of their series *Lancaster at War*. And, whilst that is so, it is not the *only* motivation that prompted my decision to "put this thing together". Nor is it the singular explanation for the great time lapse between the "events" and the written account of them.

After I had been demobbed from the RAF in 1946, I wanted, like the majority of returning ex-service personnel, to shed the last vestiges of irksome rules and restrictions of military life and to make a fresh start. And, as is the case with most young people anyway, my intention was to look forward and not back.

When I had joined the RAF in 1940, I was just coming up to nineteen, had tasted – all too ephemerally – the salad days of care-free youth and was "wet behind the ears", harbouring vague notions of "adventure".

But, now, coming home after six years, I was twenty-five and married. New responsibilities, new priorities lay ahead – finding a job, seeking some kind of career, searching for and making a home, especially after the advent of parenthood.

I also became actively involved in public life and then – particularly in the last twenty-five years of my (full-time) working experience – I was employed in occupations that were time-consuming and very demanding.

Consequently, I was far too preoccupied to seriously contemplate authorship of any kind, but then, after I retired from full-time work in the early 1980s, something – and I am now not sure what – rekindled thoughts and memories (never, in my case, completely suppressed) of the war years. And I began to read more, non-fictional accounts of the war; and to jot down some notes about my own experiences and impressions.

A further nudge towards the completion of a book was given me when I went across to Wales for a reunion with two old comrades from my overseas service days – Ray Pritchard and Gwyn Williams.

It was the second of those meetings, though, that moved me from the contemplation (of writing a book) to action; for, when I caught up with Gwyn he was suffering from that awful disease, Alzheimer's. He neither knew who I was, nor had any recollection whatsoever of the experiences we had shared. That sad encounter brought home to me the reality of the limitation of time and of mortality.

A character in one of Jack Higgins' novels says something to the effect that when she hears the phrase, "a long time ago" it is like hearing a bugler sounding "lights out".

I knew, then, that it was imperative; that I could procrastinate no longer and that I must turn all the notes I had made into a book. It didn't really seem to matter what happened to it after its completion – there was only the compulsion to write it.

The story from the days of "sprog" training; of various postings within Britain; of episodes and incidents; of overseas service, and an overall assessment of it all.

It proved to be a formidable task – all in longhand – and it took several years to complete, during which time, sadly, both Ray and Gwyn died.

In 1991, quite by chance, I discovered the existence of the Elsham Wolds Association and in that year my wife and I attended the annual reunion. And up there on the site of the old airfield and among former comrades, exchanging reminiscences, I was moved to extract from my memoirs the section covering the Elsham period and to write and produce a booklet, mainly for a readership of the Association members.

That booklet was called *The Lincolnshire Poacher* and although I feel that it was produced far too hurriedly and contained unfortunate errors and omissions, it was well received; and several people suggested that I should consider turning it into a "proper book". And that suggestion, plus the subsequent discovery of Mike Garbett's and Brian Goulding's "challenge", has resulted in this, *An Erk's Eye View* – the "proper book"!

There are people who, I am sure, will wonder why I, or any other author of stories about the Second World War, would want, still, to recount something that happened so long ago.

"Come on," they would say. "It's over, let it go. It is now a part of schools' history syllabus; and whatever you feel about it, or whatever opinion you hold, it is now purely academic."

Yes, I understand that point of view. The great Persian bard wrote that, *The moving finger writes; and, having writ, moves on.* He could have been anticipating the modern-day graffiti "artists"; but we know, of course, that he was referring to the forward-moving nature of life. But the next line is the significant one in the context of these introductory notes, when Omar goes on to say: *Nor all thy piety nor wit shall lure it back to cancel half a line, nor all thy tears wash out a word of it.*

Deeds are done, words are said (or written) decisions taken, judgements made... life walks on but the footprints of yesterday's events are left imprinted in the ground.

What the finger writes is indelibly etched on the mind even if, in places, the ink is faded and indistinct.

When one looks back on one's life from the perspective of advancing years – and I am now well into my eighties – there are, inevitably, experiences that stand out above others. And for those of us who "were there", involved, in whatever capacity, during the years 1939–1945, *that* particular experience must sit on the high ground in the patterned fields of our memories.

It seems, too, to be a feature of old age that one has a pressing desire to reacquaint oneself with time gone by, reaching out a metaphorical hand to re-grasp a time when one was young and life was vibrant.

Yes, the history books can charter the course of events in a war; evaluate strategies and tactics, and make critical assessments of leading figures. But it is only when the participants – in their many and varied roles – tell *their* stories, that it all comes to life. It is only through *their* eyes, through their remembered eye-witness accounts, that the images and the *feel* of being at war emerge.

In *An Erk's Eye View* I have chosen to tell a story about RAF Bomber Command – of the day-to-day activities in the lives of airmen – flyers and non-flyers, although, in this case, more particularly the latter – on an aerodrome in one small corner of England, at a point in time which was about the middle part of a war of massive scale.

It is my wish that in this book I succeed in conveying to the reader at least some image of and a feeling for, the atmosphere, the ambience and the culture of that RAF station.

There are other stories to be told, of other places and other experiences which may, hopefully, appear one day in another book. We shall see. But it does, perhaps, say a great deal about the impression that my seven months at Elsham Wolds made upon me when, out of all those other memories, including almost three years in foreign parts, I should choose to render priority to that relatively brief episode.

In order to dispel any assumption that might be made about me, since I write with a certain affection for a military unit in which I served, I want to say that I am not a jingoist, flag-waving, war lover. I am, in fact the opposite of these things.

Whilst I do have a great love for my country, I do not equate that with a contempt for people of other nations and of other cultures. Xenophobic nationalism is a feature of the human condition which worries me deeply. *And I have always thought that it was one of the evils we were fighting against in the Second World War.*

I am not anti-German, but I *was* anti-*Nazi* German. The distinction is important.

There has never been any doubt in my mind about the "rightness" of going to war against the vile barbarism of the Nazi creed – nor that it was necessary to defeat it.

I would like to apologise, in advance, to any eagle-eyed ex-RAF "types" who may spot errors and omissions in this book. None of us is infallible but I can say only that I have tried honestly to write faithfully and accurately. I have worked from diaries, notes, references to other authors and sources, with invaluable and gratifying assistance from ex-comrades and last – and I hope by no means least – from my own memory which is, thankfully, still serving me well.

Finally, as this is not a work of fiction, I can state that any references in this book to any person, living or dead, is absolutely intentional.

Elsham Wolds veterans and their families gather for a reunion.

Preface: *The Joy and Sorrow of Mankind*

Every year since 1979 men and women who are ex-personnel of 103 and 576 Squadrons, Royal Air Force, have gathered together in August at Elsham Wolds in Lincolnshire.

They are members of the Elsham Wolds Association and they come from all parts of the United Kingdom and from various places overseas; but more particularly from Australia and Canada.

They are all veterans of Bomber Command in World War II, who operated at and flew from that bleak and remote spot in the Wolds of Lincolnshire, between the years 1941 and 1945.

And those who were air-crew come and wonder once again at what they were called upon to do – and how they so miraculously survived.

One thousand five hundred of their comrades who flew from Elsham did not survive and they lie in cemeteries across Europe, or their names are recorded on the Runnymede Memorial in the case of those whose remains were never found.

Elsham Wolds, that isolated piece of Lincolnshire, was the last place on which they trod in England's green and pleasant land. And the surviving ex-flyers – those who were pilots, navigators, bomb aimers, wireless operators, flight engineers and gunners – will be the first to pay tribute to the ground crews, the "erks". The men and women who gave them devoted, unstinting and skilled support, often under great stress and in appalling conditions, they too are at the reunions.

Today, those who come on their journeys, their pilgrimage, to Elsham are ageing men and women, grey and white-haired. Some are bent over and slow of movement, and they recall when they were young and the deeds that were done in those far off days, so long, long ago.

As each year goes by so some of the members are missing – just as comrades went missing in the 1940s; and, like them, their names are removed from the list.

On the Sunday afternoon of our weekend we attend a simple, unpretentious open-air service on the site of the aerodrome, at the end of a now disused runway. And we remember those young, those so very young men, who did not grow old as we have grown old.

A trumpeter of the local Air Cadets – but a few years younger than we were then – plays the haunting notes of the "Last Post"; and then the only surviving, still-serviceable Lancaster, "City of Lincoln", passes over our heads on its singular fly-past.

We wave our hands in greeting and there are tears in our eyes. Of course it is a time for emotion and why should it not be?

It is not, however, a memory of glory, or of the glorification of war. Glory is not a word that sits comfortably side-by-side with the horrors, the carnage and the terror of total war.

It is, though, a memory of courage – of unbelievable courage; for if bravery is best defined as "Doing something when it scares you to hell to do it", then that is the quality to which we pay our retrospective annual tribute.

For me, it is also a time for reflection as I stand on that ground in August. To reflect that at our reunion, no one "pulls rank"; that at our Saturday night function in Barnetby Village hall, we all "sit and mix", with no regard or deference to former status or to war-time role.

And that is as it should be because it simply reflects, some fifty years on, the inter-dependence, the combined effort that was the hallmark of 103 and 576 Squadrons, and which made them what they were.

The relationships between ranks; the rapport between air and ground crews was something quite probably unique in the annals of military history. And, in fact, it is difficult to imagine how it could have worked so effectively in any other way.

It is a time, also, to ponder on the question as to why a medal, in its own right, was never awarded to the air-crews of Bomber Command – at least in recognition of the 55,000 airmen who lost their lives in that arm of the RAF.

Some of us think we know the answer to that question and it is an issue I take up in this book.

Standing here on those Sunday afternoons, many thoughts come rushing, uninvited into my mind, vying for attention; even the unthinkable whereby it would be so easy to wonder – given the continuing vicious wars, the great inequalities both within and between nations, the unremitting instances of man's inhumanity to man – if, after all, those young comrades of ours had died in vain. But, there is one answer only to that and it is, No, they did not!

They gave their lives fighting against an evil and twisted creed that threatened to engulf the world... They took the fight to the enemy when there was no other way of doing so. They died helping to ensure that the vile and obscene atrocities committed by the

Nazis were not perpetrated in this country. And they contributed, in no uncertain way, to the eventual liberation of the peoples of occupied Europe.

If the human race insists on ignoring lessons it should have learned, if world peace continues to be an elusive dream, then that is a matter for today. We who took part in the Second World War, in whatever capacity, were called upon to meet the over-riding challenge of that time. And those boys – and many were barely more – cannot be answerable for the errors of the post-war world.

Nor, in any case, is it all gloom, for most of Europe has, since 1945, experienced the longest period of peace, probably in all of its history.

So, yes, it is a time for reflection on Elsham ground in August.

Little now can be seen of the aerodrome. If you travel on the A15 road going towards the Humber Bridge, and you look to your right, you will see, in the distance, one remaining hangar of the three that once stood there. That single hangar is now a part of some commercial enterprise.

The A15 cuts a swathe across what was the outer perimeters of the airfield and, looking left from your car, you will be passing an area where the bombers stood at their dispersal points, illustrating the sheer size of that wartime base.

If you drive around some of the "B" roads in the vicinity and you stop and alight from the car, you will find the horse-shoe shapes of some of those dispersal bays, discernible even in the cultivated, reclaimed farmland. You may also find the old quarry that features once or twice in this narrative.

One runway only – the north-south – now remains of the three that made a triangle at Elsham. It is rutted, pitted and overgrown with weeds. At its north end, on the site of the Anglia Water Treatment Works, stands the memorial at which our Sunday Remembrance Service is held. And as I stand there on those poignant Sunday afternoons and the reminiscent wind – itself a ghost from the past – whips at the cord of the flag pole I go back those many intervening years and I see and hear the sights and sounds from that extraordinary experience that I shared with fine people, whom today I still count among my friends.

And I remember, with great affection, those who are no longer with us. The following poem written by John Walsh forms such a moving and appropriate end piece to this Preface, that I can wish only that those evocative words were my own.

War Days

Don't go back they told me, for you'll only find a grave,
The spirit that once inspired the field, departed with the brave.
This 'drome deserted; this sad site knows
Only tractor, maybe plough.
Windswept dispersals empty now,
Where our Lancs crouched, awaiting night.
Then through days we hoped; the nights endured
With the morrow never ours secured
On ops, those hours of living hell,
the dawn we'd never dare foretell.
Our futures thrown on dice by fate,
Dark, angry skies that flamed with hate.
And Bomber streams; the lethal flak,
Stricken Lancs with no way back.
And dying men who'd given all
With targets reached – or not at all.
Each night the fight to stay alive,
and which of us might yet survive?
War days I knew so long ago;
of yesteryear and blue clad youth;
how few survived from all that throng?
So many brave; too quickly gone.
Those martyrs, then of tender years,
Still only boys but ever men.

John Walsh, October 1988

A Brief History of No. 103 Squadron[2]

No. 103 Squadron of RAF Bomber Command has had a long and brilliant history. It operated in both World Wars.

It was formed at Beaulieu, Hampshire, on 1 September 1917 and went overseas on 12 May 1918, returning to England on 26 March 1919. It was disbanded at Shotwick on 1 October 1919, and was reformed at Andover on 10 August 1936.

Beginning with DH9s in December 1917 it was flying Hinds in August 1936, Fairey Battles in August 1938, Vickers Wellingtons in October 1940, Halifax IIs in July 1942, and Lancasters from November 1942.

The day before the war with Germany began, No. 103 Squadron took over the airfield at Challerange in France and had five other bases at various times on the continent before returning to Honington on 16 June 1940. At the beginning of July 1940, it moved to Newton, (Nottinghamshire) and on the night of 25 July sent out three aircraft to bomb the Luftwaffe in Holland. The squadron records show that the usual load was four 250-pounders.

The first Wellington was delivered on 2 October and on 23 November the personnel said goodbye to its popular CO, Wing Commander T C Dickens. There was a riotous party and the Wing Commander was 'baptised' in the river Trent.

In December, equipped with its new Wellingtons, the squadron was placed on an operational basis again and on 9 January 1941, six aircraft were detailed to attack the synthetic oil plant at Nordstern-Gelsenkirchen. Other industrial targets, including Hanover and Dusseldorf, were attacked, the Wellingtons taking four 500lb bombs and four containers of incendiaries to Dusseldorf.

On 17 April there was an attack on Berlin, seven Wellingtons taking off from a southern airfield thus reducing the petrol load. In all forty-four sorties were made on seventeen days of April without loss. During an attack on Emden, the following month, one of the

---

[2] By courtesy of The RAF Elsham Wolds Association.

Opposite page: members of 103 Squadron RAF. 1942.

squadron's Wellingtons was attacked in succession by five enemy aircraft but returned safely.

In July operations were carried out on nine nights and one day, and eighty-three sorties were claimed. On 24 July from 11am to 6.45pm the Wellingtons from No. 103 were sent out against the battle cruiser *"Gneisenau"* at Brest.

The squadron was building a reputation for accuracy and determination. On 15 August when the main railway station at Hanover was the target, one of the aircraft remained over the target for twenty minutes so as to make quite sure of its aim.

Then the Germans tried to hit back and bombed the squadron's airfield at Elsham Wolds. Besides attacks on Frankfurt, Essen, Duisburg, Kiel, Mannheim and Hamburg, the squadron bombed Turin on 10 September but only one aircraft was lost on this long flight.

A squadron, station and group record was established on the night of 28 December when seventeen aircraft operated successfully over Wilhelmshaven. Sergeants Spooner and Bray were given the immediate awards of the DFM for bringing their Wellington back after four members of the crew had baled out. A flare ignited in the rear part of the fuselage, and it seemed likely that the aircraft would go up in flames. Eventually the flare fell off.

On 9 January 1942, the squadron bombed the battle cruisers *"Gneisenau"* and *"Scharnhorst"*, and on 12 February was out trying to intercept the German Fleet in the North Sea. A DFC was warded to Pilot Officer B N Williams for his courage on that occasion.

Other highlights were the raid on the Renault Works in Paris, and the close support given to the other services at St Nazaire. By April the squadron was able to take off on sixteen nights and completed 129 sorties. In May and June it took part in the first 1,000 bomber raids.

No. 103 rested in July during a change-over to Halifaxes. the first time it used these heavy bombers on operations was on 1 August when it bombed Dusseldorf. It was a busy period for the engineering staff, for on 21 November the whole squadron had changed to Lancasters and actually had them in use that night. A letter of congratulation was received from the Air Officer Commanding the Group praising the speed and efficiency with which the conversion had been made.

In January 1943, a hundred sorties in Lancasters were made and the crews were delighted with their new aircraft. The bomb loads were now very much greater.

The 177 sorties in April 1943, included several mining trips. May was a record month and twenty-seven aircraft were got into the air on 23/24 May, which up to that time was a Bomber Command record. The bombing was mostly on the Ruhr. August 1943 is always remembered by veteran members of the squadron, for 261 sorties were made on thirteen nights. Berlin was heavily attacked.

On 17 August, Flight Lieutenant F V P Van Rollegan, a Belgian pilot, was awarded the DFC and presented with the medal at a special parade, the ceremony being performed by Air Vice Marshal E A B Rice CB CBE MC. The AOC Flight Lieutenant Rollegan also got the Belgian *Croix de Guerre*.

In September 1943 Air Chief Marshal Sir Arthur T Harris KCB OBE AFC visited the station. In September, too, 'C' Flight broke away from No. 103 to form the nucleus of No. 166 Squadron and in November a flight was posted to 576 Squadron, a sister squadron, which was being organised at Elsham. This left No. 103 as a two-flight squadron.

Thirty aircraft were sent to Berlin on the night of 26 November. Ground personnel had to meet exceptional weather difficulties in January 1944, when snow storms blocked roads and runways, and covered the Lancasters. In April and May 1944, 1,2ll tons were dropped, and in June 278 sorties were made and 1,259 tons dropped, mostly on French targets. Three enemy fighters were destroyed in July, six damaged and three probably damaged. Most of the trips were daylight operations.

Throughout the summer the squadron kept pegging away at V-bomb sites, German troops concentrations, the enemy railway systems and oil targets. August, September and October each saw 1,000 tons of bombs exceeded by a fair margin, and the latter month was the highest ever with 1,300 tons. Every bomb of this 1,300 tons was dropped on Germany.

The four months leading up to VE Day imposed a great strain on air and ground staffs especially after the strenuous effort of 1944. From April of that year to the end of April 1945, the squadron dropped 11,418 tons of bombs on enemy targets. One of the squadron's finest aircraft, Lancaster M2, concluded its operation during the early part of the year. It made 140 trips, mostly with No. 103 Squadron, ninety-seven being to Germany. Its first outing was to Dortmund on 4 May 1943. 'M2' flew for 974 operational hours and had nineteen engine changes.

The engineering section takes pride in another achievement. On one occasion they had two damaged Lancasters on their hands and within forty hours had produced a new one by joining the undamaged front and rear portions.

No. 103 Squadron has a reputation second to none and its members have overcome many obstacles. There was the story of the two Lancasters which on 29 July 1944, when attacking Stuttgart, were intercepted by night fighters. Two were shot down in less than a minute by the gunners of one Lancaster, while the other bomber dealt with a couple of fighters in almost the same time and destroyed them both.

Another crew from No. 103 shot down a JU88 over Karlsruhe on 25 April 1944, but their aircraft was badly damaged by a second JU. The rear gunner was imprisoned in his turret but a way was hacked to him. The pilot had to ditch his aircraft and the crew spent seven hours on the Goodwins before being rescued.

Pilots, navigators, air-bombers, wireless operators, flight engineers and gunners have figured prominently in the official awards lists and many DSOs, DFS, CGMs and DRMs have been gained.

No. 103 Squadron was disbanded on 25 November 1945. It re-formed on 30 November 1954 in 2nd Tactical Air force equipped with Canberras, and again disbanded on 1 August 1956. The squadron re-formed again on 1 August 1959, when No. 284 Squadron was renumbered, and was based at Nicosia in Cyprus equipped with Sycamore HR.14 helicopters operating in the Search and Rescue, Casualty Evacuation, and Internal Security roles.

The squadron disbanded at Nicosia on 31 July 1963 and re-formed in the Far East (Seletar) with Whirlwind Mk 10s on 1 August 1963. It re-deployed to Changi in 1969 and moved to Tengah in 1971. No. 103 Squadron was re-equipped with Wessex in 1972 and disbanded on 1 August 1975. The Squadron's Standard presented in 1970 was laid up in St Clement Danes, London, in September 1975.

OPERATION MANNA

I have searched through various sources to acquaint myself with the full story of *Operation Manna* but more particularly in Sid Finn's *Black Swan*; Molly Burkett's *Once Upon a Wartime III*; and *The Many*, published by Production Consultants plc, and I am grateful to them all for such a treasure of background information. The following is a less detailed summary of the story, but in essence this is what happened...

"Manna from heaven" is what it undoubtedly was for the people of the western region of the Netherlands on 29 April 1945 and for several days after, when the planes came over on their mission of famine relief.

Throughout the German occupation of their country, the Dutch people had, very courageously and had determinedly, shown their resistance. There were protests and strikes by workers, especially over the persecution of the Jews. The Nazis had responded in a typically bloody and repressive manner, even deporting thousands of workers to labour camps in Germany and elsewhere. But, even so, the resistance continued and, quite astonishingly, railway workers went on strike, when British paratroops dropped at Arnhem, to hamper and hinder the movement of German reinforcements.

In retaliation the Germans placed a complete embargo on the supplies of food from the agricultural east of the Netherlands to the more industrial and densely populated west. The Nazi also threatened to break the dykes and flood the land if the acts of defiance continued.

As the Allied Forces advanced towards Holland, the situation for the people, especially in the west, became desperate. In the bitterly cold months of January, February and March 1945, the citizens of the area suffered appalling deprivations. Coal was virtually unobtainable and families burnt almost everything combustible to try to keep warm. Furniture and even coffins were dug up to be chopped up for burning. The daily food ration was: two potatoes, three slices of bread, a little piece of meat substitute, a slice of skimmed milk cheese – a total of 500 calories. And what made the situation horrendously worse was that the Germans had, in fact, in late 1944, begun to undermine the dyke of one of the polders – land reclaimed from the sea and below sea level – so that in addition to the other privations, the sea was flooding the land.

When news of the terrible plight of the Dutch people reached the exiled Queen Wilhelmina, she appealed to the Allies to take action to relieve the plight of her people. But, what could be done? How could it be achieved? It was at first thought that it was a situation that could, and would, be solved when the Allied Forces liberated the area. But that might not be for weeks, or months; and the people of western Holland did not have that much time in which to survive. Dropping in supplies of food from the air was an obvious option, but an extremely hazardous one for air-crews, for in order to ensure minimum breakages of containers, the drop would need to be made from 500 feet only.

The RAF bomber crews were not exactly enamoured with such a prospect because they knew from bitter experience how fierce the flak was in that particular area and at 500 feet they would be shot out of the sky, if not by the anti-aircraft guns then by the enemy fighters. "Much too dicey!" was the general consensus of opinion.

Something, though, had to be done to save the starving people of the Netherlands and, without going into details, a very plain and unequivocal message was sent by the Allied High Command to the German Reichkominessor, Arthur Syss Inquart, telling him what was about to take place and assuring him that should any action be taken by the German forces against the food-carrying planes, no member of the occupying forces would, when the Allies reached the area, be accorded POW status.

Inquart hedged and attempted to reach a compromise to save face, but in the end, reluctantly, gave way.

Even so, the airmen, both British and American, who were to be involved were still not happy. (Nor was Sir Arthur Harris.) They did not trust the Nazis one little bit, and as they argued, what is to prevent the food dropped in from being confiscated by the Germans?

However, the order was given and the planning began. A co-operative operation between the RAF and the USAAF; estimating the required tonnage of food, and the nature of it; which squadrons to be involved and in which planes and crews; practice drops; bomb bay modifications (with typical ingenuity, meat hooks were used to sling the bags of food, with modified release systems) and so on. But when the crews learned that there had been no guarantee of immunity in the 'corridors' to the 'target' there was still a great misgiving about the whole operation. (And, indeed, their reservations were justified because it has been revealed since that German flak guns were manned and that some of the gunners had their sights trained on chosen aircraft throughout the operation. It would have taken only one nervous, or trigger-happy gunner to open fire and God alone knows what might have happened!)

I am not sure how many American aircraft took part but the RAF sent in 239 Lancasters, after Mosquitos from 109 Squadron had preceded them to 'mark the target'. And here I have to write with pleasure and pride that my old squadron, 103, was prominent in the operation and that Squadron Leader Ken Butler, flying "I" Item, played a leading part.

It was a superbly executed operation and over those few days of April and May the planes came in over the stricken area at the specified 500 feet by day and by night, and this is what they dropped: (12,000 metric tonnes of it), powdered egg, dried milk, soup powder, flour, meat, vegetables, cheese, chocolate, margarine, tea, salt and mustard.

The people in the locality of the drop zone had been warned to stay clear but such was the desperation for food that when any of the bags containing the food broke open on impact with the ground, some people rushed to get and eat the food there and then, and consequently there were some injuries.

When the air-crews saw for themselves the extent of the flooding and the obvious desperation of the people below they shed any reservations they may have had about the operation and knew they were on a mission to save instead of one to take lives.

This is how Squadron Leader Ken Butler tells the story:

I was with 103 Squadron at Elsham wolds and the CO informed me one day, that my plane had been loaded, not with bombs, but with sacks. I had to find out how they should be dropped. The armourers had fixed meat hooks to the bomb bays so that the sacks could be released like bombs. We practised and worked out that the safest way to drop them was from sixty feet, flying at a speed of ninety knots. We were preparing for Operation Manna. Queen Wilhelmina of the Netherlands had asked for help to save her people who were still under German occupation. They were starving.

The operation was aborted the first time. Harris refused to let us fly because he thought the bombers would be sitting ducks for the Germans to shoot down, but the Germans were instructed to stand clear and they did. The BBC put out an announcement the previous night and told the people to stand clear of the dropping zones. Then we flew in, us and the Americans, the American Eighth Air Force. Bomber Command called it Operation Manna, the Americans called it Chowhound and the Dutch called it (and still do) Food and Freedom.

We flew in and I led them. Looking back now, I think it was the best thing I ever did in my life, but we didn't think so at the time. Well we had been trained to bomb, not take food parcels and we didn't appreciate the state to which the Dutch had been reduced. The weather was dreadful, wet and stormy.

The Pathfinders went in first, the same as they did on the bombing raid. My dropping zone was Rotterdam. The one person on a Lancaster who cannot see the ground beneath them is the pilot. Once the bombs have been dropped, I would get the instruction, 'bombs away, head for home Skip' and it was the same that day. I banked to turn and that was when I saw the ground and there were thousands of people there, thousands of them, all standing with their arms in the air and written in large letters was the message, 'Thank You Boys'.

What could you say. That message got to me. It still does today, but it isn't the only thing that is in my memory. There is a little girl in a red dress standing on a rise in the ground, but most of all it is the people, thousands of them standing there with their hands raised. We'd controlled our emotions on all those bombing raids, but there were a few tears that day. The men dropped their aircrew rations, chocolates, cigarettes, anything they could find.

There were thirty-three squadrons involved with Operation Manna, 3,300 sorties were made and 12,000 tonnes of food was dropped.

A Dutchman who was a schoolboy at the time recalls: "We heard them coming and it sounded so different because this time they were low. they filled the western horizon. Each Lancaster opened its bomb doors and out came a cloud of bags like confetti. My father and lots of other grown-ups were sobbing like children. It must have been the sound because now they knew they would stay alive."

Sometimes at the RAF Elsham Wolds Reunion we have guests from Holland, Belgium and France who tell us about these things; about *Manna*, and the work of the resistance units in these countries. And how shot down RAF airmen were hidden or passed down the escape lines. They give to the RAF their heartfelt gratitude and it is always very moving.

I guess, then, that we did get some things right!

1.   The Real 'Eavy Stuff...

The posting instructions and travel warrant, when they came, informed me that my presence was required at Elsham Wolds.

'Where?'

'At Elsham Wolds in Lincolnshire.'

'Oh... right!'

Ordnance Survey maps were not readily available in security-conscious war-time Britain but I did have to consult a fairly detailed map to locate my ordered destination.

This was my eighth posting since joining the "Mob", as RAF personnel sometimes disrespectfully referred to their service. The Royal Air Force and I had first become acquainted in 1940 – at about the time that the fiasco of Norway was unfolding – and it was now November 1942.

So I was no longer a "sprog" and had "been around a bit". And yet, when that new posting arrived, I was not actually serving in the RAF, but was, instead, working in a factory in Luton, Bedfordshire.

Now, that does seem contradictory and somewhat perplexing, begging for explanation. And in the process of doing so, it presents me with the opportunity to put this book, just briefly, into context and perspective.

My induction into the RAF had occurred at Cardington in Bedfordshire and at the time of "taking the King's shilling", I really had no idea in which capacity I would serve. There were vague notions about air-crew but all I really wanted was to get into the "Raff", to "do my bit" and to just see what turned up.

The "square-bashing bit" was done at Bridgnorth in Shropshire and then pre-war employment, with the Marconi Wireless Telegraph Co Ltd at Chelmsford, would appear to have influenced the direction in which I was selected to go. For after the "licking into military shape" at Bridgnorth, I was sent to Melksham in Wiltshire where I was to grapple with the complex intricacies of aircraft instruments. I was to be trained, in RAF parlance, as an "Instrument Basher"; to be responsible for the efficient working of myriad gauges, compasses, oxygen supplies, "George" (automatic pilot) and various other aircraft accoutrements.

After passing out at Melksham, and after much sweat and tears (my sweat, tutors' tears!), I then spent some eighteen months or so, serving in Coastal Command – RAF by the sea.

In the course of that time, I was stationed at Calshot near Southampton; Pembroke Dock on the western tip of South Wales; and at Greenock on the Clyde. And I learned my "trade" servicing first Walruses, then Lerwicks, Sunderlands and Catalinas – all flying boats. It was quite an experience, which among other things, "weathered" me; and I discovered that attending to the needs of aeroplanes that sat on the sea, involved problems and required skills that were unique to that branch of the RAF.

It also became quickly apparent why Coastal Command had been dubbed the "Cinderella Command", suffering as it did from a deprivation of resources, both human and material. (I once heard an Aussie pilot describe Coastal Command as "The RAF with the arse out of its trousers!") And that, very succinctly, just about summed it up. Nevertheless – in spite of its logistical problems – there were four seas to patrol and to operate over (the North Sea, the Arctic Ocean, the Channel and the vast Atlantic) and there was a 16,500 mile coastline occupied by enemy forces. Coastal Command made a vital contribution to the war at sea and, in particular, in the desperate battle with the German U-boats.

We come now to the explanation of my presence in the factory in Luton (and I hasten to dismiss any notion that I was there to make *hats* – not even *tin hats!*) and to outline how *that* "posting" came about.

It was mid-1942 and the situation as I understand it was as follows...

In essence it was the classical economic problems of *supply and demand*, but intensified by war.

Certain dramatic and significant changes had occurred in the progress of the war; twists and turns in events that influence policy decision, and all of which demanded greater industrial production.

After the Japanese attack on Pearl Harbour, Britain found herself fighting on a new, additional front, in the Far East, thus stretching resources even further.

In the Mediterranean and in the Western Desert, very desperate battles were taking place. At home, severe bomb damage necessitated restoration and replacement.

The greatest threat of all to Britain was still mounting in the Atlantic and a greater response to the menace of the U-boat was called for – especially in equipment and supplies.

Russia had been invaded by the Nazis in June 1941 and, although that decision of Hitler's had ended – at least for the time being – any attempt to invade Britain, the initial success of the German thrust into the Soviet Union had added even *further* pressure on those already stretched resources of the Western Allies, but more particularly on this country. The further the German war machine drove into Russia, the louder came the call from Stalin to the West to relieve the pressure by opening the Second Front. But the logistics for launching an attack, on such a scale, on "fortress Europe" were simply not in place at that time.

Churchill had, however, given a pledge to Stalin that in the absence of an invasion of Europe, for the time being, a day and night campaign of bombing over Germany would be launched. And in mid-1942, that strategy was beginning to build as more of the heavy, four-engined bombers came into operation.

Consequently, there was an ever-escalating demand for greater industrial output and for supplies, further increased by the build-up towards that inevitable day when the Second Front *would* be launched.

It is certainly true that eventually the enormous resource potential of the USA would be realised; but in the meantime, an unprecedented response was demanded from British industry.

There was, however, a problem – one among many undoubtedly – and it was that there were gaps in the *human* production line; a serious shortage – if the increasing demands for output were to be met – of skilled and semi-skilled workers. (Possibly, ironically, because too many of such people had been called up into the Armed Forces!).

So, to fill these gaps, it was decided, at some high level, that the RAF should release, on a temporary basis, a certain number of personnel who had had pre-war industrial experience, to go into factories in various parts of the country.

Apparently, the "Marconi connection" identified me as a suitable candidate for service on the industrial front and, together with about a dozen other "releases" from various other RAF units, I found myself in the machine shop and then the assembly shop at Kent's plant at Luton.

We did not make hats! But, as I recall, we constructed metal casings for a variety of military equipment, which involved much hack-sawing and filing; and in that respect it provided no easy option to our duties in the RAF – apart from the somewhat warmer and drier conditions.

Yes, we did put in quite an effort and at the conclusion of our stint, towards the end of November 1942, we received the congratulations of both the Kent management and the Air Ministry.

It had been a welcome break from service life and it was nice to enjoy the home comforts of "digs" for a while. But I doubt if any of us felt really at ease in the civilian milieu during those few months. And when the recall came for us to be reunited with the RAF, I am sure that we all felt a collective sense of relief. In spite of the discomforts, the irksome restrictions, the RAF was where we preferred to be.

We were all posted to different units and, apart from a chap who came from a place near my home town of Witham in Essex, and whom I met again by chance after the war, I never saw or heard from any of those lads again.

One thing has always puzzled me about that episode and it is, given that desperate situation in the Atlantic, that RAF personnel should have been released from Coastal Command (and I was by no means the only one so released from Coastal).

Perhaps the powers-that-be simply took a holistic view of the situation and did not countenance exclusions.

But, there it was... and now to Elsham.

The story of my seven months' service with 103 Squadron at Elsham Wolds begins with another of those typically prolonged war-time train journeys in ill-lit, crowded carriages and corridors.

It was possible to imagine on such journeys that half the total of Britain's Armed Forces, plus their kit, were all on the same train at the same time. And with so many bodies crammed together it was a blessing, rather than a nuisance, that the heating system wasn't working. Hundreds of bladders must have been bursting because a "trip to the loo" up the corridor was virtually a "mission impossible".

There were several unscheduled stops and tedious delays between Kings Cross and Doncaster and it was there – or possibly Scunthorpe, I am not now sure which – that we met the *other* half of the fighting forces of this realm when we detrained and joined them in the station buffet that had become – either by design or appropriation – a Forces' Canteen.

Steam from greatcoats and mugs of tea mingled in the air with clouds of cigarette smoke. There was a great hub-bub of voices resonant with a dozen regional dialects and punctuated by guffaws of male laughter as yet another mucky joke was retold.

In order to obtain refreshment, it was necessary that you pushed and shoved your way to the counter to be served, and curses were exchanged over jogged elbows and spilt tea.

It was not an unfamiliar scene at railway termini during the war; and I recall it here because it marked my return to duty in HM Forces and also my first journey up to Elsham Wolds.

Eventually, in the evening, a second train delivered me, in the company of a group of other airmen, to the rail destination stated on my travel warrant, Barnetby.

The station name-sign was indiscernible in the gloom of the blackout and no porter had vocally identified the place.

It was the other lads on the train who were returning from leave, and with whom those of us who were "new arrivals" had become acquainted on the journey, who had confirmed that this apparently deserted station was indeed Barnetby.

We all gathered on the platform blowing soot from our nostrils in fond farewell to the engine and carriages as they disappeared wheezily into the night, heading in the direction of Grimsby.

Some of us, with misplaced optimism, had anticipated transport to the aerodrome but as mere "erks" (lower ranks) we should have known better. And so we found ourselves trudging the two and a half miles to RAF Elsham Wolds and surprisingly, since this was, after all, Lincolnshire, most of them up-hill. And, for those of us on posting who were toting full-kit it seemed a particularly long trek.

The darkness embraced us as we plodded on and in a blacked-out country, there were no twinkling and welcoming lights in the distance. Low clouds wept drizzle of the soaking kind and when the moon occasionally managed to free itself, I remember looking around and experiencing a deep sense of isolation – isolation coupled with a yearning for hearth and home, an emotion that did still emerge from time-to-time. Even after two and a half years, it was still possible to feel a sense of vulnerability.

Other thoughts, too, trailed along that road with me, triggered by something one of the "old hands" – a cockney engine fitter – had said on the train.

"It's the really 'eavy stuff 'ere mate!" And he had said it, or so it seemed to me, as if making a challenge with the implication, *Are you up to it?*

Was I indeed? I had, after all, been out of touch with aeroplanes for some months; and now coming up before me here was something quite different. Aeroplanes on *land* and big bombers at that.

Our informant had also told us that whilst there was not a lot of "bull" on the 'drome, there *was* "bags of work of the finger out kind"; and that 103 Squadron had recently converted from Halifaxes to Lancasters.

Good God! *Lancasters*! They were already legendary; in the same mould as the Spitfire; and *for* the best of planes one would surely need to *be* the best of mechanics – *wouldn't* one?

As we progressed slowly and damply towards the camp I became increasingly miserable by the minute and decidedly apprehensive. Why had I been so bloody anxious to get back into the "Raff" when I was at Luton!

It was not the prospect of working on big aeroplanes that was so forbidding for, after all, I had serviced the Lerwicks, the Catalinas and the huge Sunderlands on Coastal Command.

The cause of my disquiet had much more to do with the anticipation of the pressure under which one would work in a constantly active, heavy bomber station. And with what trepidation would I sign the *Form 700*[3] in *this* scenario? I was marching to the drum beats of rhetorical questions.

Of course, by that time, I was more of an Instrument "Basher" than I had been fresh out of training school two years earlier. But there had been that interlude at Luton and here I was destined to be groom to the Arab stallion of all the bombers in all the world! Was this *really* the ideal setting in which to pick up again the reins of aircraft maintenance?

Were similar thoughts, I wondered, occupying the minds of the other new arrivals (they were of various "trades") as we trudged up that seemingly never-ending road. Perhaps, though, and much more likely, they were of the more self-assured, *natural* technical types, licking their finger tips at the prospect of coming to grips with this new challenge. I refrained from asking them, but they *did* share my physical discomfort and comments, embracing the three "f's", with

---

[3] *Form 700* – was the document each "tradesman" signed after carrying out work and/or inspections on an aircraft declaring that, to his best knowledge and belief, the parts of the plane for which he was responsible were in good working order. The pilot then counter-signed the form, acknowledging receipt of the aircraft.

The usual practice was for the pilot to satisfy himself either by air or ground tests, before accepting the aircraft.

Form 700 certainly laid it on the line for everyone concerned.

which all ex-service personnel will be familiar, proliferated in the Lincolnshire hedgerows.

The inability of the RAF to organise a Bacchanalian celebration in a building designated for producing alcohol was also mentioned.

At least my return to service life was being confirmed step by step – that old familiar camaraderie of disgruntled and "binding" airmen.

At long last we reached the camp, its buildings blurred shapes in the darkness but, even so, instantly recognisable.

Tired, wet and travel-stained, we reported grumpily to the guardroom and from there were directed to a reception hut where a morale-boosting surprise awaited me.

The first person I saw on entering the hut was Don Boast, a short, stocky Londoner who had been an "oppo" in the early "Sprog" days at Bridgnorth and at Melksham. It was a greeting of long-lost brothers. He, too, had been on temporary release into industry and he had arrived at Elsham, on his first re-call posting, earlier in the evening.

The mantle of gloom lifted considerably as we shared experiences, reminisced and speculated as to the destiny and whereabouts of our erstwhile comrades of our training days.

Don spoke in particular of a very close friend of his of those times – and before the war – Dicky Meinke who, Don told me, had been accepted for pilot training.

I mention this because by strange coincidence I was to run into Dicky – by then a Warrant Officer pilot – in North Africa, about a year later and that meeting with Dicky was just one example of several "small world encounters" I experienced during my service days. I did, in fact, quite by the same kind of chance, and at different times, meet five lads from my home town (two when overseas) and another chap who had been a contemporary of mine at secondary school in Colchester, Essex.

The acrid smell of stove-coke fumes mingled in the air of the reception hut, with a conglomerate of cigarette smoke and steam rising from drying out uniforms and socks.

But even *that* choking internal smog could not prevent the appetising aroma of toast from filtering through as one airman thrust the remains of his sandwiches, brought from home, up against the open flap-door of the stove, on the end of a length of thick wire.

The beds were double-bunks and once again – after that recent brief reacquaintance with sheets and pillowcases at Luton – I was reunited with the rough, regulation blankets and three "biscuits" (palliasses) that were so much a part of RAF life-style. Everything, even on that night of arrival, began to slip back into place and it was almost as if I had never been away.

For those of us who had arrived late, a meal had been rustled up in the cookhouse and as I put on my greatcoat to walk over there, Don and Harry, a loquacious "Geordie" who was on Don's upper bunk, said they would join me.

"I thought they had already fed you," I remarked.

"We'll show you the way," said Don. "Don't want you to get lost!"

So taking a chance on being recognised, Don and Harry scoffed down a second helping of the warmed-up stew that was set (slopped) before us. After Don had scraped his plate clean with the thick chunk of bread that had accompanied the stew, he declared that he was *still* hungry. "I could eat a bloody horse!" he said.

"We probably just *have*, kidder!" proclaimed Harry. And he could have been right.

We swigged down a mug of cocoa and then returned to the hut, which was buzzing with speculative conversation about the future prospects at this new station.

What would the "nosh" be like?

Was there a decent Naafi?

Would there be many Waafs in a place like this?

What would it be like for getting passes to get out of camp?

What were the local pubs like? (Local? Wasn't this dump a hundred miles from anywhere else?)

In matters of that kind, I was prepared to wait and see. Other considerations were demanding attention in my mental processes, such as the lay-out of instrument panels on big bombers; automatic pilot systems; compasses, and other such items of aeronautical technology that were to be within the domain of my responsibility.

But apprehensive contemplation was mercifully short-lived as sleep came quickly and washed all such thought from my mind.

In the early hours of the next morning, still black-dark outside, I awoke to the sound that was to become so familiar and constantly present in the coming months.

It was that distinctive beat of Rolls-Royce Merlin engines as the Lancasters returned from "ops".

It was my first introduction to that truly remarkable aeroplane.

103 Squadron air and ground crews with a Lancaster.

2. GETTING ACQUAINTED

The morning of our first full day at Elsham and, as daylight overslept, we in the reception hut rose at the invitation of a somewhat impatient corporal. We performed perfunctory ablutions and then blearily followed the hordes in blue to the ORs' (other ranks) cookhouse for breakfast, which we ate with scant attention to contents. It could have been breakfast at any other RAF establishment.

Then began the customary routine for the induction of new arrivals, locating various sections of the camp and having our presence officially recorded. (They did prefer to know who was there!)

We reported to the Orderly Room, the nerve-centre of all administration and the source of all the countless and myriad forms on which the RAF depended for its very existence.

Within the precinct of the admin block were two vital departments whose whereabouts were essential knowledge for airmen. One of these was Pay Accounts; and the other was the section that dealt with the entitlement to, and the issue of, passes to the outside world.

From stores we drew blankets, and "irons" (knife, fork and spoon) and a mug.

As we traipsed around the camp we had been struck – almost literally on occasions – by an extraordinary number of people, of all ranks, who were riding bicycles.

"Bloody 'ell," exclaimed Harry in his rich Geordie accent. "We've joined the bloody bicycle corps!"

And in a sense we had, because that was the next item of issue – a bike each! We signed for them – another form of course – and they had identifying numbers stencilled on the front mudguards.

The cycles were not new and they had the unmistakable appearance of previous service. They were of various sizes and makes, mine being an upright, no-nonsense Rayleigh, a good pedigree. It was obvious that the majority of bikes on the station were designed for work rather then recreation but we were to learn that this was a misleading assumption for us to make.

We did notice, as we moved around, that there were some exceptions to the general rule; cycles of some style and distinction that, we were to discover, actually *belonged* to the guys who rode them. Such steeds had been brought to the station by airmen returning from leave. I made an immediate mental note to keep my own Elswick "pride and joy" at home. The RAF had me – they were not having my bike!

Anyway, this was a whole new experience in my own "career" in HM Air Force – but the bicycle would not have been exactly appropriate in Coastal Command. Canoes, possibly; but certainly not bikes!

Within a few days we were to discover how essential those velocipedes were on a bomber station with aircraft "parked" at great distances from the camp centre and from the hangars.

The imagery was that of cowboys riding from the ranch-house out onto the range, and that analogy is worth keeping in mind because these mounts of ours did have a social function which could also be compared to cowhands riding into town – as we shall see.

By mid-day the sullen, depressing clouds were no longer sulking over Lincolnshire but were now hurtling like sky-grown tumbleweed towards the west, driven by a biting wind which had come, unopposed, all the way from Siberia.

As Don, Harry and I wandered around the camp – left alone to find our bearings – our minds were occupied, as always when joining a new unit, with thoughts of creature comforts but not only of food and accommodation but also of acceptance into the brotherhood of 103 Squadron. We knew, you see, from past experience that on some stations of long establishment, newcomers were not always readily accepted into the fold.

Such considerations as these, however, were not unaccompanied in *my* mind, for, as the day progressed, I became increasingly aware that the base was, in many respects, profoundly different to anything I had experienced so far.

To start with the 'drome itself was so at variance. The structure at my three previous bases had been compact with no section very far from any other, whereas here, at Elsham, the 'drome stretched out into distance on all sides. Also, Calshot, Pembroke Dock and Greenock had been within urban environs but this one was set in such a rural ambience as to include two farms within its perimeters.

Three large hangars, one of them huge and wide enough to accommodate the 102-foot wingspan of the Lancaster, dominated the middle ground; and a square water tank stood up high on four iron legs like a monster alien insect.

There were clusters of huts of a great variety in size and of material construction, both at the centre and in the distance. Roads ran out from the hangars, stretching around the airfield to the scattered dispersal bays and linking the three runways that formed a triangle.

You could see the Lancasters standing "black and tan" at their dispersal bays – and unmistakably war-like.

In view, also, was the flight control tower, reminding me of the super-structure of an aircraft-carrier.

In his excellent book *Journeys Into Night* Don Charlwood, an ex-navigator (Aussie) who had been a contemporary of mine during my period with 103 Squadron at Elsham, wrote in his recollections of the station:

> ... *Like most other isolated stations, Elsham Wolds was a temporary village with its own post office, own water supply, own sewerage system, own small hospital and hairdressers and telephone switchboard.*
>
> *In its few streets the youthful, uniformed villagers went about their duties, some on foot, some cycling, a few driving.*

And Don might have added that there, too, in the "village" were the church, the cinema, the theatre, the dance hall – all under one roof, in the gym. Inside that building one could experience the physical, the spiritual and the cultural, not necessarily in that order – all in the course of one week.

Every structure on the camp was camouflaged in matt brown, black and olive green which somehow emphasised the isolation of the place. (Later on, from the air, I was to see for myself the effectiveness of that camouflage, how it blended the airfield into the surrounding countryside.)

Even on that first day I was picking up vibes. Here was *action*, an immediacy of requirement. There was a vibrancy of movement and of resounding noise. The very movement of all the figures in blue uniforms, or in dark overalls, or with leather jerkins on top of the other apparel, conveyed a marked sense of purpose and endeavour.

Merlin engines growled and roared from all directions and a variety of motor vehicles raced around the 'drome, revving their engines as if in puny competition with the Rolls-Royce foursomes.

We saw the Lancasters taking off and watched them coming in to land, and although we had, of course, heard so much about this already-famous aircraft, we had not actually *seen* them before now.

Those Lancaster bombers were carriers of death and destruction but, as they turned and banked in the sky, their aeronautically aesthetic lines were undeniable. It sent an involuntary shiver down one's spine just to watch them in flight, like giant birds of prey displaying a kind of aviatorial confidence, almost of arrogance.

But of the terrible nature of their vulnerability in the perilous skies over Germany, we were yet to learn.

There were sounds of toil emanating from the hangars and from the nearer dispersal bays – hammering, drilling, the clang of metal on metal; and raised voices sometimes filtered through.

Yes, here *was* a different scenario. Even though, in essence, it contained the same basic ingredients as in my previous stations, the *character* here was vastly at variance with the Coastal Command bases. And, above all, I think it was that tangible sense of *urgency* that made it so distinctive. Was it Swinburn who wrote about "the pulse of war"? Whoever it was, it was so apt a description of the feeling I experienced on that very first day at Elsham Wolds. Excitement and anxiety elbowed for priority of attention in my mind as I contemplated the challenge that lay ahead on that throbbing bomber station.

As the man on the train had said, "It's the real 'eavy stuff 'ere mate!" And, even if he had not implied the question as to my "being up to it" – as I had imagined – that query was certainly being raised in my own psyche.

Some time later in that day, we were allocated a hut in a remote corner of the airfield on the edge of a sugar-beet field – and a long walk, or even cycle ride, from the "village".

As we entered the hut I was reminded yet again that things were to be very different in this neck of the woods. Beds were not exactly militarily tidy and in the spaces between the beds, lay the odd boot or sock.

On a table, near the well-worn, black tortoise stove, were a couple of saucers filled with fag ends, and two cups, one of which had the letter LMS printed on its side (at some time, said cup had been the property of a London, Midland and Scottish Railway platform buffet, somewhere in Britain!)

There was a distinct smell, of soot from the stove; of concrete from the floor; of damp metal, from the corrugated roof; and of stale cigarette smoke.

There were three obviously vacant beds and we dumped our belongings and ourselves onto them rather wearily. The processes of inchoation had been somewhat tiring.

My bed, the one I claimed, was on the right, just inside the door, in a corner of the hut. It seemed a "snug little spot" and I did rather wonder why it was vacant. The answer was (of course!) its distance from the stove – but I did not discover that chilly fact until it was too late!

In the late afternoon and early evening, the incumbent dwellers of the hut began to appear, gradually filling it to its capacity of fourteen, most of whom, like us, turned out to be "Instrument Bashers". (I later learned that some people on the camp referred to our hut as the "musical box". It was where all the instruments were kept!)

It was immediately noticeable, as these "older hands" arrived, that their sartorial appearance fitted in perfectly with the condition of the hut in which they lived. Stained and crumpled uniforms, ditto overalls, scarred jerkins, greasy caps and lustreless boots. Dishevelled was the word that came to mind but DISGRACEFUL was the adjective that would have radiated at great volume from the mouth of any self-respecting Drill Sergeant in such places as Cardington, Padgate, Bridgnorth (and Calshot) – as I remember them! Idle on parade indeed!

Even though, in all my previous stations, the appearance of most aircraft mechanics had been, because of the very nature of the job, less than pristine, here at Elsham Wolds the degree of scruffiness had a quality all of its own. But, as is often said, appearances can be deceptive; and it was no less so in this situation – as I will show in due course. Indeed, as we saw that very night, when some of the lads were going out on a pass, the transformation as they got into their *best blue* and shining footwear, was quite stunning.

Any fears we may have harboured about *attitudes* towards newcomers were quickly dispelled as we were greeted most amiably by our predecessors, who welcomed us and gave us, unsolicited, useful "gen" about the camp and the Squadron. In fact, the coming together of old and new hands was quite spontaneous and to this day I recall with great warmth of feeling, the reassuring nature of that initial introduction. And I was to learn that immediate cordiality was a true measure of the comradeship I was to share in the course of the next seven months.

I do not, now, recall the names of all the occupants of our "cabin in the clearing" but of those whom I do remember more will be written later on. For the moment I shall just say who they were:

Frank Wain from Sheffield – who was to become a particularly close "oppo";

Wally "Bud" Senior from Manchester;

Doug "Pop" Tylor from Leicester;

Alan Dilks a Nottingham lad; and also

Harry Batty, Freddy Lloyd, "Lofty" Bartlett, none of whose places of origin I now recall. And there was "Paddy" – who was from the southern half of the Emerald Isle, but in his case, it is his surname that escapes me.

However, as I say, I will acquaint the reader a little more closely with their characters as the narrative proceeds.

I asked Frank Wain, who occupied the next bed to mine, how they managed to get away with the hut's distinct lack of military precision and presentation.

"Oh," he told me. "They don't worry too much about all that stuff here. Keeping the 'kites' in the air is what counts. There are occasional purges but we usually get wind of it; and then we *tidy up a bit.* Don't worry about it, just make yourself as comfortable as you can. It can get bloody cold out here lad."

3. THE WAY IT WAS (I)

The ablution block was situated in the centre of the camp and a long enough cycle ride from where our hut was situated. Thus our inner and outer cleanliness would be achieved only after that early morning ride, although should one be desperate – either during the night, or at the time of rising from slumbers – then one was obliged to stagger into the undergrowth; a great joy in winter.

On the morning of our second day at Elsham we rode up to the ablution block in driving rain. As we pedalled along the muddy cart track, Don Boast commented that we now had no need to wash. When we entered the washhouse and found water sloshing about on the floor, he observed that he was quite impressed with the facilities at Elsham Wolds since he could shave *and* wash his feet at the same time!

The place was crowded and we had to queue for access to the communal basins and taps; and we noticed that the lads were all shaving in front of small pocket mirrors – or bits of mirrors – which were obviously their own property. A little reminder of something we had forgotten in our temporary absence from the RAF.

The water was cold – but *that* was no surprise. And nor was breakfast – lumpy porridge, chunky slices of bread, sausages of indeterminate content, powdered egg. (Real fried eggs were reserved for air-crews and that was fair enough, but sometimes, especially if you won the favour of a cookhouse Waaf, and if you came in off a late or extended duty, a "pukka" (real) egg might just be found somewhere!)

A large tin of jam stood on each long table; and, of course, there was that precious mug of tea. Breakfast over, you trooped outside to the great vats of water into which you dunked your mug and "irons" – the first to wash off the residue of your meal and the second to rinse. Naturally, according to when you got there, and depending on the number of airmen who had "dunked" before you, the waters would be decidedly greasy and no longer hot.

And now! And now to the Instrument Section. This was *it* then. *My moment of truth!* The Section was situated in a corner of the biggest of the three hangars, just to the left of the massive sliding

16

doors. Voices echoed in the hangar and blue-overalled figures were already clambering all over the Lancaster that stood there, awaiting one new engine. Scaffold trolleys were pushed up against the vast wings and chain and pulley lifting gear stood adjacent to the "tooth stump" where the old engine had been.

And, as we had entered the hangar that old, familiar aerodrome aromatic mix of oil, aviation fuel, metal and aircraft "dope", wafted into our nostrils. We were "home" again.

In the Section there were work-benches along the walls on which lay aircraft instruments of great variety, some intact, others disembowelled; and a selection of tools, laid untidily around. A couple of vices were fixed to the benches and piled up at the back were a number of portable oxygen bottles in webbing "holsters". Laid along another wall were two long oxygen cylinders.

To me, this encounter was rather disquieting, for although we had covered the oxygen "bit" on the course at Melksham I had never, in Coastal Command, had occasion to put the theory into practice. Seaplanes simply did not fly at such altitudes.

(Those oxygen cylinders also gave a little nudge to my latent home-sickness because there was a British Oxygen plant quite close to where I lived back home; and it had been a frequent sight there, to see the cylinders going in and out of the gates. Were *those* cylinders, at Elsham Wolds, also natives of Witham?)

Stuck on the walls were two grubby but strident war-propaganda posters; and two others displaying the silhouettes of German and Allied aircraft.

There were also various dog-eared diagrams of aeroplane instruments and of other aviation equipment.

At the far end of the Section was a narrow "inner office" and this was the sanctum of the NCOs in charge, Flight Sergeant Willmott, and Corporals Clifford and Simpson.

It took very little time indeed to become aware that here was a trio of NCOs who knew their job, who were confident in it; and would expect similar application from others.

Nevertheless they all greeted us amiably and it was rather more like being welcomed by a somewhat serious but kindly foreman in a factory, and by two amiable charge-hands. And that is an appropriate analogy because, although there were obvious and constant reminders that we operated in the military milieu, the working practices and relationships at Elsham were, in many respects, reminiscent of the civilian work-place. In fact, that is precisely what made the servicing of aircraft work in the way that it did.

Most of the other lads from our hut were there and although the general bantering, friendly atmosphere in the Section was in itself reassuring, my unease was not totally allayed.

How would I meet the new challenge? Was my level of competence adequate for the demands that would most certainly be made here?

Why this insecurity? Had I not nearly two years of air base experience behind me? Had I not, during that time, moved up from AC2 (Aircraftsman second class) to AC1 (Aircraftsman first class) and then to LAC – Leading Aircraftsman? It may not have been the dizzy heights of promotion but incompetence would not, surely, have been rewarded at all?

Perhaps this would be the opportune moment to explain and clarify the state of uncertainty which beset me.

There are, basically, two inter-related factors which combined to undermine my self-belief. The first, as I have previously hinted, was a lack of *natural* technical competence. It is ironic that life had, perversely, pushed me in an engineering direction, in spite of my lack of proclivity for it. Somehow I had won a scholarship to a *technical* secondary school; soon after leaving school – where English, History, Geography and Art had been the only subjects I had enjoyed and in which I had shone – I found myself working as an electrician's mate, followed by my employment at the Marconi Company. It was the way it was in the 1930s when employment was difficult to find and when one was encouraged to try to find a "safe" job, even if it wasn't what you really wanted to do.

And, once again with irony, it was the Marconi connection that had enhanced my acceptance, as a volunteer, into the RAF; and had also determined my designation as an Instrument Mechanic.

So it had been a story, really, of the archetypal non-artisan square peg in the technological round hole.

As I have said, the instrument course at Melksham had been hard work for me as had my initiation into servicing aircraft. (The story of my very first D.I. – Daily Inspection – is well worth the telling and it will feature further on in this book.) But I am not stupid, and by dint of effort and the invaluable help of many "oppos" – God bless their memory – I "got by", and achieved a sufficiency of competence. Yet, I lacked that "sure touch", that self-assurance of the natural mechanic, of which ilk the RAF was so generously possessed.

The second factor would, in any case, overlay that non-technical feature of my make-up because it is a life-long deficiency in self-confidence, *per se*. It is something I have always had to combat and overcome, even in the areas of life where I have achieved at least a modicum of success.

Sometimes, I have been able to conceal my uncertainty from people with whom I interact, both socially and at work. But it is always there, lurking in the corridors of my psyche.

Twice during my service with Coastal Command I had volunteered for air-crew, deliberately throwing down the gauntlet at the feet of my unconfident nature, trying, I guess, to prove something to myself, rather than in pursuit of heroism. But, as it turned out, I was rejected on both occasions on the grounds of colour blindness.

And so, I had soldiered (or rather "airmanned") on as an "Instrument Basher", doing the job to the best of my ability; and always conscious of the serious responsibility involved.

Given all that, I hope that the reader will have some understanding of the state of unease I was experiencing on that first day, reporting for duty with 103 Squadron, on an active bomber station in December 1942. Remembering, also, that I was coming to this demanding situation after a few months out of touch with aircraft altogether.

Little did I know at that moment that I was, at Elsham Wolds, to grow in confidence – and competence – and now, to recall it as the period in the whole six years of the war which pleased me most.

My first assignment turned out to be a remarkably fortunate one, for I was sent out to assist one LAC Ron Grantham, a thin, almost gaunt (he was then, he isn't now!) affable Yorkshireman, on a major service of that Lanc. that stood in the hangar.

I wonder if Flight Sergeant Willmott was aware of the vital importance and significance, as far as I was concerned, of that allocation of duty.

4. THE WAY IT WAS (II)

I worked with Ron Grantham in the hangar for just two weeks but in that short time I learned so much.

It is true that a great deal of the instrumentation on the Lanc. was the same, or very similar, to that on other aircraft I had worked on previously; but there were variations and additions; and there, also, were differences in layout.

From the estimable Ron, though, I picked up the "feel" of the Lancaster, and the requirements of *our* job on that rather special aeroplane.

Our main task on that particular Lancaster in the hangar was the fitting of a new "George" (automatic pilot) system, but during that process Ron passed on so many invaluable tips about inspecting, checking and remedying faults.

I recall how surprised I was when first entering that big aircraft, to discover the paucity of space in its interior. It was so narrow and seemed to be bristling with metal protuberances and obstacles. One needed to be something of a contortionist to reach – sometimes almost inaccessible – parts that needed investigation or attention.

How, I wondered, did the air-crews move around in the close confines of the Lanc. when wearing all their flying gear? A more pertinent question would have been: "How did they get out when circumstances demanded that they should do so in a hurry?" The grim answer to that question was to be revealed later.

As far as I could tell, there was no way that "Chiefy" Willmott could have been aware of my unease on that first day in the Instrument Section, so I guess it was purely fortuitous that he should assign me, that morning, to be Ron Grantham's "mate". But whether by design or chance, the fact is that when, at the end of the second week, I was switched to the "D.I. Brigade" (the Daily Inspection team) I was, as they say these days, "up for it". Certainly I was still wary and very conscious that I was now about to become responsible for the instrumentation efficiency of *two* Lancasters out on the Flights. (The airfield was divided into three sections called Flights, each one consisting, on average, of eight aircraft. Each

Flight, A, B & C had its own Commanding Officer, air-crews, and "resident" ground staff.)

Whereas Don and Harry had been allocated to B and C Flights, I was now to join the "A team".

In the case of the engine and airframe fitters, they were normally "one kite men", responsible for just one aircraft; but those of us who, in a sense, attended to the accoutrements – electricians, radio and instrument "mechs" – had a more plural obligation.

It was the job of every "trade" out on the Flights to carry out a daily inspection of those parts of the aeroplane for which we were responsible – and accountable – and to remedy any faults or to repair any damage reported or discovered, that was within our means. Major repairs, engine changes, modifications, all such extensive work would be within the domain of the "hangar boys" – such as Ron Grantham.

Even with the bigger tasks, in the hangars, there was a degree of pressure, because the "brass" wanted the Lancs out on the dispersals and ready for action, not languishing in the hangars. But, out on the Flights there was an *ever-present* time-pressure awareness, especially when "ops" were scheduled.

So, yes, even though, thanks to Ron, I *was* more ready to meet the challenge that lay ahead, I was not totally devoid of trepidation as I rode out to "A Flight" on that morning of my "D.I. debut".

But, once again, fortune rode alongside me; fortune in the chunky shape of Frank Wain, who had been *asked* to show me the ropes.

Like Ron Grantham, Frank was a superb mentor and from him I learned "what to look for"; "where problems most frequently occurred" and the most efficient way in which to conduct the D.I. "Dents, kinks, leaks and connections – those are the things to watch out for," Frank advised. And he was right, so right.

"And Gremlins!" said one of the other "erks", working nearby. "Turn your back and they're in there, causing 'effing' havoc!"

(Gremlins? Minuscule hobgoblins, lived in the entrails of all aeroplanes in the RAF. They had emigrated from somewhere out in the world of sprites and imps and had decided for some perverse reason, to take up residence in an aviatorial environment. Their sense of humour was malevolent and what they enjoyed most was to cause damage in the most inaccessible areas of an aeroplane's anatomy; or, even more entertaining (for them) to launch an attack on an item of equipment, just recently repaired or replaced. Sheer vandalism!

In odd, and rare, moments of silence on an aircraft, you could just hear the high pitch of the Gremlins' manic laughter. Nonsense? Think that if you will; but you won't find an ex-aircraft mechanic who doubted their existence, nor one who did not, at some time, suffer at their evil little hands. *Honest!*)

There was, of course, a servicing manual for the Lancaster. But I made out my own, like a shopping list. On a piece of paper, torn from a school exercise book, I wrote down the order of inspection, annotated with "jog notes", reminders of "snag points" and tips passed on by both Ron and Frank. That piece of paper, greatly dog-eared and smudged, was my mantra, my single-page bible, and was a constant reassuring companion in my pocket.

I wish I still had it, for it would be a treasured memento of those hectic times. But, alas, it was in my kit-bag stolen in the night in North Africa sometime after leaving Elsham. And it may well be, now, an item of great curiosity in some Algerian household!

Day-by-day, I progressed from my tentative beginnings to an acquirement of a measure, at least, of self-assurance and confidence always helped along with the knowledge that Frank – and Bud Senior and "Pop" Tyler, who were both also in "A Flight" – were available should I need a hand, or advice.

After a few weeks I could sign that once-dreaded Form 700 with the confidence of knowing that I was on top of my job – an inestimable, morale-boosting milestone of personal development.

It was not that I signed the Form 700 with contemptuous familiarity – I was far too aware of the responsibility involved to do that. But there I was, an accepted part of a team, helping to ensure the air-worthiness of one of the RAF's elite aircraft. It was the "*feel good factor*" and a far cry from that day at Calshot, back in 1940, when my aircraft inspection virginity was broken on that most unlikely of flying machines, the Walrus flying boat.

I was fresh out of training school, then, and very much "wet behind the ears". The contemplation of carrying out my very first D.I. on a real aeroplane was sufficiently disturbing; but the prospect, also, of doing so on planes that bounced up and down on choppy water intensified my trepidation.

Clutching my toolbox and inspection lamp I went down the slippery steps of the wind-and-spray-swept quay and clambered awkwardly (one becomes more adept at that in due course of time) into the motor dinghy that ferried both air and ground crews out to the seaplanes riding at their buoys on the Solent.

As we set off, a strong gust of wind separated my cap from my head and I could only sit and watch it – much to the merriment of the other "erks" in the boat – floating off in the general direction of France, as if to serve notice to the Nazis of further things to come.

The loss of the cap did nothing to improve my already-shaky morale because in the short time I had been at Calshot, I had discovered that this pre-war RAF station – home of the Schneider Trophy seaplanes – was rather fond of "bull"; and the impression I had gained was that the loss of any item of uniform apparel could be almost a court-martial offence!

Once on board the Walrus, I carried out what should have been placed in RAF Records as the aircraft D.I. of the longest duration *ever*. I checked every item of equipment for which I was responsible – and probably others for which I was not – many times over. I tightened nuts, screws, connections which were already absolutely firm. I scrutinised tubes and panels for the slightest nick or dent; no compass had ever been inspected with such distrust. I even rubbed instruments with the sleeve of my overalls as if to ensure their efficiency.

Many of the other "bods" on board had hailed the dinghy and had gone off to another "kite" and I was still beavering away at my D.I. when the air-crew came aboard.

The "Skipper" wanted to know who I was and when I gave him my name he informed me that my *name* was of very little interest to him. What he *did* want to know was what I was *doing*. And when I told him, I was informed in no uncertain manner that I should sign the Form 700 and go! And then, when I said I was not sure if I had finished, he pre-dated Ken Wolstenholme by declaring "*You have now!*"

So, I signed my very first Form 700 – with a shaky hand – and together with the Engineering "Chiefy", who had come out with the air-crew, I boarded the dinghy and headed back to shore.

I stood on the quay, watching the Walrus revving up its engine, taxi-ing further out into the Solent and then saw it take off. And it was at that moment that I realised, in horror, that I had left my inspection lamp on the plane!

Oh God! It would slide about and get jammed in the controls and cause the Walrus to crash! And I would be shot at dawn, probably without trial! The Walrus, however, completed its test flight and returned safely. *Thank you for that God! I owe you!*

I later retrieved the lamp. And the cap? Our "Chiefy" had a spare, which fortunately fitted. Another piece of divine intervention!

Well, since that unforgettable debut, I had signed the Form 700 on numerous occasions but had now graduated from the Walrus through a variety of other seaplanes to the imposing Lancaster bomber.

It is highly probable that being made responsible for individual aircraft at Elsham was a contributory factor in the growth of my self-confidence for that, also, was a new experience for me.

In Coastal Command I had worked in a rather haphazard, non-specific system of "kite allocation". But at Elsham, having one's own charges to look after gave one a more proprietorial attitude to the job.

Also there was the familiarity – and the banter on a daily basis – with the lads in the other "trades" who formed each "kite's" team. Plus, of course, there was that other vital incentive to conscientiousness (and of "wanting to give of one's best") and that was the regular contact and rapport with the air-crews, about whom we became proprietorial also.

There is no doubt that in a short space of time – about two months I guess it would have been since my apprehensive arrival at Elsham – I had come a long way.

I had no idea, during that time – nor I suspect did any of us – that the campaign in which we were so committedly engaged was to become the subject of such great controversy in later years.

We were involved in a desperate war against a formidable and ghastly enemy and we were, as we collectively saw it, contributing in a purposeful manner to the ultimate defeat of that enemy.

And, on a personal level, I felt good about myself, as a cog in the wheel.

I had not been able to be accepted for air-crew, but I was coping well at the next best thing, helping to keep the Lancasters flying; and supporting the boys who *did* fly. And importantly, I was basking in the warmth of reassuring comradeship. I was, indeed, among friends.

5. THE WILD WOLDS

I little knew when I arrived at Elsham Wolds that memories of my time there would sit so pleasantly in the storage section of my mind. It seemed to be the most unlikely place for which one would feel nostalgic.

In 1991, a booklet was published by the Elsham Wolds Association to mark the 50th Anniversary of the opening of Elsham as a RAF bomber station in 1941.

Air Chief Marshal Sir Hugh Constantine was the first Station Commander and in the booklet he wrote:

> *Wars are stupid and bring misery to so many people but when you stand alone against an arrogant dictator, ordinary people pull together and suffer hardships far better than in times of peace. This was certainly true of Elsham where conditions were none too good, with few luxuries and little relaxation, but morale and team spirit between all ranks remained high. Yet there was still time for some fun and laughter.*

The Air Chief Marshal was so right, on all counts, for certainly that aerodrome in the north of Lincolnshire was not the most comfortable place to be.

The weather there was a mixture of the most unpleasant meteorological elements – sometimes all of them visiting themselves upon us on the same day – and there was always that prevailing ambience of bleak isolation.

Lincolnshire is, for the most part, a flat county (hence its appropriateness for RAF bomber bases) but Elsham Wolds stood exposed on top of an uncharacteristically high stretch of land.

In his superb book, *Journeys Into Night*, Don Charlwood quotes his "Skipper" Geoff Madden writing in his diary:

The Station is situated on top on an escarpment and is open to the cold winds off the North Sea and anything that may come overland from the west.

Yes, and out at the dispersal bays where the Lancasters were "parked", when the wind howled across that escarpment, it threw at us, in climatic turn, rain, sleet and snow. And when those elements took time out for respite, there then lay upon us a cloying mist, shrouding everything – buildings, aeroplanes and people – into ghostly shapes.

Those winds really hit us in the March of '43 and their ferocity is recorded by Sid Finn in his very readable history of 103 Squadron, *Black Swan*:

> *The closing days of March (1943) brought equinoctial gales. Winds howled and gusted through the woods near the billets, scattering small branches along the roads. Every few hours a Tannoy blared forth with storm warnings and cancellations of planned "ops": Upon the Wolds the full force of the winds sweeping in from the North Sea was felt. Hangar doors banged and windows rattled. Even the big Lancasters strained and surged against their chocks – wing tips moving, eerie whistles coming from gun ports in the turrets.*

We in our Nissen hut expected to see the corrugated roof take off at any moment; and even the tortoise stove shuddered with apprehension!

According to my diary, "ops" were scrubbed on eleven nights in that month. But, even so, four Lancs. were lost on the nights when "ops" were on.

(Is it any wonder that I am reminded of such times when I attend the 103 Squadron Reunion and, with reminiscent frequency, even in August, the wind still gusts across the Wolds!)

I had been at Elsham only a couple of weeks when it snowed – and snowed – and snowed some more! There were tons of the stuff; and although I recall very little of our Yuletide celebrations up there – whether because of memory lapse or over-indulgence, I am not prepared to say – I do know that we had a distinctively white Christmas.

In one respect, the snow at Elsham was worse than that at Greenock in the awful winter of '41, because in the wide open spaces of Lincolnshire it piled up in great high drifts. And I remember, too, how we "erks" – together with some of the air crews – worked like the canal navvies of previous centuries, clearing the roads and runways, only to see the snow engulfing those thoroughfares again, when we came on duty the next day.

An Aussie instrument "basher" who was attached temporarily to our unit when I was in Scotland, and with whom I formed a close friendship, had never seen snow before that winter of '41. He was so enthralled that he wanted to ...*put it in a box and take it back to Oz. What a souvenir. What a beaut!*

Well, "Lofty", my old "Digger" mate, you are welcome to it all! Not since childhood have I cared for the stuff. It always reminds me, not only of less than pleasant times on airfields (even in Italy!) but also of the scourge of chilblains! In a word association game I would respond to "snow" with "chilblains"!

Anyway, the latter part of December saw another spate of "ops" cancellations, including one scheduled for Turin on Christmas Eve.

Santa Claus may have been airborne that night but 103 Squadron RAF was not, which must have been one hell of a Christmas present for the good citizens of Turin. Even so, it was not just the snow they had to thank for their reprieve, but 10/10 cloud over the target area.

I am now not sure where I came across the following lines written by Henry Trace and entitled, *Lincolnshire Bomber Station*, but it seemed so very apt to quote them in the context of this chapter:

Across the road the homesick Romans made
the ground-mist thickens to a misty shroud;
Through flat, damp fields call sheep, mourning their dead
in cracked and timeless voices, unutterably sad,
suffering for all the world, in Lincolnshire.
And I wonder how the Romans liked it here;
flat fields, no sun, the muddy misty down,
rusting sword and helmet, wetting the feet
and soaking to the bone, down to the very heart...

Such evocative lines. The Roman Legionnaires and RAF personnel, centuries apart but linked by kindred spirits in the discomforts of a posting in the bleakness of winter in north Lincolnshire.

So, there was the weather. And there was our accommodation, our "des res" as Frank Wain had named it.

Set in a dip where three muddy fields converged, it was impressively air-conditioned, or put another way, decidedly draughty; and we had to keep its black tortoise stove well fed with a great variety of fodder in order to achieve any semblance of warmth.

That stove – converted from Stephenson's Rocket according to "Bud" Senior – was of a temperamental nature and was, depending on mood, just as inclined to puff out smoke into the hut as it was to push it up the chimney stack.

And those fumes, combined with all the cigarette smoke that pervaded the air, created an internal pollution that was not exactly conducive to good health. But, in those days of ignorance (and innocence) we were oblivious to such hazards.

Although, given the general circumstances, even if we had been well-informed on matters of unhealthy environments (and practices) I doubt whether we would have acted very differently. It is though, an indication of how strong and prominent the olfactory sense is in our nostalgia, for whenever I now catch a whiff of acrid smoke, I return in my mind to that Nissen hut in a corner of a Lincolnshire field.

Amenities in the camp were rather basic and, with reference to Henry Trace's poem, I would be less than surprised to learn that the Roman Legionnaires were provided with ablution blocks somewhat superior to ours when they were stationed in Lincolnshire!

Certainly there were signs of improvement during my sojourn at Elsham; but initially, and for at least three winter months, conditions, as Sir Hugh Constantine wrote: ... were *none too good*. (The RAF has a tradition for understatement).

They even waited until after I left before introducing organised inter-section, inter-unit football on the station. And I am sorry I missed out on that. I would have enjoyed soccer at Elsham.

In the matter of food, I retain only a hazy and limited memory of the victuals placed, or rather "slopped" before us at Elsham; a lapse of memory shared, it would seem, by ex-comrades with whom I chat at our reunions. And, on two counts, that is not surprising.

Firstly, because food – unless repetitively menued on a daily basis, or is outstandingly enjoyable or absolutely awful – is not exactly on the top floor of our memory bank. (Can you remember what you had for dinner on a Wednesday, the week before last?)

Secondly, "service nosh" was, generally, so "appetizing" as to be utterly forgettable anyway.

I do, most definitely, recall the atrociously poor fare we were obliged to put up with overseas – a diet dominated by dehydrated meat and veg with the texture of sliced rubber and the taste of soggy cardboard – but that will come up (an appropriate term!) in another, future book.

At Elsham the cookhouse "bods" did the best they could; and I guess that at least in quantity, if not in quality, we probably fared better than the majority of the civilian population on their meagre rations.

But what we were given was never sufficient, for, as we were young and often cold, we were always ravenously hungry. Thank God for the Naafi in which we could supplement the "RAF issue" with sausage and chips.

For some reason, as mentioned in a previous chapter, I do recall the breakfasts, but have only vague recollections of other meals.

Stews feature in these somewhere; spam and corned beef too. Sausages of indeterminate filling (sawdust according to Don Boast) and root vegetables – and why not, in Lincolnshire!

We did have "afters" – although none of my contemporaries seems able to recall what form they assumed – but I only know that there were desserts because the one certain gastronomic memory I do retain is of lumpy custard with the distinct flavour of something that has stood in a pot over a high flame for far too long!

Overall, I suppose one could say that the "nosh" we received "filled a hole", temporarily at least, which is a comment appropriate to most institutional meals. It is probably how we all recall school meals; or hospital food – or possibly, too, in-flight meals on airlines.

Of course, we "honked" – "binded" (i.e. grumbled) – about the grub, but we did that about so much else as well. That was our prerogative; our "relief valve". Mind you, although we did pass derogatory comments about the meals, we seldom did so when the Orderly Officer came round requiring to know if "Any complaints?"

A response to that challenging question was always regarded as (a) a waste of time and (b) traditionally inadvisable!

So, yes, we "honked", a feature of daily life in HM Forces; and it did help to sustain us, for, as most ex-service personnel of lower rank will undoubtedly confirm, we had little faith, when we had a grievance of any kind, in the processes of "official channels". That procedure was regarded, with justifiable cynicism, as a theoretical sop which, in practice, rarely worked to one's advantage.

So, instead, we compensated by "binding"; and there were innumerable targets for our opprobrium quite apart from the culinary fare. There was ...the weather; the billets; the ablutions; duty rosters; officers and NCOs; "snoops" (service policemen); "snags" on aeroplanes; gremlins; letter from home; lack of letters from home; bullshit printed in the newspapers; Hitler; the war; Churchill's cigars (when we could often get only inferior war-time fags!); weak beer in the Naafi; each other... and so much else. It was almost an obligatory litany; and an outside observer may have been persuaded that we "erks" were engaged in one big collective whinge.

But, if the same observer had listened carefully, he would have realised that his initial conclusion was somewhat erroneous.

A great deal of the "binding" was, in fact, laced with humour – of diverse nature: laconic, sardonic, acerbic, wry, "music hall", and was simply a continuation of the rank-and-file grumbling tradition that has been there throughout military history.

> *Bloody wind! There is more wind up here than at a conference of baked bean woofers!*
>
> *My granny could drink ten gallons of this gnat's piss they call beer and still thread 'er needles!*
>
> *I met a Waaf yesterday who preferred the "erks" to the aircrews. Then I woke up!*
>
> *I said to the Chiefy, "Hey Chiefy, I was on night duty last week and now I'm down for guard roster. That ain't fair," He said I was being secretly trained as a night fighter pilot!*
>
> *Three weeks I waited for a letter from home. Then I got one today, posted a fortnight ago. Bloody post! I got a big surprise – it was from me dad! Know what he said? He said, "Dear Son, your mum has hurt her hand so I am writing instead of her. Can't send you a postal order this week because I'm cooking the dinner! Hope you're enjoying yourself. All the best, Dad." Silly old sod. And now I'm skint!*

Just a few examples of the kind of things one would hear on a regular basis. And not infrequently the "binder" would be exhorted by others to, *Wind it down you honking bastard, We'll get you a posting to the wailing wall at Jerusalem!*

And those of us who had volunteered to join up were promptly reminded, whenever we were "binding", that, *Only us conscripts are entitled to have a gripe. You shouldn't've joined, mate!*

But on that basis, perhaps the voicing of discontents was a prerogative of the vast majority of us, for after all, we were essentially civilians on loan to the military; and we were not time-serving regulars. Not that they, the "old sweats", were any less averse to having a good grumble. Indeed, they had acquired more practice at it!

So yes, RAF Elsham Wolds could have been called, "Much binding in the Wolds." But I doubt very much if it was distinctive in that respect. Grumbling in the ranks has been a feature of military life from time immemorial, and it plays as I have said a vital part in maintaining morale.

6. THE ETHOS OF ELSHAM

Throughout the book I endeavour to evoke a feel for the general ambience of a war-time bomber station – and of one in particular. In this chapter I want to portray, as I remember it, the ethos that existed there.

It was, in fact, a culture, or way of life, gestated and reinforced by the prevailing circumstances, and it manifested itself in various ways and with interesting facets of which all that "binding" was just one.

Although *An Erk's Eye View* is devoted, essentially, to the ground crews of the RAF, their role cannot be seen in isolation from the men they served – the air crews. The ultimate purpose of the bomber station forged a link between air and ground crews and that interlocking, inter-dependent feature of life on the station, was, in itself, an integral part of the culture. But, because of the nature of the more hazardous job they had to do, it is necessary, in the first instance, to say something about them – and their place in the culture – and to pay my own personal tribute to them.

One of the most revealing aspects of air-crew attitudes is that of their reaction – and interpretation of – discipline. I write more specifically about the subject in a later section of this book, but it is important, too, in the context of this chapter.

Discipline did not, for the air-crews, operate totally on normal military lines. And, in the circumstances how could it?

Naturally, when they flew on "ops", there was an imposed discipline in terms of target, altitude, navigation, timing, etc., etc.; but it was inside the bombers where the departure from the norm was given emphasis.

The Lancaster bomber carried a crew of seven – pilot, navigator, bomb-aimer, wireless operator, flight engineer and the dorsal and rear gunners. In almost every case, that crew would consist of a variety of ranks but no matter what the pilot's rank may have been – or whatever the rank of the rest of the crew – he, the pilot, was the "Skipper". He was the boss; the man in charge; the decision-maker, and that position of leader, of authority, would not be questioned.

So, it was not at all unusual for the "Skipper" to be a Sergeant and for the navigator or bomb-aimer – or both – to be commissioned officers. Even the other NCOs in the crew might have been Flight Sergeants or in some cases, Warrant Officers.

Thus disciplines on board the plane was not based on, or imposed by superiority of rank or status, but by the role expectation of each member of the crew. And, on the ground, the "Skipper" would also speak for his team whenever that became necessary. And, since it was common practice for the crew to pick themselves, it is not surprising how close-knit they invariably became.

How, then, could such "teams" be separated socially – except by residence – when they were so bonded in action, sharing so much danger and discomfort?

So, immediately, we can see how that self-perpetuating variance on the traditional military rules of hierarchial command could have a significant bearing on the "way of life" on the bomber bases. And, undoubtedly, it was an "enigma variation" as far as some of the die-hards of the "old school" were concerned.

It was a development in the evaluation of the RAF protocol that was bound, also, to escalate as the strategic bombing campaign built up and the casualties mounted – and consequently an ever-increasing number of pilots were of NCO rank.

Off duty, it was something akin to King Canute and the incoming tide for the "system" to keep the air-crews under anything but minimal control. They showed, in no uncertain manner, a collective hostility towards anything resembling "bull"; and indulged themselves in irreverence at every opportunity. It was not that they were a "rabble" – they were far from being that – but were, when not in action, somewhat non-conformist!

That old fatalistic cry: *Eat, drink, and be merry, for tomorrow we die!* could have been the air-crews' theme song for their grasp on life was so tenuous.

In John B Hilling's very readable book, *Strike Hard*, in which he describes the development of the life on and the operation from another bomber station, Downham Market in Norfolk (which has a passing place in this book also) he, too, brings out the air-crews' acute awareness of life when the living of it was so precarious. He quotes the comments of Flying Officer B J Sherry, DFC, 608 Squadron:

> *Bomber air-crews, raiding over Occupied Europe led a strange schizophrenic existence. By day, in the quiet English*

countryside; by night engaged in a running fight in the cold and dark over enemy territory; and then coming back from this bad dream to the calm of the Fenlands. It was two totally different worlds that we moved between. In the dark side could be a hell, then daytime, largely by contrast, become a bit of heaven. Morning came, you were still alive, and very conscious of being alive. Everything tasted better... jokes were funnier... colours were brighter... birdsong was sweeter... nature lovelier... all girls were beautiful...

There was heightened intensity about the daytime half of the equation as well as the night-time part, and very little excuse was needed to have a celebration. The unspoken reason was that we were still here, still in the land of the living.

We had some memorable parties, both on the station and in the pubs of the surrounding villages, and enjoyed some marvellous hospitality from the local people.

Death does indeed remind us of our own mortality and at the wake after a funeral, in the midst of sadness and sense of loss, talk among the mourners is often loud and animated. Death has knocked on the door but it was the turn of someone else, this time, not yours.

To reach any understanding of the air-crews' perspective it is necessary to grasp the reality of their situation. At the time of my arrival at Elsham in December 1942 not one air-crew of 103 Squadron had completed a tour of "ops" (thirty missions) in recent weeks.

In the course of the seven months I spent there, thirty-three Lancasters were lost, of which two only were written-off in flying accidents. (Other accidents did occur but in those cases the aircraft concerned were "restored".)

Thirty-one Lancs. did not return from "ops" in those seven months, which meant that 217 air-crew members were killed, wounded and/or taken prisoner. (The total operational losses at Elsham were such that between 1941 – when Elsham Wolds opened up as an operational bomber base – and the end of the European war, 1,500 air-crew of 103 and 576 (which was formed after I left) Squadrons were killed in various operational sorties.)

In Bomber Command, as a whole, during the war, there were over 55,000 fatal casualties to which must be added the thousands more airmen who were wounded, mutilated, burnt and mentally shattered. (Counselling was not part of the military agenda in those times! In fact, what was in vogue was the rather indiscriminate tendency to level the charge of "lacking moral fibre" – cowardice, in plain English – at some unfortunate flyers who simply cracked up. "Lost it" if the modern idiom is preferred.)

Only one branch of HM Forces in World War II sustained a proportionately higher casualty rate than RAF Bomber Command, and that was the RN's Submarine Service.

Of the total of 7,373 Avro Lancasters built (and the similarly grim statistics for all the other makes of bomber used by the RAF would add emphasis to the appalling reality of it all) 3,400 were lost on operations – an average of twenty-two a week – and a further 200 were destroyed in crashes when not on operations.

In the course of operations throughout the war, of those who were Bomber Command air-crew at the beginning, eighty per cent became casualties of one kind or another.

In due course I want to turn to the ground crews and their attitudes and expectations; how they saw their role in the culture of 103 Squadron, Elsham Wolds. And we will see then, more potently, how the link-up between air and ground crews formed a crucial ingredient of the whole ethos of the station.

But, for the moment, let us stay with the air-crews and just consider who and what they were.

For the most part they were little more than boys, and those who had received the benefit of a secondary education, not long out of school. Most were not yet old enough to vote (at twenty-one in those days) and many – including some of the pilots – had not even learned to drive a car! Most of the veterans of numerous operations were only just into their twenties. I think, somewhere, someone has written that ... *they came to war as boys and died as men.* Yes, and you would have to mature pretty quickly in that situation!

Without exception, they were volunteers. No one who joined the RAF was conscripted into air-crews.

So, there they were, young men with a tremendous lust for life, overshadowed by the awful knowledge that the threat of death was in constant attendance, blanking out plans for the future.

The young believe that they will live forever, but even the optimism of youth is difficult to sustain in an environment so polluted by carnage. And even that crumb of comfort, the belief that others will be shot out of the skies, but you will survive, became somewhat dubious. There were just too many deaths in the family.

It was true that in many cases – although it carried no gilt-edged guarantee – that a crew's chance of survival increased with the

number of "ops" completed. *Complete five and you stay alive.*
Experience on "ops" did widen the odds. But, after all, even with five
completed, there were still twenty-five to go – on the first tour, that
is.

They were truly remarkable young men – from a wide range of
social backgrounds and from places overseas – and you had to
wonder at their courage and durability.

Today, when I hear people say, "Well, they did it only because
they were ordered to. They wouldn't have done it if they hadn't been
forced to do it... ", I can only reply, "Please don't insult them. You
were not there. You didn't know them. In fact, you simply do not
know."

How could those who diced with death on such numerous
occasions come to terms with it? Or with the dread of horrendous
burns and of being crippled for the rest of your life – which many
feared more than death itself?

How did they cope with those fears? Night after night, with nerve-
ends stretched like piano wire. From whence did they dredge up
such reserves of inner strength?

The story of the bombers in action has, I know, been told many
times but let us remind ourselves of what was involved.

First, there was the discomfort – the ear-shattering noise of the
aircraft itself; the cramped position of the crewmen; the bone-
numbing cold; the terrible eye-strain, not only on alert for night-
fighters but also to avoid collision with other bombers when there
would be hundreds of them in the approach to, and over, the target
(collisions were not uncommon occurrences); the breathing in of
oxygen – as if on a airborne life-support machine; and the problems
of bladder and bowel relief. (How often is that aspect mentioned in
the stories?)

Second, the exacting navigational skills, the disciplines of altitude
position and time-schedule in the approach to the target.

Third, the flak, concentrated and intense, through which the
bomber had to run the deadly gauntlet, on the "bomb run". (Would
you say that thirty seconds is no time at all?) Well, any ex-RAF
bomber crew member will tell you that it was an eternity of nail-
biting time on that – *left, left, right a bit, right a bit more, steady...*
approach to target with bomb doors wide open and with jagged
chunks of hot metal whistling around you.

Fourth, night fighters guided by radar, deadly efficient. Every dark
shape, every shadow, even every friendly aircraft, must be seen as a

potential threat. Eyes straining to penetrate the blackness of the night.

Up ahead; to port; to starboard; above; to the rear. But no bloody eyes when they are most needed – your blind spot is underneath...

and the first thing you will know about a JU88 coming up at you will be a cannon shell exploding somewhere on, or inside, the plane!

Fifth, the journey back home. Another three, four or five hours; icing up; maybe a hole in the side, an engine gone, a crewman wounded (or dead); the possibility of enemy fighters all the way across Europe and over the sea.

In a way, given that the bombers were required – whether they were attacking general or specific targets, or laying mines – to maintain a designated approach course and height through a hail storm of flak before releasing the bombs, the air-crews could be compared to the infantry in the bloody battlefields of World War I when they were ordered to walk towards the murderous machine-gun fire from the enemy trenches.

There has to be something special about men who can take on all of that, night after night – doesn't there?

Well, we who served them thought so; and we do still.

Individually, the air-crew members handled those demands – and themselves – according to their own characters and personalities; and as individuals they ranged from the "Errol Flynns" (there were very few of these, as I recall!), the "Richard Todds" (yes, they were very much a part of it) and the just "ordinary" blokes, of whom there were many. Ordinary, yet extraordinary!

Roistering and irreverence were all part of the psychological protective armour worn against emotional turmoil when so much had to be suppressed – anxiety, fear, the pressure of responsibility and grief at the loss of friends and comrades.

As always, the Bard of Avon had words for it:

...Give sorrow words; the grief that does not speak
Whispers the o'er-fraught heart, and bids it break.

But, sorrow, bidden with such frequency, cannot find the words. Not, anyway, the words of convention that would have to be uttered so many times. (And think of the COs and Adjutants who had to write those many letters of condolence to wives and to parents.)

So instead, the outlets for both strain and grief were expressed in that irreverence, that defiance, and in euphemisms.

Euphemisms seemed, somehow, to deflect the tension and the horror.

Comrades who had been shot down had "bought it!". Or, "Had it!" Or, "Gone for a Burton!"

Going over to the relentlessly fearsome skies above the Rhur was described as, "Another jaunt into happy valley!"

Even the most horrendous crash was, simply, a "prang". (Old Smithy pranged his kite. Made a mess of his pancake (landing). Looks like a write-off job. Smithy and his flight engineer are in dock. Poor show!")

Triumph and disaster were, indeed, treated as imposters just the same. Or, at least, accorded similar understatement. "Bad show"; "good show"; "bit of a dodgy show". It was all part of the cultural norm to understate, to play down, everything.

I recall a pilot, flight sergeant, surveying his badly damaged "kite", the morning after a trip to Essen.

"You know," he said, the bloody Jerries are getting increasingly inhospitable!"

His mid-upper gunner, standing near-by, commented, "Getting friggin dodgy by the bloody minute if you ask me!" (Their wireless operator had been badly wounded.)

It would be wrong to assume that such laconically dismissive remarks were confined to the "Flying Officer Kite types".

In fact, I do not recall coming across any air-crew member of that stereotype in the whole seven months I spent at Elsham.

Nor did one hear the "gung ho", "death or glory" language so beloved in so much of war fiction. It seemed not to be part of the lexicon of Bomber Command.

The air-crews had no need for flamboyant orations. The exhortation to "be ready to lay down your life for King and Country" would, in the circumstances, have been somewhat inappropriate. An occasional pat on the back, a few apposite words of encouragement, would not, on the other hand, have gone amiss.

It would be ridiculous to suggest that the air-crews of Bomber Command were impervious to any attempt to boost their morale. Of course they needed that. But the degree of acceptance would have been in direct ratio to content and to the presenter.

Whilst the stirring words of Will Shakespeare's *Henry V,* rich-voiced by an Olivier or a Burton, sends shivers up and down the spine in the theatre, I doubt if it (or its like) would have cut much ice at the average pre-ops briefing on a bomber station, during World War II.

Now set the teeth and stretch the nostrils wide.

"And suck up that oxygen Jock!"

37

Hold hard the break and bend up every spirit.
"You can say that again boyo!"
To his full height. On, on you noble English.
"Noble? You don't feel very friggin noble with a JU88 up your arse!"
Noble English!
How about the Scots, Welsh, Canadians, Aussies, etc. etc. then? What are we, ignoble?"

The kind of advice that would have been more appropriate – and better appreciated – would probably have been something on the lines of...
You are going to Berlin where the flak is thick.
So unload your bombs and get out quick!

It would have been their immediate commanders and senior officers whose words would have counted most. For those men would have been there – and still were, in some cases – and who would know the score. Men who would know the grim nature of the job; who had learned evasive tactics and techniques of execution coupled with a capacity for survival. They led by example.

Looking back to those times, I cannot help but wonder at the rationality of the air-crews. From conversations with the flyers – out on the Flights; on casual encounters; sometimes in the pubs or cafés – I realise now, I didn't so much then – how "everyday" and conventional the exchanges were.

Apart from the subject of an aircraft and its performance (and "snags") the conversation ranged over the weather, the camp, food, pubs, sex, places of origin, sport – everything in fact – except "ops", references to which tended to be rare.

Whether or not that is surprising is a matter of conjecture. After all, sometimes people handle their pressures by talking about nothing else.

That the air-crews did reveal and discuss their anxieties and fears – and speculate on their chances of survival – amongst themselves, is apparent from the reading of so many books in which their stories are told. Just, also, as they compared notes on aircraft performances, various aspects of the jobs they had to do and the technical factors involved. But even from the reading of those books, one has to be struck by the ordinariness of so much of their verbal exchanges. Perhaps by holding to mundane, everyday topics, the air-crews retained their sanity and their grasp on normal life.

I did not, of course, ever attend a pre-ops briefing but from what I have gleaned, at the time and since at the Elsham reunions, (and have also read), these gatherings were more likely to have been circumspect, prosaic and pragmatic rather than dramatic.

It was the way it had to be.

~ ~ ~

And what of the ground crews?

One thing above all drove those who served on the ground. It defined their sense of duty, and marginalised all of the other demands made upon them.

It was the giving of maximum effort in support of the air-crews.

Aware as we were with such constant reminders of those daunting casualty rates among our air-crews, and the awful dangers into which they flew, how could we have given anything less?

The least we could do for our air-crews – and by God were we proprietorial about them! – was to widen the odds for their survival by providing them with aeroplanes that performed efficiently and reliably.

That was our *raison d'être* in the war-time *milieu* in which we found ourselves.

NEVER LET THE AIR-CREWS DOWN, should have been a maxim written in tablets of stone; and if not in stone, then that rule was certainly etched into the minds of those of us who serviced the "kites" and revered the men who flew in them.

But the spirit, that dedication – and if that is a superlative I make no apology for using it – went right down the line among the ground staff, from the engine fitters through the petrol bowser drivers, the WAAF drivers, parachute packers, R/T operators, etc. to the general duties "bods" and right along to the officers' batmen.

In any work situation you will find people less committed than others, and you cannot always legislate for the "skivers". But at Elsham, I recall very few of the Squadron's personnel who came in that category and who would give anything less than their best effort to provide the back-up that the flyers so richly deserved.

Those of us who actually serviced the aircraft did, of course, spearhead that support for, apart from actually working on the Lancs., we saw them off on "ops" and, according to duty roster, were there to receive them on their return – whatever kind of mess they, and their crews, were in.

We did not see the results of their raids over there. Nor were we aware whether or not they were effectively contributing to a successful conclusion to the war. But we most certainly hoped that they were if those grim casualty rates were to be justified.

It was that concern to do a good job for our crews, that dependency factor, that had a great bearing on our attitude towards discipline. It shaped our disposition towards that and to so much else as well.

Our discipline was imposed, not so much by the rules and regulations and the demands of a militarily-orientated hierarchy, but rather by our sense of responsibility. And we resented anything – in the shape of "bull" – that impinged upon that singular commitment or interfered with it.

Of course, we needed to be reminded from time to time, that we were a military establishment, and we were willing to accept that. But, not unlike the air-crews, we were hostile to "spit-and-polish-type bull" for its own sake.

However, let us be fair about this. The truth is that those in command were not, in the main, at variance with the emphasis of the ground crews. For they, too, required (and demanded) that nothing less than a maximum number of aircraft should be available for action. And there was, therefore, a mutuality of priority between the hierarchy and the rank and file of the Squadron.

Indeed, as I will demonstrate in a further chapter, the top brass did not countenance unnecessary intrusions into the "working life" of the aerodrome. Hence, also, the blind eyes that were turned to the sartorial inelegance of the "erks" at work; and the partial tolerance of the less than pristine appearance of places of accommodation.

If the ground crew lads "honked" or kicked over the traces on occasions; or, like the air-crews did a bit of roistering off camp; or were overtly irreverent where military symbols and protocol were concerned, it was not because we were "bolshie" *per se* – although there was some of that in our attitude to authority; (and rightly, and healthily so.) It was much more to do with our lack of inclination to reconcile the imposition of normal military procedures – which some of those of higher rank preferred – and handle the pressures that emanated from the job we had to do.

It would be an entirely erroneous impression, in view of what is written here, to conclude that the ground crews on the station were – no more than the air-crews – an "undisciplined rabble". Such an extreme departure from expected behaviour within a military context would never have been tolerated. Nor could the Squadron have operated so efficiently had it been so. It was all a matter of checks and balances; and an understanding, a tolerance, that by mutual consent, enabled the prioritised job to be done.

So, yes, we had our pressures too, not least of which was the responsibility of servicing these big, heavy bombers. It required close scrutiny; attention to detail; checks and double checks; dexterity and, in certain situations, strength. It involved the exercise of patience and the handling of frustrations.

There was a lot of work on aeroplanes carried out in an atmosphere of tension as a race against time – approaching operation take-off time – intensified. And so much of it was happening in all kinds of adverse conditions. But, there was something else in there too.

How would anyone suppose we felt when a "kite", on which we lavished great care and attention, and its crew with whom we had formed such a close rapport and for whom we had such genuine respect, failed to return from "ops"? Had "gone for a Burton"?

Make no mistake, those losses were felt very badly; but the ground crews were no less inclined to "stiffen the upper lip"; to set up their defence mechanisms.

So, in place of tears there was swearing and a façade of, not indifference, but of imperviousness. It seemed to be a part of the folk-lore of a bomber station to eschew any form of sentimentality; a tendency to scoff at any hint of it and to mock.

Off duty, any talk about work, with the exception of requests for guidance (or a "bind" about some kind of frustration) or reference to a lost "kite" and crew, was usually discouraged with the exhortation, "For Christ's sake, close the bloody hangar doors!"

Everyone on the station indulged in the game of "mistranslation", which, it would seem, was another aspect of the tendency to turn seriousness into flippancy. The symbol (logo nowadays) of 103 Squadron was the Black Swan, but to us it was the "Mucky Duck"; and whilst few, if any, of us – and I suspect, including the air-crews – were fluent in Latin, we did indulge ourselves in cod-Latin. So, for example, the RAF motto, *Per ardua ad astra* translated as "Through bullshit to the stars!". The Squadron motto, *Noli me tangmere* (Touch me not), I seem to remember being expressed as, colourfully, an invitation for someone to vacate one's space. And we all knew that *nil desperandum* meant "Don't let the buggers grind you down."

Some of the emotional reticence we displayed, the disdain for sentimentality, was attributable to traditional plebian male machismo with its admiration for toughness and its contempt for "softness". Perhaps the conditions and the nature of the daily life (and death) on the bomber station simply reinforced that "hard" *persona* that the "erks" brought with them into the situation.

Certainly it helped to deflect the emotional reactions to events which they were so loath to display.

But, when you knew these lads, as I did, when you worked, played and lived among them, then you were aware of the rich vein of caring and kindness that lay beneath the surface of their, apparent, sceptical and irreverent behaviour. You would be aware, too, of their generosity, of spirit as well as materially; of their awareness of responsibility and sense of loss; yes, and of pride in their skills, in being a part of the team, and their contribution to winning the war!

They would have scoffed at words like pride and team spirit, considering them to be affected. They preferred phrases such as "Getting stuck in" or "Mucking in" and "Helping out your 'oppos'".

Above all, though, what I recall as the quality – and I use the word deliberately – that sustained us all was that lovely, reassuring, morale-boosting sense of humour, brought into our huts, out on the Flights, on nights out – wherever and whenever – by natural comedians and given extra sharpness by a dozen regional accents. A sense of humour that was not only sustaining but also the cement of our comradeship and camaraderie; the thread that knitted up our sense of belonging.

That extraordinary entertainer of modern times, Billy Conolly, takes hold of so many of the things in life that give us anxiety or embarrass us, or distort our dignity and, in his coarse way, makes us confront those "troubles" and laugh our heads off at them. Makes us laugh today at those things we might have been in tears about yesterday.

And that is precisely what our "Billy Conollys" achieved for us, fifty-plus years ago at Elsham Wolds.

As one of my "oppos" up there, "Bud" Senior used to say in his lovely Lancashire accent:

If ya don't laff lad, you'll cry. When ya lose tha virginity, enjoy it. But if ya lose yer sense of humour, you've lost everythin'.

And when we were all having a good old collective "bind" about some irritations, when the grumbling reached its peak of discontent, "Bud" would say,

Ee up lads. It's bein' so cheerful as keeps us goin'!

Mood switch then ensured.

Thus I recall something of that ethos, that culture of RAF Elsham Wolds. For it was not a village simply in the sense of its structure or of its in-built, self-providing services. It was, too, a community and a way of life with a mixture of formal and informal rules – or ways of doing things – that somehow worked.

It was a community in which most of the "residents" knew each other, if not by name, then certainly by recognition. And like a village it had its fair share of gossip, rumour, squabbles and antagonisms.

It was a military establishment in which distinctions of rank were often blurred and variations on the norm of protocol sat across traditional lines.

Although, today, when I attend the Reunions I find the veterans more ready to display their emotions and sentimentality, they do so still, somewhat self-consciously and in a self-effacing manner.

We all, though, share the same fond nostalgia of our time spent on that bleak and so often cold airfield.

It is difficult – at least I find it so – to put one's finger on exactly why we old men and women remember our time at Elsham with a kind of affection. Whether or not the contents of this chapter will enlighten the reader on that question, I have to leave open.

I know only that, although there were other memorable experiences during my six years' service in the RAF, and I shared them with equally estimable comrades, I never, ever, felt the same degree of self-esteem, of belonging, of affinity with the air-crews as I did at Elsham. Possibly, the ensuing chapters will demonstrate the reasons why I make that statement. We shall see.

~   ~   ~

Footnote: I am well aware of the retrospective judgments that have been made about the strategic bombing campaign against Germany; and, later on in this book, I do express an opinion on that controversy.

However, I do feel that I should say at this juncture that, whatever the "rights" and "wrongs" might be on the subject of that bombing campaign, nothing can diminish the extraordinary courage of those young airmen who flew the missions. I think the casualty rates in RAF Bomber Command, to which I have referred, demonstrate that fact. Nor should any retrospective debate demean the dedicated service that the RAF ground crews gave to the men who deserved nothing less.

7. ME AND 'DONALD DUCK'

I have written in the previous chapter about the proprietorial attitude we "erks" took towards our "kites" and their crews. And I use the possessive pronoun "our", because that is *precisely* how we felt about them.

It is highly probable that the engine and airframe "bods" were more possessive about their charges than anyone else because they were, in the main, "one-kite" men, responsible for a single aircraft, whereas those of us of other trades had to divide our care and attention between two or more. Nevertheless, we, too, could entertain a strong sense of "ownership"; and the Lanc. that became rather special to me was ED 417 PM (103 Squadron identification letter) "D" Donald, or sometimes "D" Duck; or, even, "D" Donald Duck.

That close affinity arose from a friendship I struck up with "D"s' Flight Engineer, Sergeant Pat Brechney, a quietly spoken Scot from Broxborn, West Lothian.

Pat and I hit it off immediately when, one morning, he came aboard "D" as I was fitting a replacement instrument into "her" flight- deck panel and we conversed about instrument performance and degrees of reliability.

We established a mutual regard for each other and then, through Pat, I came to know, also, the other crew members. Obviously, we were already acquainted on a recognition, nodding, "passing the time of day", basis. But after Pat's introductions, I began to feel a close affinity with the whole crew – and, indeed, with the aircraft also. There were longer chats at the dispersal bay, chance meetings on the camp; and an easy exchange of greetings and conversation.

I also had several air trips with "D", of various kinds, and on each occasion I was welcomed aboard and never, at any time, felt in the way.

The crew of "D" were:

- "Skipper" Carey, pilot, an easy-going Canadian. Easy-going but very serious about the job he had to do.

- Navigator – Sergeant Dick Rolands.

- Bomb-aimer – the affable "Rich" Talbot.

- Wireless Op/Air Gunner – Sergeant "Tiny" Lewin, a guy larger than life in every sense of the term.

- Dorsal (mid-upper) Gunner – Sergeant Burch, known to one and all as "JS".

- Rear Gunner – the "tail-end Charlie" – also a native of North America, but in his case from the USA – Sergeant "Yank" Montgomery.

- And, of course, there was Pat Brechney, Flight Engineer.

"Yank" Montgomery, as I understood it, had joined the RAF before the USA came into the war, and had then opted to stay with the "Brylcreem Boys", even after his country entered the fray. Whether that was because he preferred to fly over Germany at night, rather than in daytime, or had developed an affection for the RAF, I am not prepared to say. But, for whatever reason, there he was; and he was most conscientious about his role as a gunner, and meticulous about his guns. He had a kind of Clark Gable look about him but he was not at all like the "Yank" of popular imagery.

It was "Yank's" thumbs-up sign that was the last contact I had with "D"s' crew when I was present to see them off on "ops". It was a kind of ritual as "Duck", released from her chocks, edged out from the dispersal bay and headed out towards the runway.

I should hasten to say, here, that the special rapport I had with "D" and her crew did not mean that there was an absence of care and conscientiousness towards any other Lanc. to which I was assigned. That would have been unthinkable. It was just that there was something extra as far as "old Duck" was concerned – and my high regard for that crew was to be reinforced and enhanced by a later incident, when I found myself on a charge; and about which I will write in another chapter.

For various reasons, it was not always possible to be at the dispersal to see "D" off on "ops", or to be there when the "kites" returned. But, there or not, I always wished her well; and she was the first "kite" I enquired about, on a morning after "ops" had been on the night before.

"Duck" was still operating at the time I left Elsham to go overseas. And I was to learn – although not until more recent years – that she and the crew did complete that first tour, just a few weeks after I departed. Pleasing news indeed.

Unfortunately, however, I have, at the time of writing this book, been unable to ascertain what happened to that "magnificent seven" of mine, after they completed that tour. All, that is, except for Pat Brechney.[4]

Pat survived the war but, most regrettably, died back home in Broxborn some time after – and before I started to make enquiries. How annoying one's own procrastination can be.

Unfortunately, also, I was informed that there were no living relatives. It would have been so nice to have contacted someone just to say, "I knew your Pat. What a lovely man he was. And a quietly brave one, too." Yes. I would like to have done that.

So, it would seem, the crew of "D" Duck are now lost to me. But, I do, however, retain a tangible item of memorabilia appertaining to them.

During the period about which I have been writing, a notice went up on a board in one of the Squadron's offices, stating that prints of an oil painting by the artist John Salisbury, entitled "The Briefing", were available for sale. As the title suggests, the painting depicts a briefing of air-crew prior to an operation. It tended to be rather idealistic but it was nevertheless symbolic.

Anyway, I purchased one of the prints and then took it out onto 'A' Flight where I managed to obtain on the base of it, the signatures of "D" Duck's crew; and of several of the "erks" who were around at the time.

The picture – but more particularly the signatures on it – thereafter became a prized possession. And some kind of talisman, for, when I was posted overseas, I rolled it up and put it in my kit-bag. Wherever I went, it would go too!

Then a few weeks later, much to my dismay, and disgust, I very nearly lost it in North Africa when, one night, some exceedingly stealthy – and one must say, competent – Arabs crept undetected into our camp and stole a number of items of equipment, "RAF for the use of"; and then slid away as silently as they had come. Among

---

[4] Apart from Flight Engineer Pat Brechney, I have, at the time of publication of this book, been unable to ascertain what happened to the rest of 'D' Duck's crew, with the exception of 'Skipper' Carey. I have recently discovered that Flight Lieutenant Douglas Minto Carey, later flying with 12 Squadron was shot down and killed on the Nurembourg raid on March 31st 1944. He was 22 years old and lies in a War @raves Cemetery in Hanover.

the purloined articles was my kit-bag – containing my two cherished mementos of my sojourn at Elsham Wolds – the picture (and those signatures from my comrades) plus that "aircraft servicing memo list" to which I referred earlier.

To quote the ex-England football team manager, Graham Taylor, "Was I not pleased!" No, *I was not*; and we went out with an armed search party, intent upon reclaiming our lost property.

None of the *equipment* was recovered, only some empty kit-bags including mine, *and* – I could hardly believe it – my painting, which, having been discarded by its thief, who obviously had a somewhat different taste in art, was plaintively clinging to a grape vine!

Never mind the bloody equipment – I had got my signed picture back! But not, regrettably the servicing memo list.

"The Briefing" stayed with me after that and, eventually, came home with me from Italy; and by then, in a rather crumpled state. But then, in the settling-back process after demob, the picture went into a cupboard and was – sad to tell – largely forgotten.

Forgotten that is until I discovered the Elsham Wold Association and then I was moved, in 1994, to have "The Briefing" restored and framed. I then presented it to the Elsham Association.

In a sense, "The Briefing" has "gone back home" – after its travels and adventures – because "Halltop" sits up on another of Lincolnshire's rare hills, and what *was* our old aerodrome lies within the panoramic view from up there.

I am glad the picture is there. So pleased that those, now fading, signatures will mark the presence of those friends of mine, some fifty-plus years ago. And thanks to the photographic skills of my cousin, Roy Poulter, a veteran of the Normandy Landings, I can, still, savour the significance of the painting in my home, for Roy produced a near full-sized copy for me.

It is not, now, easy to fit faces to names. Some countenances remain quite clear in my mind but others have diminished. It is, after all, a long, long time ago.

~ ~ ~

"D" Donald Duck, unlike her crew, was not rested after the completion of her thirty missions. She carried on, going into action with another crew.

Sadly she did not survive the war. She "died with her boots on" when returning from a raid on Berlin.

In the early hours of the morning of 27 November 1943 – four months after I had left Elsham – Duck collided with a Halifax over

Middleton St George aerodrome, near Durham. She and all of her crew were killed.

I am so glad that I was not at Elsham when that happened.

> *She ran out of luck*
> *Poor old "D" Duck,*
> *Having just been to Berlin.*
> *She made it back home*
> *On the way to the 'drome*
> *But the way that she died was a sin.*

8. THE JOB OF THE GROUND CREWS

The daily scene, both in the hangar and out on the Flights, was one of RAF "worker ants" scrambling all over and inside the Lancasters, each mechanic with his own responsibility and assigned task. This chapter is devoted to a description of that scenario as I relate to the reader an account of a "typical" day on an RAF bomber station in World War II.

"Typical" is, of course, a relative term in this context for, as I have written earlier, unpredictability was the hallmark of the course of events on any day. "Ops" could be scheduled and then scrubbed – even at the last moment. Stand-downs could be ordered in the midst of intense activity. Weather forecasting was not quite the more exact science it is today and, in any case, northern European weather has always been renowned for its capricious nature. Incidents and mishaps on the drome could disrupt the numerous routines that were being pursued in the various areas of activity. No two days were ever quite the same, but whatever the extraneous circumstances might be, there were basic, essential procedures and my evocation of a "working day" is engendered by that essence of "normality". The picture I present will be as seen through my eyes as an instrument "basher", going through the routines and procedures of my particular "trade"; but the general activity of the airfield, and its ambience, are embraced also.

After some reflection I have thought it advisable not to insert into this chapter an indulgence with technical detail. It is not because I no longer carry such minutiae in my memory – which is true – for, after all, I could easily find appropriate manuals to provide the relevant information; but my decision is based much more on my belief that technological preciseness would be an unnecessary intrusion into the "atmospheric" nature of the narrative. Whilst I know that the option I have taken will disappoint some readers who have a predilection for aeronautical engineering, it will, I feel certain, come as a relief to others who find it irritating when reading, to have their "flow" disrupted by unfamiliar language or by esoteric technical jargon.

And I feel sure that there will be sufficient material in the ensuing description of the "job" for the readers to "get the picture".

Although we instrument "bashers" of the "D.I. Brigade" were assigned to the regular inspection and maintenance of two Lancasters each, we were required, also, to accept a degree of flexibility. Much depended on prevailing circumstances and contingencies. If, for instance, a colleague was absent because of incapacity, or being on leave – or for whatever reason – each of us would be expected to cover for our absent "oppo". And, similarly, should a major "snag" arise on any of the aircraft that necessitated extra hands, then our presence would be required to help sort it out. It was called "mucking in".

On the days when "ops" were scheduled, all ground crews worked under some pressure, and the intensity of that pressure would vary according to the nature of the technical problems that had to be resolved. And the skills, patience and tenacity of the aircraft mechanics were often severely put to the test. Sometimes, too, frustration would cause patience to snap – especially if a mechanic was being badgered by someone of senior rank; and I recall angry utterances issuing from the mouths of "erks", when being so pressurised, that bordered dangerously on insubordination. But invariably such outbursts were let to pass because the readiness of aircraft was a priority that superseded military protocol. For an aircraft scheduled to go on "ops" and then to be withdrawn because of some technical fault was regarded as something akin to breaking the Ten Commandments!

I think it is true to say that as far as my own "trade" was concerned, the part of the aircraft equipment for which we were responsible, most likely to create last-minute problems, was the *oxygen supply*. It was vital that the source of oxygen sustenance should function with the utmost efficiency; and I will give emphasis to that as this chapter proceeds.

So many things could go wrong with the aircraft and with its component parts. A pilot was once heard to say something on the lines that, since the Lancaster was assembled from 50,000 separate parts, that meant that 50,000 things could go wrong with it – which of course was true! And even though there is no question that the Avro Lancaster was a fine piece of aeronautical engineering, built by the best of craftsmen (and serviced by dedicated mechanics) even it could not remain impervious to the harsh treatment dished out to it when going out on those bombing missions. Being up at high altitudes; buffeted about in the most adverse weather; hit by shrapnel and being pulled and thrown into all kinds of evasive contortions – it is hardly surprising that the aeroplane was "all shook up" and in need of care and attention! And what we "erks" were there to do was to give our "kites" that necessary care and attention; and to restore them to "fighting fitness" in order that they could go up and do it all over again.

~ ~ ~

At this point, I think it might be appropriate to say something about "Chiefy" Clacker, mentioned in passing in a previous chapter.

Flight Sergeant Robert Clacker was the formidable, omnipresent "Chiefy" of all the "erks" who serviced the "kites" on 'A' Flight. He strode the dispersal bays, a sharply vigilant overseer, seeing much and missing little. "Clickerty" Clacker, as he was – out of his hearing – sometimes referred to, was not just an omnipresent figure but was – in the matter of aircraft maintenance – also omniscient. He had probably forgotten more about aeroplanes than most of us "erks" would ever know, whatever our "trade" happened to be.

He had joined the RAF in 1933 as a "Brat" (apprentice) when he was about fourteen years of age. Posted to 103 Squadron in 1936, he was to serve with the squadron – including during its period in France in 1940 – until the end of the war.

The lads used to say of him that "… He's been in the 'RAFF' since Pontius was a pilot!" And, of course, to most of us who were so young, I guess he must have looked like a man of "advancing years" although he could have been only in his mid-twenties! But he did have that "mature" bearing. "Chiefy" would prowl around the dispersal in 'A' Flight, checking on progress of the work in hand, and keeping an eye out for hazards to which he was very alert. He was acutely aware of arguments that might get out of hand and discouraging of any horse-play that happened to start up among the energetic "erks" – regarding that, also, as dangerous in the vicinity of aircraft. (Dangerous to us or to the aircraft, I am not sure; but probably to both!) "Chiefy" could exhort everyone to greater effort in no uncertain terms, but he could be equally encouraging. "Keep at it lad. It will come; it will come!"

There was a good "team" of all the trades on 'A' Flight, and "Chiefy" Clacker knew that, and appreciated it. He was liked by some and not by others – a position not unknown in any work situation – but I guess he did have the respect of most of us.

After the war he went into the civil aviation business and in 1969, in partnership with two friends, he founded Monarch Air Lines, starting with just two planes. Bob Clacker was Engineering Director of the company, a position for which he was eminently qualified. He attended the 103 reunions at Elsham but, sadly, he recently died, breaking another link in the chain of old comradeship.

~ ~ ~

"Keeping at it!" was what we did at Elsham. There was no alternative; and procrastination was not permitted to be a thief of time. "Tomorrow" simply would not do – not when "ops" were scheduled. Servicing aircraft instruments was an exacting responsibility. No more, of course, than any of the other "trades", but all the component parts of an aeroplane that gave indications to the pilot and his crew as to its performance were within the instrument "basher's" domain: height, speed, direction, position of the aircraft in relation to the horizon, engine temperature, fuel and oil content and various others.

In a sense we were responsible for the "white sticks" that guided the air-crews through the blackness of the night. And, in addition we provided and serviced that vital oxygen supply, the automatic pilot, and the bomb-sights.

It was not a responsibility to be treated in a cavalier manner, and it was not. It did, in fact, concentrate the mind in no uncertain manner.

~ ~ ~

A Day in the Life Of ... "Openers"

It begins in the early morning, still dark outside in the winter months. We rise from our slumbers in our "tin-roofed" *des res* and sit up growling in disbelief at the brevity of the night.

It is not a time for pleasantries; any hint of *bonhomie* at dawn's early light is discouraged by oaths and footwear projectiles.

In our "neck of the woods" there has been no bugle call, nor any form of broadcast *reveille* to rouse us. Apart from the occasion of CO's Parade and the fortnightly pay-parade, our first assembly will be in the Instrument Section, where we are expected to report in on time. And this is another feature of the prevailing ethos at RAF Elsham Wolds – the reliance on a sense of duty, rather than a call to duty. (One of the lads in our hut did, once, have the temerity to bring back off leave a very offensive weapon – an alarm clock. It was not a popular addition to the accoutrements and, soon, mysteriously disappeared. On the other hand, when another of our residents established a wireless set in the hut, we offered no resistance. And that became our favoured introduction to the new dawn, when switched on by any one of our number who could be relied upon to wake before the majority.)

We are stirring from our slumbers to that aromatic cocktail of coke-fumes, damp concrete, condensation, stale tobacco and even staler blankets. There is "light" music from the Light Programme of the BBC crackling through the speaker of our wireless set. It always crackles!

Some of the lads sit on their "pits" (beds) in their RAF-issue underwear and light up a "fag" to cough-start the day.

The night duty lads are returning and we learn that two Lancs "bought it" on "ops" last night, one from 'B' and the other from 'C' Flight. It means that a couple of our "oppos" will have lost a "kite" and a crew each. But there is little comment except, "Christ! Not them!" There is always the hope that the missing aircraft may have force-landed elsewhere; and we have all grasped at that particular straw. I am relieved to learn that "my two", "D" and "E" are back.

Most of us are unable to postpone bladder relief until we get up to the ablution block and we run out into the undergrowth. All around us stand skeletal trees and bushes, shrouded in grey mist.

We pick up our bikes, wipe the cloying dampness off the saddles and ride up the rutted track towards the centre of the camp.

We are attired, variously, in "working blue" (uniform), jumpers (not all of service-issue!), overalls, leather jerkins, or greatcoats. On our feet are either Raff boots or "wellies" with long white fishermen's socks pulled over the tops. We do not exemplify the Ux-bridge/Cardington image of ultra-smart airmen, but rather resemble a group of Tito's partisans!.

It is misty now but we know that this condition will not last; and that that Siberian bloody wind will soon howl in off the North Sea, blowing the low cloud away. It will be "brass monkeys" out there on the Flights; and those winds constantly remind me of what the "old boys" in my home town used to say. "Tha's a lazy owd wind boi. That'll goo roight thru' ya, instead 'of round ya!"

The ablution block is not a place to linger and from there we move on in mumbling semi-silence to the cookhouse. (As we "erks" are, in the main, proletarian, we prefer the term *cookhouse*; and we consider the official nomenclature, "Other Ranks' Mess", as rather affected; and an identification of lower order status!)

Breakfast is consumed with automaton disregard for content and with indigestion-inducing speed. "Chiefy" Willmott does prefer us to report at the Section on time. On the way to the hangar we pass a group of Waafs of our acquaintance going about their various duties and there is an exchange of banter in which they give as good as they receive. And so we gather in the Instrument Section.

Most of us are there, apart from those who were on night duty, or on leave – or "skiving with a sick chitty!" "Chiefy" checks us in ... Frank Wain, Dougie "Pop" Tyler, Wally "Bud" Senior, Don Boost, Harry the Geordie, Bas Lowe, who has joined us more recently, Harry Batty, George Turner, "Kenny" Kennington, Freddy Lloyd. My early mentor, Ron Grantham, is there, of course. And so too is "Organ Stops" – a lad so-called because of his wide, staring eyes, giving the impression of permanent surprise. (His actual name is now lost to me.)

We are now awake and more exuberant, exchanging banter and listening to stories – "stretchers" as Huck Finn called such tales – about the previous night's jaunts and conquests. There are a couple of new mucky jokes too, to be guffawed at. "Chiefy" Willmott brings us to order and he and Corporals Simpson and Clifford brief us as to our allocation of duties for the day. We learn about damage sustained on last night's "op'' and repairs and replacements that are down to us to carry out. One of my two charges, "E" Edward, requires a new altimeter; and I discover also that in addition to "D" and "E" I have a third Lanc., "F" Freddie, to cover for a D.I. But hopefully, "Bud" Senior should be able to help out on that one.

It is not known, yet, if "ops" are "on" again this night but we have to proceed on the assumption that they will be. (Or scheduled only to be subsequently "scrubbed".) We are told that the two missing "kites" are confirmed as lost; but again it evokes little response.

We check our tools, draw instrument replacements from stores, collect our required number of portable oxygen bottles and check that they are at full reading on the dials; if not, they must be topped up from a cylinder. (The purpose and function of the portable oxygen bottle? In their various positions inside the Lanc. the aircrew members are plugged in – via their face-mask – to the main cylinder's oxygen supply. But if, for whatever reason, a crewman needs to move around the aircraft, he "puts on" the portable bottle, held by a strap around his neck. Each bottle has a nine and a half minute supply of oxygen, so it can be immediately seen why we gave such close attention to the whole business of oxygen supply.)

The portable bottles, at least a dozen, are wrapped around the handlebars of our bikes and, carrying also our tools and replacements, we mount up and ride out onto the "range" where our allotted aeroplanes await us and sure enough, with the first real light of day, the icy-tipped wind is sweeping across the "prairie", driving the mist away. And, apart from the cold blast of it, it makes hard work of pedalling the heavy bikes – and the load we carry – into the teeth of it.

I ride out with Frank Wain and "Bud" Senior, but, in effect, each of us is now on his own as we approach the Lancaster bombers that earlier had stood spectrally in that early morning mist.

There they stand – "O" Orange, "P" Percy, "Q" Queenie and all the others – all, that is, except the two that have gone and will not be seen again. And, in the empty dispersal bays where they once stood, their ground crews are aimlessly gathered in a huddle of forlorn hope. It is not an uncommon scene in the morning, on an RAF bomber station in 1943.

On all the "kites" that are in place, some of the "worker ants" are already busy; and the sounds of toil have begun to resound around the vast and wide-open airfield. The sudden clang of metal on metal disturbs a flock of starlings, their wings crackling like the sound of bursting shrapnel as they rise *en masse*.

Frank and "Bud" peel off to go to their respective charges and I head for "E" Edward. I go to her first because I have to fit in the new altimeter. (Even though the aircraft were, in the main, identified with male names – "D" Donald, "E" Edward, "C" Charlie, "T" Tommy etc. etc. each of them was, as with ships, referred to as "she" or "her".)

Now then, to begin the day's work, the length of which is unspecified and can finish some time in the afternoon, or may not terminate until take-off time. And, in my case, I will usually be there for that if I can – assuming "ops" will be on again this night.

As I dismount and lean my bike against the sand-bagged wall of "E's" dispersal bay, and unload the portable oxygen bottles, I am greeted with the customary – and obligatory – insults from "erks" of the other trades who are already there.

"Look out lads. Here come the 'gash (spare) trades' to bugger everything up!"

"How can I make a bigger balls-up than you lot have already made. Now, move aside and let the real tradesman get to work!"

"Oh, 'ark at 'im! We've already done a day's work by the time you instrument 'bashers' get 'ere!"

"In that case mate, shove off and give us a bit of space!"

"Up yours!"

"And a good morning to you too!"

It is a good-natured exchange but the engine and airframe "bods" do consider themselves to be the elite of the aircraft servicing trades. And in a way, I suppose they are: but we never concede that to them.

It is cold inside the Lanc. and even though she has been cleaned out, there is still the lingering odour of a bomber that has been in the night skies over Germany just a few hours before. (It is a smell that can be quite overwhelming in some cases, immediately after landing and vacation by the crew. The reader must use his/her olfactory imagination!)

The Lanc. when standing on the ground forms a fairly steep incline from tail to nose and it is something of a climb up to the cockpit – or flight deck if you so prefer. One has to squeeze past various metal protuberances and it is also an obstacle course, especially climbing over the transverse central hump that is the mid-section of the wing spar. It is my experience as an instrument "basher", that very few aircraft are constructed with any consideration of access facility for maintenance. In fact, as I mentioned earlier, contortionists would possess distinct advantage on the job. Slimness, as opposed to rotundity, is also advantageous!

The paucity of space inside the Lanc. is a constant reminder of the problems faced by the air-crews when they need to exit in a hurry from the aircraft. Apart from the pilot, who sits on his parachute, all the other crew members put their 'chutes in the storage bay along the fuselage. And so, if the order to "bail out" is given, the crewmen have to vacate their position in the aircraft; make their way to the parachute storage; don their 'chutes, and then seek exit from an aeroplane which is rapidly losing height, and, probably, also on fire. And all of that in bulky and cumbersome flying gear. There are miraculous escapes but the stark truth is that in many such situations air-crews do not make it. What the hell must it be like in that terrifyingly desperate situation? Knowing that this is the moment when you will die! God, it doesn't bear thinking about: and I bring my thoughts back to the job in hand – and it does require concentration.

It is now very busy inside and outside the aircraft, and space is even more at a premium:

"Oi! Stop shoving. I'm not in your way you 'Brummy' bastard!"

"You're in every bugger's way. Shift over and let the dog see the rabbit!"

Other exclamations proliferate:

"Sodding nut!"

"Not another friggin oil leak!"

"How the hell are we supposed to get our hands in there!"

"The bloody war will be over by the time we get this 'kite' sorted!"

Whereas earlier it had been cold inside the Lanc., the press of bodies going about their tasks has now pushed up the temperature and there is even a smell of sweat.

Sounds accompany our presence in the aircraft: banging, clanging, drilling and that awful scrunch of metal on metal which sets the teeth on edge. And, if things are running well, there will be some of the "erks" who will "whistle while they work" – including the inevitable one who is tone-deaf and completely out of tune. The popular war-time songs are, naturally, much-favoured: "Blue Birds Over...", "We'll Meet Again", "Quartermaster's Stores", "Roll Out the Barrel". Or, the melodies from the big bands are featured too – the great dance music from Glenn Miller, Artie Shaw, the Dorseys *et al*.

The whistling will reflect the mood of aircraft mechanics at work, for, if there is a "sod of a snag" that is proving defiantly resistant to solution, then, for some reason – psychologists please explain – there will be the shriller renderings of the "mucky songs" so beloved of the military – and of rugby clubs!. And if some person of higher rank has come aboard and expressed some kind of criticism, the whistler – whilst the "critic" is still within earshot – will strike up with "Colonel Bogey" or "Bless 'em All". (Did the Roman Legionnaires express their resentments in such "bolshie" ditties, I wonder?)

~ ~ ~

I decide that, prior to carrying out the D.I. on "E" Edward, I will remove the offending altimeter and fit in its replacement. This is accomplished – not without difficulty in the confined space behind the instrument panel – and now I can begin the inspection routine.

It is a routine which, by this time, is well known to me; but I still refer to my "shopping list", mentally ticking off each step as I proceed. Familiarity cannot be permitted to breed contempt in this business; and neither can a casual attitude be tolerated.

Despite my enhanced confidence, there lingers still the nagging doubt that I might, just, overlook something; or be too easily satisfied with face-value evidence.

On several occasions I have returned to the Section after completing my D.I. only to cycle out to the Flight again just to make sure – and to reassure myself. It is not paranoia but the thought that a part of the aircraft for which any one of us is responsible could, because of undetected, unremedied attention, impair the chance of a crew's safe return from "ops", is a constant reminder of what we are about.

Did I make that reconnection?

Did I check every one of the portable oxygen bottles?

Did I top up the 'George' oil sump?

Better safe than sorry. A most apposite slogan for aircraft mechanics.

~ ~ ~

The D.I. – and other things

As stated earlier, the instrument "basher" is responsible for the checking and day-to-day servicing of a variety of components on the Lancaster. Any serious and obvious malfunctions of any of those pieces of equipment will have been reported by the pilot or the flight engineer after returning from last night's operation. And such faults will have to be remedied, such as, on this occasion, the requirement for an altimeter replacement on "E" Edward. (The existing instrument is "duff" or "u/s" i.e. unserviceable).

But even if nothing untoward has been reported, it cannot be taken for granted that everything is in working order. Some instruments are very sensitive and delicate and spotting early signs of defects now can prevent more serious problems – and save precious time – later. There are numerous instruments on the Lanc. and it takes time to check through them all. Most of the instruments can be properly tested only in flight, or during engine run-ups; or bench-tested in the Instrument Section. But, on the D.I. we can check for needle movement, security of connections and, as far back from behind the instrument panel as possible, to look for those "breaks, kinks and dents" in the tubes wires and capillaries.

Sometimes, though, such damage can have occurred in a "line" further away from the panel, somewhere along the wings and/or up to one of the engines; and this will then incur an arduous and time-consuming trace job, involving the removal of panels. To do that in the hangar with the "kite" stripped down and with, at least, some time to spare is one thing; to do it out on the Flights when the time schedule is already very tight anyway – and not to mention the weather – is never a welcome chore. But, today, at least on "E" I am fortunate and I can proceed with the routine.

Before leaving the actual instruments and moving on to our other allocated accoutrements, there is one check that can be made which has some resemblance to the situation in flight; and this relates to the air-speed indicator. There is a short, metal covered tube that is located usually on the outside body of the aircraft, just below the cockpit or sometimes protrudes from the leading edge of the port wing. This is called the *pitot* tube, through the open end of which air flows, and then passes through a connecting tube to the air speed indicator. And my next job on the D.I. is to ascertain that the *pitot* is not blocked in any way and that air flows freely through and up to the instrument. To do this I have to blow into the *pitot* (yes, I am well aware of the ribald connotations here!) but as the Lanc. stands some twenty feet high, I have to borrow a scaffold trolley from the engine and airframe "wallahs" to achieve it – always to the accompaniment of those jokes!

I need assistance from someone inside the "kite" to check, when I blow, that there is a reading on the dial of the air-speed indicator. (Imagine what fun and joy it was carrying out this "little" test on flying boats in Coastal Command with everything going up and down!)

There are a couple of important points about the *pitot* tube that need to be borne in mind, the first of which concerns its heating element. This is, of course, built into it to prevent it becoming iced up at high altitudes; or, even on the ground when there is a sharp frost. And, in the latter case, it is necessary to switch on the *pitot* heater (in the cockpit) to defrost it before carrying out the "blow-test". Great care is required in all this, as one can burn one's mouth if the heater is inadvertently left on too long – or if one forgets to check. But omission to warm the *pitot* first could result in frost-burnt lips.

The *pitot* tube does have a protective cover but it is not always remembered to put it on when the aircraft returns to the dispersal bay after a flight. However, what would be unforgivable, and potentially calamitous, would be to forget to remove the cover prior to flight. There would be some consternation on board a Lanc. thundering down the runway at 90 mph, fully bomb-laden and with 1,500 gallons of petrol in the tanks, but no reading on the air-speed indicator dial!

If I find a blockage in the *pitot* that cannot be cleared, a replacement will have to be fitted. But if the obstruction proves to be somewhere between the tube and the instrument on the pilot's panel, then again, a major tracing and repair – or capillary replacement job – will be involved. But today, fortune continues to shine upon me.

The wind is now throwing squalls of cold rain across the airfield and the engine and airframe "wallahs" are intent upon their tasks, either on the aircraft or working from the scaffold trolleys pulled up alongside. Engine nacelles are off and heads and arms are thrust down into the entrails of the Rolls-Royce Merlin engines. There is quite a display of overalled bums and the icy wind whips at the mechanics' clothing. A "tilly" (utility truck) driven by a Waaf, pulls in to the dispersal to drop off a couple of technicians from the Photographic Section, coming to set up the cameras for tonight's raid. The Waaf driver is greeted by one of the "erks" from up on the starboard wing.

"Hello, Darkie. Got your 'passion killers' on today?"

"That's secret information, Harry," she shouts back.

"Well," rejoins Harry. "I can't uncover your secret today – me assets are frozen!"

She laughs and drives off.

The engine and airframe mechanics are a tough and weather-hardened breed; and they just "get stuck into" their work whatever the weather happens to be.

We all have our share of frozen fingers and of getting very wet, but the engine and airframe "bods" do the bulk of their work on the outside of the aeroplane. (A physical feature of so many of those lads which I noticed – and still recall – was that they tended to have big, square and capable hands; and finger nails that could double up as screwdrivers!)

I have a choice as to the next step in the D.I. process. I can either check out "George", the automatic pilot system, or give priority to the oxygen supply. And I decide on the latter for two reasons. The first is that a "kite" will never be withdrawn from "ops" because "George" is not functioning; but some failure in the oxygen system, unless it can be corrected, will jeopardise an aircraft's participation.

Secondly, there is a time factor involved here. The earlier a "snag" is discovered with the oxygen supply, the sooner it can be remedied. So oxygen gets the nod, and I begin by once again checking that the replacement portable bottles are reading full, and then place them in their various positions in the aircraft and I gather up the used bottles from last night's "op" for return to the Section.

The main oxygen supply in the plane comes from containers that stand upright under the air-crew's "rest bunk", a bed that is more likely to accommodate a wounded or even dead airman, than to provide a place of respite. I inspect the containers and their valves for leaks and for damage, then run a similar check on the supply lines and connection hoses.

The task of refilling the main oxygen-supply bottles is allocated to whichever instrument "basher" is "duty oxygen wallah". His assignment is to go out to all the "kites" that are scheduled for "ops", driving a tractor behind which are trolleys carrying long oxygen cylinders. And the "wallah" has to "get his finger out" in order to accomplish the "refuelling" process prior to the arrival of the armourers who will be coming to "bomb up".

The connecting valve for receiving the replenishment of life-preserving gas is located in the thirty-three-feet-long bomb bay and therefore it does present something of a problem to connect up when the bomb bay is loaded with bombs – one of which is a 4,000 pound "cookie" blast bomb. And we other "bashers" keep our fingers tightly crossed that there are no last-minute "snags" with the oxygen supply at that end of the line. It is an arm-breaking, "feeling rather than seeing" struggle to get at that oxygen intake point when the 4,000 "cookie" is hanging over your head. And should it fall off – a not unknown occurrence – then it is purely academic as to whether or not it explodes, for you will be imprinted into the concrete anyway!

On this day I complete my oxygen check-up and move on to "George" and its mechanism, ensuring that it operates smoothly and topping up its oil sump as necessary.

Some pilots claim that they never engage "George", preferring to be in control at all times, whilst others say that they do use it for a little respite, at least on the return journey from a raid. But whether or not they employ "old George", it is part of our duty to ensure that "he" is going to be reliable should "he" be needed.

~ ~ ~

A shout goes up. "Char wagon" and the "Sally Army" van draws up nearby. It is time for a break and the vehicle – rather like a hot-dog stand and manned by two ladies – each of whom could be any one of our mums at home – is immediately surrounded by a crowd of grimy, overalled and leather-jerkined "erks", lining up for a "char and a wad" i.e. a mug of tea and a cake, the latter being something akin to a scone but of somewhat harder consistency. (The "wad" was a universal item of culinary fare in HM Forces in World War II and, in spite of the uncomplimentary jokes made about it, it was consumed voraciously and, in its way, it was a morale booster: even though some cynics were of the opinion that if the "wads" were dropped over Germany instead of bombs, they would kill or stun more of the enemy. Or, failing that, would tempt the severely rationed populace of the Third Reich to eat them and then endure indigestion so severe as to cripple war production!)

It is a short break, just time enough to warm one's hands on the mug of hot tea, drink it, put one's teeth at risk with the "wad" and snatch a quick smoke. "Chiefy" Clacker does not allow us to linger and reminds us that there are Lancaster bombers awaiting our services.

I go back into "E" Edward and the next item on my "shopping list" is the D.R.C. (Distance Reading Compass), which is arguably, next to the Gee and Oboe navigational radar systems, the most sophisticated item of aeronautical technology on the aircraft. It is obviously of vital importance and it must be maintained for ultra-reliability. Should there be a serious malfunction with the D.R.C., then it will have been reported by the pilot or navigator, and if this occurs then the unit must be removed and thoroughly investigated. It will also mean that, when restored, the aircraft must be "swung" to re-establish the magnetic readings. The D.R.C. which is suspended adjacent to the rear door, is housed in a drum-like container, inside which are banks of wires, connections and contacts. The compass readings are electronically transmitted to repeaters on the navigator's and the pilot's panels. Thus the name, 'distance reading'; and the reason for that distance is to cancel out interference from the aircraft's engines.

(It was a complex system – well, it was to me – and "Bud" Senior said it reminded him of fishing; with all those wires it looked like a "tin of worms!" And since it was so electronic I often wondered why the D.R.C. was not a part of the electricians' domain. Interestingly, too, the RAF opted for the cautious, "belt and braces" approach for even though the D.R.C. was the acme of instrument sophistication, the aircraft still had on board and in place the old long-tried "bowl" compass.)

In the absence of any reported faults, the D.I. consists of a check for broken or loose connections and a cleaning of contacts; the smallest speck of dirt can cause problems, rather as it can on the points in a motor-vehicle engine. Today all is well, which again is a relief.

The morning is ticking away and we now are *officially* informed that "ops" are on again this night, an "item of news" that merely confirms our own earlier conclusions. There are certain signs – the sealing of public telephone boxes, for example, and a "buzz" (hint) coming out from the bomb and petrol dumps. But, we just know. Call it instinct – or a "feel", born of experience. The petrol bowsers are now out and the chug, chug of their pumps join the myriad sounds of airfield activity. The sharp smell of petrol vapour wafts in the wind and somehow the refuelling process re-emphasises that pulse of war I referred to earlier. The bowsers are pumping in the life-blood of the Lancasters that will sustain them throughout their journey into combat over Germany and, hopefully, back home again. The vapour rises and spreads. For God's sake don't strike a match or cause a spark at this juncture in the proceedings!

The full capacity of petrol in the wing tanks on the Lancaster is 2,154 imperial gallons; and if those tanks are filled up we all know that tonight the target is probably Berlin – or even northern Italy. Two other things we all know. One is that it will be a long haul this night; and the other is, as on all nights of "ops", those petrol tanks will be a prime target for a deadly Germany night- fighter.

Engine tests are commencing and all round the airfield the Merlins are spluttering and then roaring into life. Sign language is now in vogue. There can be as many as thirty engines running up simultaneously, a combined ear-shattering chorus of 1,280 hp motors. The corporal fitter on "E" Edward is running "her" engines and the plane vibrates along its full length – especially when the "corp" pushes the throttles up to the "gate" to full power. The noise and the shaking of the Lanc., straining at its chocks, pounds at your head – and sends a strange thrill up your spine at the same time. I watch the gauges – fuel, oil, temperature – and exchange a smile of relief with another of the engine "bods" when they all respond correctly.

Three small jobs, and the D.I. on "E" is complete: an inspection of the bomb sight for any obvious damage; and replacement of the height scale from last night's raid with one issued for this night. (The height scale enables the bomb-aimer to calculate bombing height and velocity.) Then check that the gun-sight illumination bulbs are in place and working. I now sign the Form 700, leave the aircraft, pick up my bike and move on to "my baby" ("D" Donald Duck), which stands in the next dispersal bay, and I will now repeat the D.I. process on her. It is raining hard.

They have already carried out the engine run on "Duck" but that is not a problem because I will be promptly informed if any of the gauges are "duff". I find one or two minor faults to be sorted out, such as a loose oxygen valve, but thankfully both "D" and "E" have been kind to me today. I sign my second Form 700. (It is, of course, not always as straightforward as this; and it is all so unpredictable. By the very nature of the strains the Lancs are subjected to, serious "snags" can crop up for any one of us, whatever our "trade" – engines, airframes, radio and radar, electrics, instruments and armourers. Today, however, I am lucky.

~ ~ ~

And after the D.Is?

Two relatively straightforward D.Is. such as I have described would occupy a full morning after which I would ride back to the section, report in and then go to the cookhouse for dinner. But, on "ops" days, if one or more serious, and seemingly intractable, problems are to be tackled, such as I have indicated in the foregoing, the meals can be at any time. And even on the "typical" day, there might have been a third D.I. to cover owing to the absence of a colleague, which again would delay one's "lunch hour", and it is so on this day, for "C" Charlie requires a D.I.

There are various "options" open in the afternoon ... helping out on another Lanc., where there was a major snag; jobs in the section – from bench-testing to tidying things up – or even assisting on the Lanc. currently undergoing "major surgery" in the hangar. Another task was the unloading and stacking of a new supply of charged-up oxygen cylinders in the oxygen bay of the hangar. If any of us found that we were down for night duty, of any kind, then we might be released for a few hours' break. But everything was determined by contingencies and personnel availability. My personal preference in the afternoon was to be out on the Flights, even if the weather was unpleasant – although even more so in the warmer months – and to be involved out there. Apart from the continuing activity, I enjoyed the banter and the camaraderie; and having a mug of tea with the lads in the flight hut.

I liked to be at the dispersal when the air-crew came out to do their ground and/or air tests. If "ops" were not on, the crew would take up their "kites" for "circuits and bumps" – take-off and landing exercises – or "cross country" trips; or, simply, to do a flight test on some new item of equipment or bodywork repair that had been carried out on the aircraft. Such exercises gave the ground staff the opportunity to fly with our air-crews; and also to talk with them. There were exceptions, but in the main, air and ground crews and officers, NCOs and ORs mixed easily together at these times. Of course, the condition and performance of the aircraft was a central feature of the conversations but there was "small talk" too, such as opinions on local hostelries; film shows coming up in the gym; WAAFS; camp rumours; and enquiries about places of origin.

"What's is like in Aussie then?"

"How do you Canadians get on with the Yanks?"

"How the hell can you actually live in Scotland – 'brass monkey' place that is!" (As if Lincolnshire was a paradise of continuous sunshine!)

And as we talked we all knew – air and ground crews – that each time we "socialised" in this way it could well be the last of such gatherings for any of the former. The last of all this, and – no more nights in the pubs or out on the town. No more dates with Waafs; or going home on leave. It was an unspoken thought; a grim awareness pushed to the back of everyone's mind. But not unthinkable because the reality of the situation could not be denied.

Others came out to the "kites" too. Personnel from the Photographic Section and the armourers who, by their presence, reminded us of the terrible end-product of all of our endeavours. But more of them in a later chapter.

When the pilot had tested his "kite" and found it to his satisfaction – and only then – he counter-signed the Form 700 accepting the aircraft. His signature on that document of responsibility always came as a relief to the mechanics. We liked to satisfy our customers!

9. THE "ERKS"

The term, "RAF ground staff" defines itself: they are Air Force personnel who are not flyers. But it is an all-embracing term and the description of a large body of men and women whose roles and functions are many and diverse; and each of those functions is categorised under the heading of a "trade".

In today's RAF, it is highly probable that the "trades" are differently defined and labelled (advanced technology will inevitably have been accompanied by appropriate nomenclature) but on an active aerodrome, or sea-plane base, during the Second World War, the "trades" would have included the following:

Aircraft servicing mechanics of various kinds; armourers; administration staff of equal variety (they formed the RAF's "hands on" bureaucracy); transport drivers and mechanics; stores personnel; radio and radar operators and technicians; medics and ambulance drivers; fire crews and crash teams; postal clerks and telephone operators; cookhouse staff and mess orderlies; S.P. (Service Police); units of the RAF Regiment; carpenters and allied trades; batmen; parachute packers; petrol dump attendants and bowser drivers; and general duties staff, who were the "dogs'-bodies" of the RAF.

I have not listed the above in any value-judgement order of importance, but simply at random as they come to mind. And if I have omitted to mention any other categories of employment in the war-time Royal Air Force, I apologise, in advance, to irate protestors!

Every "trade" was important in its own way, right through the system of that vast organisation, sometimes referred to as the "Air Works". Whatever the role, no matter how menial the task, each was a link in the chain and an integral part of the RAF's war against Nazi Germany. And the collective function of all the ground staff "trades", directly or indirectly, was to provide maximum back-up to those who did fly – the air-crews.

Without that support, and the spirit in which it was given, the operational efficiency and effectiveness of the war in, and from, the air could not have been sustained.

That old cliché that states something on the lines of: *"...the efficiency of the whole, is only as good as the proficiency of its component parts"*, has never been more appropriate than it is when applied here.

It is interesting at this point to look at the distribution of personnel on a typical heavy bomber station during the war.

On average, the total establishment would have been 2,000-plus. At Elsham Wolds at its peak of operations, the figure was 2,500, of whom about 400 were WAAFS. Of the 2,000 men, no more than 200 were air-crew who were, for obvious and grim reasons, the most transient of the station's population. And that means that for every one flyer there were twelve members of the ground staff, who, in their various ways, ensured that the organisation was in place to put the aircraft into the sky.

And, if the number of ground-staff officers and Senior NCOs is subtracted from the station's establishment, then it can be seen that "other ranks" (or "lower ranks") constituted about four-fifths of all personnel; and that is a pertinent statistic in the context of both this chapter and the whole book.

The "other ranks" were: the corporals (and more about them in a moment), the LACs, the AC1s, and the AC2s, who were the lowest rank in the RAF and who were known as the "AC plonks". WAAFS had equivalent ranks.

These, then, were the "bods", the "bashers" and the "wallahs". They were the "erks", a slang word of description that immediately raises the question as to its origin.

Unlike the Army's "Tommy" or "Squaddie", or the Navy's "Jack" (or even "matelot") the derivation of "erk" is not self-evident. It does, in fact, have a place with some other words in the jargon of the Services, in that there is some conjecture as to its entry into the lexicon of "RAF speak". (I recall a rather lengthy debate in the letter columns of a national newspaper over the origins of the Forces' exhortation, "Two – six – heave!" (instead of "One, two, three...") when a group is engaged in the effort of pulling, pushing or lifting. There were many theories but the issue was never satisfactorily resolved.)

I do not propose to offer a selection of theories on the "birth" of the appellation "erk" but instead offer the result of my enquiries into, on the face of it, such a puzzling term. My contention is that "erk" is a corruption of "airk" which is shortened from aircraftsman. And if I am wrong I will be most surprised if someone – or many – will not promptly tell me so!

I have no recollection of WAAFS being referred to as "Erkesses" and they were, in any case, "erks" in their own right. And I will be paying my own personal tribute to the "girls in blue" in a later section of this book.

The Corporals? Did they belong in the "great family of 'erks'?" Their "membership" depended on two factors: location and relationship. At "square bashing" camps and at training establishments, corporals were definitely and prominently seen as a part of authority, but on active aerodromes or on seaplane bases, if the two-stripes were integrally part of the "team", and mucked in with the lads, then they too were in the "erk" fraternity. But, even so, corporals, in whatever situation, were akin to charge-hands in certain work places – not quite management but still with one foot in that direction!

So then, we can see that ground staff is a general and vague term, necessitating a more distinguishing definition, and that O.Rs. and "erks" are synonymous.

~ ~ ~

What is my own memory of the "erks"? First of all I must stress that I have retained an appropriate respect for all ground staff, no matter what their role happened to be; and I would never demean any of thei functions. But, inevitably I suppose, whenever I think of the "erks", I immediately associate them in my mind with the ground crews, i.e. the aircraft servicing mechanics, who more directly, "kept 'em flying"; and who had that close rapport with the "fly boys". They were the "erks" who spearheaded that long line of support that the ground staff provided to operational viability. They were the engines and airframe fitters, the flight mechanics, the electricians, instrument repairers, radio and radar electricians, and the armourers.

Those ground crew "bods" were the airmen with aircraft dirt under their finger nails; and with the aroma of petrol, oil, glysol and aeroplane metal about their persons. The men who carried out their exacting tasks in all kinds of circumstances and climatic conditions. They serviced aircraft, brought them to operational readiness, partly in hangars, but mostly out in the open in cloying mist or in howling wind; or when soaked in driving rain and with frozen fingers on icy winter days. In places overseas the ground crew "erks" kept the aircraft flying in spite of clogging sand and dust, and under searing heat that made metal burn the flesh, turning also, the interior of airplanes into sauna baths.

RAF ground crews fought their particular corner of the war with extraordinary tenacity and with great ingenuity. They were superb improvisers who, when confronted with a shortage of equipment, or of components, just "found ways around it"; and, if necessary, made what they couldn't obtain.

"Necessity is the mother of invention..." should have been the official motto of those who serviced aircraft in World War II. The aircraft mechanics of the Royal Air Force may not have performed heroic deeds, but they did, without question, work heroically and often against the most challenging of odds.

The following article by Basil Cardew appeared in the *"Daily Express"* during the war and it speaks volumes in support of my personal tribute to my erstwhile comrades.

> *The only part of his name he will allow me to use is Bert, and he will not let me give his address. In peacetime he was a London milk-roundsman, a fact which may have something to do with his patience and his methodical way of working.*
>
> *He is now a flight mechanic fitter in the RAF – that is to say, he can do any repairs which one man can do to an aircraft engine.*
>
> *Bert has just been mentioned in despatches, and he now wears a little bronze oak leaf on the left breast of his tunic. "Mentioned in dispatches?" he said, when he was told. "M.I.D.? What in 'eck for?"*
>
> *Bert had one ambition. To see "B-Beer," the heavy bomber on which he worked at a North of England station, complete 71 trips.*
>
> *The record for the squadron was 70 and Bert was certain that "Beer" could break it. "Beer" was his work, his play and, at times, something very like his whole life. No one had ever taken so much pride in a bomber as Bert took in "Beer". He would clean the engines with the same care that others would give to a fine collection of Sheffield plate.*
>
> *Long after his colleagues had left he was still there, checking up – "Making sure", as he called it. And afterwards they would jokingly taunt him with those RAF words, "Bull" and "Flannel".*
>
> *"Bull" means unnecessary, or purely ceremonial work, and "to flannel" means to ingratiate oneself with one's superiors in rank.*
>
> *"More bull today?" they would say, "Trying to flannel, eh?"*

Then, when "Beer" came back with a bad oil leak, and the port outer propeller feathered, they would say to him, "She's getting old, Bert."

When "Beer" had 65 yellow bombs painted on its side, they began to call it "An old bag of bones". "She'll never make the record," they added.

Bert disagreed. And the station began to lay bets on "Beer's" chances.

Bert made no bets, but he worked through last winter as if cold, frost and rain meant nothing to him. He began to develop a cough. But there he would remain, perched on the trestles, cleaning a contact breaker on a magneto, putting in a split pin here, tightening a bolt there, or just peering into the engine's innards, trying to guess where the next fault was likely to originate. Slowly his cough grew worse.

Chiefy, the flight-sergeant, started to worry about Bert. He offered him days off. Bert refused them. He tried to make Bert see the doctor. "E'd 'ave me in dock," was Bert's reply, "and there's time enough for that when "Beer's" made it."

To renewed accusations of "bull" Bert said, "I keeps 'er clean and I see the oil leaks – see?"

Bert began to advise the aircrew. The pilot was a flight-lieutenant and the flight-commander as well, but he understood Bert.

"Take 'er easy – see?" Bert said to him. "No need to 'urry 'ome. I've seen kites what's bin first 'ome. And the engines 'ave 'ad it. Now, 'Beer'..." The pilot would nod, and agree, and nurse his engines home just as Bert had stipulated.

The day came when "B-Beer" had to have an engine changed only six hours before it was due to take off for Berlin. Covered from sparse hair to matt black boots in oil, Bert worked on, missing his dinner, and then his tea.

Chiefy ordered him to rest, and Bert became obdurate. "I'm finish' this 'ere job" he muttered. "You can do wotcher like abaht it." Chiefy knew that exactly 70 bombs had now been painted on "Beer" and what it meant to Bert. So he hadn't the heart to insist, though he did not like the look of Bert at all.

"Beer" took off punctually with the others, and I saw the flight-commander, who was piloting it, shake hands with Bert. "You made it, Bert", he said. And the little fitter replied, "You'll make it too, sir."

The next morning Bert was seen running down to the flight. He had left his breakfast half-eaten on hearing that "Beer" had not come back. "It's not time, it's not time," he mumbled to anyone who would listen. "Mark my words – she'll come in."

It was easy to see that Bert now had a high temperature as well as his usual cough. He went and stood by himself, shivering, with his grey face turned to the sky.

About midday the telephone bell rang in Chiefy's office. Chiefy answered it and called Bert. He said: "Bert you were right. "B-Beer's touched down at..."

Bert was silent. He threw his cap into the air and then fell to the ground, unconscious. He was a long time in hospital. And when he came out and heard the news – "M.I.D.? What in 'eck for?"

Bert was an exemplary aircraft mechanic but there were many of his kind and I met them in Coastal Command, Bomber Command and on various bases overseas. I worked alongside them, lived among them and socialised with them; and, although I was one of them, accepted in their "terms", I was never quite as they were because I was not imbued, as the great majority of those lads were, with the inherent artisan skills and instincts that were their distinctive hall-mark.

Indeed, it is due to so many of those airmen that I reached my own level of competence and confidence.

So, who were these "erks" about whom I write with so much retrospective warmth? What was their background? What were they like as people?

They came, with few exceptions, from the working-class and from every corner of the United Kingdom. To be with them in any number was to have one's ears assailed by a polyglot of regional dialects and accents – and subtle variations on each of those also. "Brummy", "Scouse", "Cockney", "Taffy", "Jock", "Geordie", the counties of north, south east and west. You name it, you heard it, a lingual *pot pourri* of pronunciation and enunciation, some so thick as almost to require translation!

The "erks" were, for the most part, in their late teens or early twenties; but there were, in their midst, some older men who were in their late twenties or into their thirties. (On one or two bases during my time in the RAF I did come across a few men of even more advanced years i.e. in their forties, who in civilian life had been watchmakers or employed in similar precision trades. The RAF had, wisely, been prepared to "bend the rules" to allow those "old boys" in, for they were ideally qualified for calibrating and bench-testing instruments).

Academic education for many of the young aircraft mechanics had been terminated at the age of fourteen, an abrupt conclusion of nine years' schooling which was in no way connected to any collective lack of intelligence on the part of the pupils. It was something that happened to the vast majority of children of the working-class pre-war, in an educational system that proceeded on the assumption that as most of the working-class young were destined for plebeian employment anyway, any extension of school learning would have been surplus to requirement!

Secondary education was not, as it now is, free and compulsory and was available only by fee-paying or by scholarship. The former was out of the question for the overwhelming majority of families and even entry by scholarship – with books, uniform etc. to pay for – ensured a limited entry. And, in any case, in so many families, especially in the poorer areas, there were urgent economic reasons for the kids to get a job and contribute to the meagre coffers – if a job could be found that is. But, some of the "erks" had made it to Grammar or High Schools or to Technical Schools (as in my own case), and others, especially those serving apprenticeships before the war, had enhanced their prospects by attending the Evening Institutes that flourished in those days.

Nevertheless, as I say, those who had ended their academic education at fourteen were far more numerous, even though they most certainly did not lack intelligence. Of course, as in any group of people – undoubtedly even at Eton and Harrow – there were some lads whose cerebral mechanism was slow to get in into gear; but generally I found my fellow "erks" to be sharp and perceptive; lumpen proletariat they were not!

Before the war, those who were to become members of the RAF's ground crews had been factory hands, postmen, shop assistants, building trade workers, railwaymen, roundsmen, clerks, draughtsmen and apprentices to a variety of trades. Or, in some instances, they had come into the Service straight off the dole queue. It was usually though, an industrial and technical background that had brought about their presence in the RAF as aircraft mechanics.

What were they like as men? Although they did have a great deal in common – about which more later – they were, as any other body of men, the usual mixture of characters and personalities. And during my six years' service I think I met them all: the extroverts and the introverts (i.e. the brash and the withdrawn); the loquacious (known as loud-mouthed bastards!) and the taciturn; the aggressive and the placid; the "line shooter" and the modest; the excitable and the dour; those quick to take offence and others tolerant to a fault; some who talked tough and a few who really were. There were young men whom I could have loved as brothers, and others who "got right up my nose"; whereas, quite possibly, they found me offensive to their nostrils also!

It was an early lesson, important to learn in HM Forces – the recognition of the diversity of human persona and how to react appropriately to each kind. And that proved an invaluable social lesson for me in various occupations in the post-war years.

~ ~ ~

There are intrinsic problems associated with nostalgia and they are:
(i)   the temptation to idealise the past, and
(ii) the tendency – especially if the intervening years are many – to "place retrospectively, old heads on young shoulders". By which I mean that in our mature and advanced years it is easy to imagine that we thought and acted then just as we do now; and, in the main, it was just not so. In those famous words of L.P. Hartley: *"The past is a foreign country. They do things differently there."*

And of course we did. The framework of our perceptions was different
as was our "world view". We were young, with all the callowness of youth; naive, opinionated, quick to judgment. We were skittish, oft times "silly", very "laddish" and sometimes boorish in our behaviour. "Men behaving badly" in fact!

It was expected that one should be "manly" and even awkward manifestation of sentimentality caused embarrassment because we all felt uncomfortable in its presence.

With few exceptions male chauvinism reigned supreme but we could hardly be blamed for that since that was the norm in society in those days.

Sex was prominent in the choice of conversational topics ("topic normal" as we used to say) and although there were womanisers, "crumpet chasers"; "love 'em and leave 'em" types among us, much of the claims to sexual conquest was wishful thinking and adolescent fantasising.

73

So, yes, we were in so many respects a collective personification of callow youth with half-baked ideas and with obvious immaturity. But yet, that was not the total picture for, in some respects, we had been obliged to grow up quickly. We showed a mature sense of responsibility towards our job of servicing the aircraft; and to the men who flew in them. The war itself, whilst in some ways intensifying our lust for life and the seeking of enjoyment, also had its own sobering influence. Many of us had experienced the "Blitz" in various places, and had families, wives, girl-friends, living in areas that were more often targeted for attention by the Luftwaffe. And some of the lads had, in fact, lost relatives and friends in air raids.

There was, therefore, a kind of dichotomy going on whereby we became partially matured by impinging aspects of the war (plus some influence from the older men in our midst) and, conversely, our determination (or natural predilection) to indulge ourselves in the waywardness of youth. We were, it could be said, "mixed-up kids", 1940s style!

When I look back and reflect on the general nature and behaviour of the "erks" (including myself of course) in those far-off days, it is not my intention either to canonise or to demonise them. I merely tell it as it was, or, as I remember it. By and large for reasons I have already hinted at – and will now emphasise – I count myself fortunate to have known and to have served in the war with my fellow "erks".

They were real people with no pretensions and what you saw was what you got. Whilst some were shallow – there are, inevitably always exceptions – most of the lads had more to them than appeared on the surface. And one discovered many interests among them in which they were impressively knowledgeable. In quieter moments, a one-to-one conversation would reveal a whole range of hobbies and fascinations. There were music enthusiasts who surprised one with their knowledge of the classics or of jazz. There were philatelists and railway "buffs"; anglers (and poachers!); some were political and well-informed; sport featured high on the list of the "erks'" interests and I recall young men with something approaching encyclopaedic knowledge of football, rugby, cricket, boxing – whatever.

Many discussions in the billets, or the NAAFI were loud-voiced slanging matches on the subject of sport, sex, politics etc. but interlaced with all that, there were more measured, thoughtful exchanges of opinion about the future. (Would it be another broken promise of *"...a land fit for heroes to live in..."* as had been the case in 1918?)

Ideas and opinions about how life should be in post-war Britain were already forming. Also, there were explorations into the realms of philosophy, asking those age-old questions. ...Why are we here? What is life all about? How did it all start? Where the hell is it going...?

Our part-earnest, part-facetious exchanges may not have reached the levels of the hallowed, intellectual cloisters of academia, but we were asking the same questions and exhibiting similar curiosities which are the precursors of contemplative learning.

I have written that, although the "erks" were a collection of diverse characters and personalities, they did, also, have certain things in common. And some of these I have already pointed to in this book, such as: pride and confidence in their individual skills and abilities; a very serious awareness of their responsibilities; the work-ethic – not so much the traditional "doing a good day's work for a good day's pay", for, after all, the ground staff's fortnightly remuneration was hardly a princely sum! – but rather the ethic of doing a job well. What, nowadays, we would call work-satisfaction.

Yes, there were those manifestations of homogeneity among the ground crews, but let us enlarge a little on some of the other shared "norms" to which I have also hinted.

First, an unwritten code about acceptable and unacceptable behaviour; axioms that were tacitly understood, even if not voiced. And honesty was an integral part of that code.

There was an openness and frankness whereby the lads were very much inclined to speak their minds. To say what they thought and to call a spade "a bloody shovel" (a characteristic, incidentally, not as conventional wisdom would have it, confined to natives of the north). It was not in their nature for the "erks" to dissemble or to be disingenuous; and their bluntness could, at times, be quite devastating before which the more sensitive souls would quail!

Honesty, too, in the matter of theft. Whilst it was acceptable to "win" (i.e. acquire) extra items of equipment or clothing from the "firm" you did not steal from your own kind.

"There were three kinds of Robin... Robin Hood, Robin Red Breast and Robbin' bastards!"

The "erks" were very judgemental on that issue and unforgiving. And an incident, which I will relate in a further chapter, will demonstrate the kind of behaviour that met with such opprobrium from the rank and file.

Little "victories" against the system were, again, regarded as "fair do's": a wangled pass; "going round twice" for an extra meal" a "skive" out of sight for a smoke when things were quiet; or a clandestine trip to the Naafi. But habitual "skivers" or work dodgers, were not exactly popular. Worst of all though, and absolutely beyond the pale, would be any act or omission that "dropped a mate right in it". You did not cause an "oppo" extra work or additional duties by not being there when you should be – unless you were genuinely sick or injured, in which case the lads would willingly (even if cursing your hide!) cover for you; and even fetch and carry for you. As for allowing someone else to "carry the can" for your misdemeanour, well, that was on a par with a capital offence!

Secondly, generosity, both in the material sense and that of spirit. The "erks" had that in abundance. It was an integral part of the comradeship I remember so well, and cherish:

"We're going to the Naafi. Comin' Tom?"

"No, I'm skint mate."

"Get your soddin' coat on, you big girl's blouse! I think we can manage a half-pint for you between us."

Chorus: "Yeah. Come on you miserable git!"

"OK lads, thanks. But my treat next – !"

"Oh wind your neck in for Christ's sake and get your finger out or the bloody Naafi will be shut!"

Generosity was spontaneous and unconditional, unaccompanied by sentimentality, an emotional expression that, like sympathy and concern, came out awkwardly and with embarrassment. But those lads, with their tough demeanour, imbued in so many cases by working-class socialisation, possessed an uncanny instinct for knowing when an "oppo" was in trouble in some way. (Bad news from home, perhaps; the receipt of a "Dear John" letter; the loss of a well-liked air-crew.) Solace would be offered in the same rough way; or a directive would be issued in no uncertain terms – "leave him alone!"

And if one of us found ourselves on a disciplinary charge for some misdemeanour, or alleged dereliction of duty, then the support of our comrades was needed, and it was given unequivocally.

Standing by – and with – your mates was a basic ingredient of comradeship. Perhaps, though, the cement of comradeship was laid by that shared, enduring, morale – sustaining sense of humour. Gags, quips and repartee for all occasions and for any kind of situation.

Humour that eased tension and turned grumbles into smiles. Laughter that mocked pomposity and put anxiety in its proper perspective.

Picture the scene...

"Ops" are on. It is late afternoon and a Lanc. stands ready to go to the hostile skies over the Third Reich. She is "bombed up", "tanked up" and bristling with pugnacity.

A ginger-haired, LAC airframe fitter is walking around the kite, satisfying himself that all is well with her, when, suddenly the 4,000-pound "cookie" blast bomb falls out of the open bomb doors. It thuds down onto the cement base of the dispersal bay, right beside the "rigger's" body. There is but a moment's contemplation of this extremely unnerving turn of events and then "Ginger" lifts his head and yells at whoever is in the cockpit. "FOR CHRIST'S SAKE – DO I LOOK LIKE BLEEDIN' BERLIN?!"

~   ~   ~

Patriotism? I encountered very few "erks" who could be described as patriotic in the overt, jingoistic way. The tendency was to "take the mickey" out of all that. But, the vast majority of the lads did possess a great love for their country, even if, in some instances prior to the war, their country had done little for them or their families. But no matter what criticisms or grievances any of them may have harboured about this "Sceptred Isle", none of them was predisposed to countenance Nazi jack-boots stomping all over it. And they knew, well enough, the nature of the enemy and the vital necessity of defeating him.

As far as militarism was concerned, I have earlier on in the book, outlined what I consider to have been the "erks'" attitude to that: but its pertinence needs to be stressed. It could be summed up as ambivalent. They were not stupid and they understood the need for discipline and order in a military situation. What they did find "difficult to accept" – and I stress this again – was:

a)   "bull" for bull's sake, and

b)   "bull" that intruded and, as they saw it, disrupted their military *raison d'être*: serving the need of the air-crews. It was, always, a bone of contention "among the ranks".

The roulette wheel of chance and the vagaries of conscription and recruitment, had placed the "erks" down in that particular form of war-time employment. Had those wheels of chance delivered them into some other role – as infantrymen, gunners, army engineers, sailors, whatever – I know (because I knew them so well) that these young men would have given of their best in these situations as they gave to the RAF.

Some of them had – as in my own case – volunteered for air-crew but had been turned down for various reasons. Others simply did not see themselves in that role and with their usual candour would say, "Not for me mate. Too bloody dicey!"

I think it was Southey who wrote, "Men do less than they can unless they do all that they can..."

There is no doubt in my mind that, as a body and as individuals, the ground crew "erks", who self-deprecatingly referred to themselves as the "penguins", did, indeed, do all that they could to perform the duties for which they had been selected, with maximum commitment. And I believe that the RAF was blessed by the presence of such men.

Whatever they were like as individuals or how "wild" their male bonding behaviour could, sometimes, be, my enduring memory is of men who showed a lot of the qualities and values which really count and which I personally admired.

It is high time that their story was told and this book endeavours to relate at least a part of that story. And it is why I dedicate it to them, the war-time "erks" of the RAF.

10. "CHOCKS AWAY"

It is late afternoon, nearing dusk in winter. The weak sun that has made brief and ineffectual appearances in the course of the day has now withdrawn to be replaced by a pale moon heralding the night.

Out on the Flights small groups of ground crew "erks" huddle together and stamp their feet against the cold as they wait beside the Lancaster bombers in the dispersal bays. In each group there is at least one mechanic from each aircraft servicing trade standing by to give urgent attention to any last-minute snags that (gremlin inspired) do have a habit of cropping up. And, indeed, from over on 'B' Flight we can hear the sound of a Merlin engine having a "coughing fit".

"Ops" are on tonight and 103 Squadron is at a state of readiness. Ground crews, their concentrated efforts throughout the day (as described in Chapter 7), are now – apart from those eleventh-hour "hiccups" – awaiting the arrival of the air-crews.

The Lancasters also stand and wait, large, inanimate structures and yet, as you look up at them, they take on a life form of their own – black, sleek, combative, sinister and predatory. And, earlier in the afternoon, came the men who transformed these aeroplanes into killing machines ... the armourers.

There is something about the armourers' trade that sets them aside from the other ground crews. Their work is at once menacing and esoteric with skills and knowledge secretive and exclusive. They come on the job like specialist sub-contractors given a franchise by the main company. They arrive on the scene bringing with them the deadly merchandise that will, this night, be delivered by the Lancasters to enemy territory.

The bombs and the cans of incendiaries are carried on long trolleys pulled by tractors and some of the armourers, wearing belts of .303 Browning machine-gun bullets draped around them, evocative of bandolier'd Mexican bandits, sit with studied nonchalance on the 4,000-pound "cookie" blast bombs.

The tractors and the trolleys drive right around the Lancaster and then back in, beneath the 33 foot-long open bomb doors. The armourers prefer that we keep out of their way whilst they are at work and we are only too happy to oblige; and whilst two of them go into the "kite" to lay in the belts of bullets in the feed channels to the guns, their "oppos" "bomb up".

First to be cranked up is the 4,000-pounder, followed by six 500-pound, "general purpose" bombs, or by cans of incendiaries. It is hellishly hard graft and even on the coldest of days, the "bomb boys" sweat profusely. Perversely, too, as they toil away the armourers are only too well aware that even at the very last moment, "ops" can be "scrubbed"; and the whole demanding process will have to be repeated (plus de-fusing!) all over again – but in reverse!

There is no gloating among us "erks" at the sight of all this grim and terrible weaponry that is to be launched, once again, against the citizens of some luckless European city. *"Some more poor buggers are gettin' that lot tonight!"* is a more likely observation.

But, there is no moralising either. "They bomb us. We bomb them. We are at war and the sooner the whole bloody thing is over and done with the better!"

~ ~ ~

Other things have gone on board too: cameras that will take high-altitude photos as the bombs fall; "Window" – thin strips of aluminium which are scattered over enemy territory to jam and confuse German detection radar. And, on occasion, propaganda leaflets designed – with misplaced optimism – to influence the citizenry of the Third Reich against their Nazi rulers.

But do the leaflets not burn in the fires below? Is it not a severely punishable offence in Germany to be caught actually reading a leaflet thus delivered? Would not the average *herr* or *frau* who might just pick up one or more of those tracts, secrete them quickly and take them home to supplement the almost non-existent toilet-roll supply! Isn't that what happened in the case of Nazi leaflets dropped over here? My friend on "D" Duck, Flight Engineer "Jock" Brechney, is of the opinion that the leaflets would probably have more impact if dropped still tied up in bundles – together with the Naafi wad! War has many facets.

~ ~ ~

The scene out on the Flights, described above, stand at the end – or near to the end – of a long chain of command. The whole strategic bombing campaign against Germany (and Italy) is jointly orchestrated from the War Cabinet (policy) and Bomber Command

HQ at High Wycombe (executive). Targets are selected and bomber strengths decreed at the latter centre and then passed to Bomber Group HQs where the organisation is set in motion to implement the requirements of the "top brass". And every time, for every raid, every sortie, a meticulous and complex exercise in logistics is involved: the number of bombers to take part; which bases and which squadrons; pathfinders and target markers; selections of attack leaders; intelligence and photographic reports on target approaches, the nature of the target, and the known deployment of air and ground defences; consideration of met. reports and so much else.

Each station and each squadron in the various Bomber Groups will have been notified of their place in the scheme of things and provided with as much information as Group is able to convey. Then, at the airfields, the air-crews have been briefed and the ground crews set to work to prepare the bombers for action. And we, who have done our job, and now wait for the arrival of our air-crews, have not been privy to all of that decision-making and planning that has been the exclusive preoccupation of the "back-room boys"!

We do not know, either, the 'target for tonight'. But we do have certain indicators that enable us to make at least shrewd guesses, as to the distance of the target, and whether it is to be a long or short haul. If it is to be a long flight then the wing tanks of the bombers will be filled to their capacity of 1,254 gallons of high-octane petrol. Also, take-off time is earlier for these long-distance trips.

Tonight, the bets are on Berlin or, possibly, northern Italy; but we know that the leaflets going out tonight are all printed in German. But, then again, they could be intended to be dropped *en route*.

Take-off time is always earlier in winter anyway for the *raison d'être* of RAF. Bomber Command is to bomb at night, whilst the USAAF goes over there in daylight. The consequence is that in war time, double-summer time, the night bombers must delay their departure in order to enter the skies over enemy territory in darkness.

I often wonder about this and what might be the reaction of the air-crews. Did the later take-off in the summer prolong the tension, the anticipation, or did it mean another, longer day to be enjoyed and to grasp at every extra minute that is free from danger? I must ask "Jock" about this, sometime...

~   ~   ~

Elsham Wolds is in No. 1 Group of Bomber Command where HQ is at Bawtree Hall, just south of Doncaster. As well as Elsham the other stations in the Group are all in the northern section of Lincolnshire: Binbrook, Blyton, Ingham, Dunholme Lodge, Faldingworth, Goxhill, Hemswell, Kelstern, Kirmington, Lindholme, Ludford Magna, North Killingholme, Sandtoft, Scampton (to become famous as the Dam Busters' base) and Waltham.

A similar number of bomber bases are spread over the south of the county and, it is said by some of the locals, that: *"Lincolnshire is noted for tulips, potatoes and sausages first – and bomber bases!"*

And now, as take-off time for tonight's "big show" operation inexorably approaches, the same scenes that have unfolded on the airfield at Elsham will be duplicated right across, not only Lincolnshire, but also Yorkshire, and Cambridgeshire and Norfolk. Eastern England is resounding to the sounds of the dreadful intensity of 20th Century warfare.

But every aspect, every facet of the activities of this day, has constituted the prelude, the overture to what is now unfolding.

"Here they come!" someone shouts and through the gathering gloom we can see the "tillies" (utility trucks) WAAF-driven, coming out from the centre of the 'drome, heading for the dispersal bays and the waiting aircraft. The air-crews are on their way.

There is feverish activity in one of the bays just a short distance away, where someone has noticed that an engine cowling on "F" Freddie is not seating properly; and it is not responding to immediate remedial treatment. "Chiefy" Clacker is there (of course!) and so, too, is the Engineering Officer, who never misses a thing!

The engine "bods" are under pressure to get it sorted. *"Come on you blokes. The bloody air crew are on their way!"* And I know about the pressure because I have experienced such last-minute, unexpected problems; especially with an oxygen-system fault.

A "tilly" swings into "D" Duck's "parking space" and her crew, my friends, jump down. They are in their flying suits, wearing their "Mae Wests" and their flying boots; and carrying their parachute packs.

"Skipper" Carey has a brief word with the corporal engine fitter and then goes aboard. It is still an hour before take-off time but pilots, especially, like to get inside the plane to check things out. In fact, many air-crew lads choose to board the aircraft straight away as if making a statement: *"Come on. Let's get this thing done!"* But others prefer to delay their embarkation, some to chat with their ground crew and there are several also who perform a variety of pre-op rituals.

One gunner is known to walk around his Lanc three times; a navigator who taps seven times on the aircraft fuselage. And a big Aussie wireless op/air gunner on one of the "kites" on 'A' Flight always pees against one of the wheels, oblivious of the presence of the WAAF driver who has brought him to the dispersal.

There is a great deal of superstition among the air-crews of Bomber Command. And a belief that no matter how great the skill and the experience they may possess, "Lady Luck", too, has a part to play in all this mayhem. So thus, apart from the rituals to call in the angels of fortune, they also wear "lucky rings", a girlfriend's silk scarf, a grubby and crumpled pullover, or carry a talisman such as a cigarette lighter, a pocket knife, a photo – whatever. And they carry these "charms" as another shield against flack and *Luftwaffe* night fighters.

Four of "D"s' crew, Dick, Rich, "Tiny" and "J.S.", do not hang about before going aboard but all exchange greetings with me. Rear-gunner "Yank" Montgomery goes to "Duck's" tail-end and looks up as if to check that his turret is in place! And, as always, he then turns to look out over the darkening fields, perhaps imagining the country back home in the USA and wondering if he will ever see it again. He spots me and says, "Hi kid" before going up the ladder into the aircraft's door.

Flight Engineer "Jock" Brechney has had his usual "wee word" with me; and his ritual parting comment: "And your instruments had better be working correctly laddie!"

Everyone is tense – air and ground crews – for different reasons and it is handled in a variety of ways. As each minute ticks by that acutely tangible tension builds and builds.

The accumulator-trolleys are now being pushed up to the aircraft and plugged in. Engines fire, propellers turn and wheeze and then spin in response to ignition. Inner starboard, outer starboard; then inner port and outer port – always in that order.

All across the aerodrome the Merlins are bursting into life and "F" Freddie, now "sorted", joins in a chorus of throbbing power. It is a *crescendo* of sound as these powerful motors are revved and a tremor runs along the ground that must be stirring even the long-dead in Elsham's church-yard.

"Chiefy" Clacker is chasing around the 'A' Flight dispersals ensuring that all is clear and that the accumulator-trolleys are unplugged and withdrawn. "Those boys," he tells us, "have enough to worry about without having a dirty great acc-trolley dangling down when they take off!" It is a standard Clacker comment but errors of omission are not entirely unknown.

"Chocks away!" and the Lancs are moving out onto the link roads that lead round to the runway.

I see "A" Apple go, followed by "B" Beer, on board which is Aussie navigator Don Charlwood, who in later years will be the author of several books, among them the outstanding accounts of Bomber Command operations – and the men who flew in them: *No Moon Tonight* and *Journeys Into Night*.

Now it is the turn of "D" Duck and as she eases out the slip-stream whips at the clothing of ground crew lads caught in its wake. We exchange the thumbs-up sign with "Skipper" Carey and "Jock" Brechney and then, as "D" turns onto the road, "Yank" Montgomery sitting in his turret, gives us the same optimistic (hopeful) parting symbolic signal.

Dusk is already turning to dark as the black shapes of Lancasters, their movements traced by glimmering wing-tip lights, are converging from various directions towards the runway that is to be used tonight and forming queues. It is, this short terrestrial journey, the first of a night that will be filled with strain for the pilots. There is little space on either side of the planes as they negotiate the unlit link roads, and the slightest misjudgment can result in a wheel bogged down in the soft earth of the verges. It is a manoeuvre further complicated by the tail-to-nose angle of the aircraft, which limits forward vision. The pilots are only too well aware as they "drive" on engine and brakes, that if they should veer off and get stuck, this can cause a "tail-back" of the Lancs coming on behind; a "right cock-up" that can throw the take-off schedule completely out of sync; a situation not exactly popular with the "brass".

The resonance of engine noise is now concentrated at and near the runway. In each aircraft are seven young men who are about to dice with death and endure severe discomfort. At 20,000 ft it will be 40 below and even at 5,000 ft, in winter, a plane can ice up. So the flyers wear several layers of clothing under their flying suits, including thick roll-neck pullovers and scarves. And some will wear silk socks (or even stockings) inside their fur-lined flying boots. But the guy who will suffer most from the cold will be the rear gunner as a result of the modification that has removed a section of the perspex screen from his turret, in order to enhance his vision. It is hardly surprising, therefore, that the rear gunner's turret, already dubbed the "blood bucket" because of its vulnerability to night-fighter attack, is now also called the "ice bucket"!

The lead plane is now on the runway, engines revving and the Lanc straining impatiently against the restraining brakes. Further along the runway, in the distance, the aldis lamp beside the chequered control caravan is showing red. They wait for the light to change to green and to that moment of truth – take off. And everything that has gone before, from the planning to the issue of the orders; from the organisational procedures to the briefing, and through to the effort of the ground crews, has been leading towards this moment, this point in time.

The atmosphere is compelling and sends involuntary shivers up the spine, that emotional reaction which the French call *frisson*. No matter what your feelings may be about the bellicose nature of what is going on here, the excitement, the expectation is overwhelming. The fact that this is also history in the making, and another grisly chapter in the sorry story of human warfare, does not really register. Nor that all this carnage and blood letting is occurring just some twenty years or so, a generation only, since another global war of attrition tore the heart out of the youth of many nations.

But it is history in the making; and it is non-fictional drama too. Dramatic scenes are being enacted here in a remote corner of Lincolnshire that if a musical score was to be added, one would, ironically, turn to Wagner!

Fifteen Lancs of our squadron are lined up to fly on this night, just one part of an air armada of 600 bombers that will cross the North Sea. And strangely it is highly probable that the crew of any one aircraft will not see, on the approach to, over, or on the return flight, another RAF bomber – unless, possibly, one caught in the cone of searchlights, or is seen falling, on fire, out of the sky. Nor will a crew see, until it is too late, the bomber with which they collide, in the vicinity of the target. (That too is not an uncommon occurrence.)

~ ~ ~

Cockpit drill now in the leading Lanc, a routine to be duplicated in the other fourteen. A drill familiar to the members of ground crew, too, for it is the same pattern on non-operational flights also, but the difference here is that the crew are sitting, not only in a 57,000-lb aeroplane but also with wing tanks full of highly inflammable 100-octane aviation petrol, a batch of potentially explosive oxygen bottles in place, and a bomb load of at least 10,000 pounds of TNT and incendiaries.

No room for take-off error here; mistakes, mis-judgements are unforgiving in this scenario.

Radio silence now, just inter-com. Pilot and Flight Engineer by his side, in dual control. Interchange of checks between Pilot, Flight Engineer and other crew members:

- Brakes on?
- Brakes on.
- Check pitch control.
- Check pitch control. OK
- Check magnetos.
- Mags checked. OK
- Green light
- All clear forward?
- All clear forward, Skip.
- All clear aft?
- All clear aft, Skip
- Clear all round?
- Chorus: All clear Skip.
- Flaps 30 degrees?
- Flaps 30.
- Flight Engineer checks all relevant gauges
- Brakes off.
- Brakes off.
- Right, here we go.
- Throttle forward, gathering speed, aircraft eager for flight, like a bird of prey on a falconer's arm.
- 80... 90... 110 mph. Four Rolls-Royce Merlins in full song. Aircraft wheel tyres screaming.
- Throttle 'up to the gate', full revs but just a little in re-serve, through the gate, for emergency.
- Tail up, aircraft shaking and bouncing.
- Watch that damn swing to the left!
- Compensate! Aircraft lifting.
- Chorus: Come on you beauty, up you go.
- Undercart Up?
- Undercart up.
- Undercart locked?
- Undercart locked Skip.
- Flaps up?
- Flaps up.
- Airborne and going
- A chorus of relief: *Well done Skip!*

It has taken skill, nerve and strength to get the huge Lancaster bomber into the air and they have all come through that particular moment of anxiety, but fear will ride with them throughout this faintly moonlit night.

And so they go, one after the other. The Lancs roar and scream down the runway, the sounds pounding in the watchers' ears and the smells of aviation wafting into their nostrils.

There is no hanging about, for the "powers that be" require a compliance to operational time schedules and also they want the airfield restored to complete blackout.

As the noise of our aircraft dies away, we who stand around pick up the sound of other bombers from near and distant bases throbbing their way to the east coast. They fill the sky with their thunderous resonance and it will be *nessum dorma* for anyone in Lincolnshire hoping for an early night. But then, perhaps the good citizens of the county have by now become accustomed to it.

Suddenly, however, all is quiet and the sky is empty save for clouds racing as if to catch up with the planes; and stars seemingly reappear as if they had been taking cover.

There is an eerie stillness settling on the land, broken only by the sound of a dog barking in the distance; a motor-vehicle starting up and muffled voices from a nearby dispersal hut. It is then that you realise that this is the first time in the past twelve hours or so that Elsham Wolds aerodrome has been at peace; and it is a quiet so tangible as to convey a distinct feeling of anticlimax.

But, there will be no sense of peace, no tranquillity aboard those Lancasters as they pass through the night: and nothing but terror and another nerve-shattering endurance test for the citizens of Berlin. *"The Tommies are over again tonight."*

~ ~ ~

Sometime in the early hours of the morning the Lancasters begin to return and the fire trucks and the "blood wagons" (ambulances) are standing by.

Some of the planes are passing over, going on to other airfields. "Ours" come home intermittently, one singly, then another, then three in close succession, followed by another on its own. They circle the 'drome before lining up for landing and, from one or two, at least, a "darky" radio signal will have been sent out. This is the "I am in trouble" signal and a notification that the landing might well be "dicey".

An engine, two engines gone; tail damage, maybe, or wing badly holed; undercarriage damaged or jammed up; coming in on one wheel only, or at worst, no undercart at all. Nor is it unknown for a plane to return with a bomb, or bombs, stuck in the bomb bay!

All of these hazards are on the cards for any of the crews and it is a rare event for all the aircraft that go on an operational sortie to return unscathed – a grim fact that applies also to the crews themselves. And the inside of a bomber that has been "shot up" is not a pretty sight. Nor, too, are the wounded and the dead members of the crew.

Some of the Lancs – a remarkably durable aeroplane – make miraculous landings; others are not so fortunate. And all the runways of RAF Bomber Command during the Second World War lay as monuments to the carnage among the bombers returning to base. A wartime song, *"Coming In On a Wing and a Prayer"*, could have been their anthem.

~   ~   ~

Two of our aircraft have failed to return on this particular morning. Neither is written off, yet, as "lost". Either one, or both, could have force-landed elsewhere; and only time will confirm either the good or the bad news.

"D" Duck has made it – and in one piece – and I am thankful for that.

All the air-crews disembarking from the returning aircraft show the unmistakable signs of the indescribable endurance test to which they have been subjected. They light up cigarettes as they clamber out of their "kites" and their sheer weariness shows as they climb aboard the "tilly" trucks that the WAAF drivers bring out to pick them up.

There will be no immediate rest though, for they first must go for their debriefing procedure. But there, there will be richly sweetened cups of coffee, more cigarettes and later, a bacon and real egg breakfast. Scant reward for what they have been through but, nevertheless, a token recognition that is very welcome and much appreciated.

Perhaps they will be on "ops" again tonight. Possibly there will be a break for a couple of days. They don't know. And nor do we, their ground staff support group.And so another day dawns and the whole business will start all over again...

Noel Coward wrote the following words in 1943 and it sits so well at the conclusion of this chapter.

Lie in the dark and listen
It's clear tonight so they're flying high,
Hundreds of them, thousands perhaps,
Riding the icy, moonlight sky,
Men, machinery, bombs and maps,
Altimeters and guns and charts,
Coffee, sandwiches, fleece-lined boots,
Bones and muscles and minds and hearts
English saplings with English roots
Deep in the earth they've left below.
Lie in the dark and let them go;
Lie in the dark and listen.

NOTES

1. Pilot Ken Wallis, writing in the Elsham 50th anniversary booklet, described an experience which emphasises continuing hazards, even when over 'friendly' territory:

> *I remember well on the 22nd October 1941, the "Welcome Home" to a very sick Wellington by the Immingham Balloon Barrage.*
> *Our radio had been struck by lightning on the way to Mannheim.*
> *Both engines had iced up after leaving the Dutch coast on our return and only came back to life just before ditching in a very stormy North Sea. Our first welcome was to be shot up by the Harwich defences (not up to enemy standard!) so we turned north and, eventually, briefly west. Then we learned the effectiveness of our balloons. We were very lucky to crash land in the dark, just on the edge of the quarry face at Elsham Wolds and to get away with it.*
> *It was a surprise, subsequently, for all the crew to be invited to a party laid on for us by the balloon operators at Grimsby. There they said how pleased they were to have a crew with whom to have a party; they had brought down over forty British aircraft in the Command and some seven German!!*
> *They also said, quite rightly, that they were preventing low altitude bombing. Each of us was given a piece of the cable that caught us!!*

2. In December 1990 the *"Evening Telegraph"* published in Lincolnshire, issued a special edition, one in its series of *Bygones*,

covering the war-time history of 1 Group of Bomber Command. The history was also published in three books, *Maximum Effort: The North Lincolnshire Bombers; Maximum Effort: 1 Group at War; Maximum Effort: The Untold Story.* The compiler was a journalist, Patrick Otter.

I quote from the section on Elsham Wolds and 103 Squadron:

> *Its Lancasters, initially, went "gardening", laying mines off the coast of France, Holland and Germany. Sometimes they ranged as far as the Baltic. It was universally hated by all who took part.*
>
> *Crews spent long hours, often flying alone, trying to locate a particular area in an estuary, a reference point in a sea lane. The nature of the mines they were carrying meant they had to fly low. They had to cope with terrible weather, lack of navigation aids, flack ships, fighters and the nerve-wracking discomfort of long flights over water for no visible results...*
>
> *...only a few of the mines did what they were supposed to do.*
>
> *And then they returned with the knowledge that their trip did not count as a full sortie towards the completion of their tour.*
>
> *(On reflection that was absolutely incomprehensible. Diabolical in my view. Author)*

3. THE DISPLAYING OF OPERATIONAL SYMBOLS

On the planes that have returned, just below the cockpit on the port side on the airframe, will be painted another small yellow bomb, "Chalking up" another "op". If an enemy fighter has been shot down then a swastika will be added; an ice-cream cone if they have been on the long haul to northern Italy!

Such is the very quirky humour of warfare.

4. It may occur to readers to ask: "How about those gremlins – did they go on "ops" with the bombers?" You really must be joking of course! Mischievous, troublesome, irritating they may have been but stupid they were not. But, you can be assured that as soon as the planes returned to base and were parked back in their dispersals, those pesky gremlins were ready and waiting to wreak their own version of havoc, just to add to whatever problems the night's operation had thrown up. They could be counted on. Ask any ex-ground crew "erk".

11. Bits and Pieces

There is no question that the Avro Lancaster was a superb flying machine and much favoured by the air-crews of Bomber Command who flew in them.

Don Charlwood in *Journeys Into Night* describes the scene when Squadron Leader Fox announced to the 103 air-crews that the Squadron was to be the first in 1 Group to convert from Halifaxes to Lancasters.

> *It was impossible for him (Fox) to continue for cheering, whistling, stamping, nor could he conceal his own delight. To the men he had become someone exalted, a Moses assuring them of deliverance to the Promised Land.*

Of the Lancaster, Don Charlwood wrote...

> *They are the most beautiful kites imaginable to fly – they climb like a bat out of hell, very light and responsive to the controls... Quite easy to land – you feel them down like a Tiger Moth.*

It may seem inappropriate to describe a heavy bomber as a "beautiful kite" but Don Charlwood was so right to enthuse about the Avro Lancaster. Its purpose was deadly but its performance as an aeroplane was, unquestionably, among the very best in aviation history.

Just a few statistics about the Lanc., and we must remember that we are talking about an aeroplane that was flying over fifty years ago and is not to be compared with the sophisticated, technologically advanced civil and military aircraft of today.

> *The four Rolls-Royce Merlin engines of 1280 to 2400 HP drove the plane fully loaded, at a maximum speed of 275 MPH at 15,000 feet. It could climb to a height of 24,000 feet and operated, usually, at about 20,000 feet.*
>
> *The Lanc. had a wing-span of 102 feet and some bomber bases were obliged to instal bigger hangars to accommodate it. During the course of its operational life, this extraordinary*

aircraft carried bomb loads that ranged from 8,000lbs to 22,000lbs according to modification.

The Browning machine-gun in the three turrets – front, dorsal (upper) and rear – could fire 1,150 rounds of .303 bullets per minute.

The Lanc. was constructed of 55,000 separate parts and it took 30,000 jigs and tools to put it all together with the help of a workforce of 40,000.

Each of those bombers cost £24,000 and each engine alone came in at £2,500. One propeller cost £350 and a radio set £250... a collection of figures just to give some idea why it was that the Second World War cost this country such a hell of a lot of money! And it is "old" money we are talking here.

~ ~ ~

During the six years I served in the RAF I found the great majority of aircraft captains, and their crew, most amenable to having ground crew lads on board their "kites" when on non-operational flights – testing, on "circuits and bumps" or on cross-country runs. And, indeed, in some places it was positively encouraged in order to add another incentive to conscientious workmanship!

My own flying experience was not extensive and I never actually kept a "log", but I guess, over those years, I did clock up a cumulative, fair number of hours in the air; and in a great variety of aircraft. From the time of my "maiden flight" in the "flying pig", the Lerwick flying boat, I had a few short and longer trips in the redoubtable Short Sunderland and the American-built PBY Catalina whilst serving in Coastal Command. Overseas I was on a squadron that we sometimes called the "Bassetts" because of the "all sorts" of aircraft we found ourselves servicing; and consequently I can now say that I can include, Dakotas, Hudsons, a Mitchell, a Baltimore and a Cessna (the latter piloted by my friend Dick Meinke, from the Melksham days whom I mentioned earlier in the book) among the great variety of aircraft in which I have flown. And, of course, there was the Avro Lancaster at Elsham.

Sometimes the trips were legitimate and authorised (especially those involving air tests of instruments or other equipment for which we "Instrument Bashers" were responsible) but, thanks to friendly relationships with air-crews, there were, also, "scrounged" and less "legit" flights. And blind eyes were sometimes turned to allow that to happen.

But there is no question in my mind that, apart from the Sunderland flying boat, the Lancaster was the aeroplane in which I felt the safest and most at ease. It simply had the feel of reliability and of belonging up there in the sky.

It is important to mention that, not only to echo the air-crews' admiration for the Lanc., but also because of my own attitude to flying. I was in the RAF – yes – and I had twice volunteered for air-crew, certainly; but during my service I had, always, a decidedly ambivalent relationship with the business of flying; an attitude I retain still to this day. I can thrill to being in flight... absorbing the sheer power of it, the movement in the air, the passing through and above clouds; seeing the Lilliputian transformation of the world from up there. I know, too, enough about the theory of flight to understand how it all works, yet, I cannot, and never could, bring myself to believe it! The whole damn thing of flying machines – especially the bigger ones – registers in my mind as taking liberties with nature! Birds belong up there – but do we?

However, since I do carry this mental "conflict of interest" around with me, it is, perhaps, understandable that I should have more confidence in some aeroplanes than in others. And the Lanc., as I have said, rates very highly on the scale of reliability.

~ ~ ~

During my seven months' service with 103 Squadron at Elsham, I had several "flips", most of them in "D" Duck, and my confidence in the Lancaster grew with every flight, reinforcing the widely shared affection for the "kite" throughout the squadron. There were, however, three incidents that put my personal approval of that bomber severely to the test.

The first, which was at once exhilarating and "hairy", quite positively demonstrated the aerobatic versatility of the fabled Lancaster, about whose performance in the air I had heard so much.

For some reason, now forgotten, I went up one morning on an air test with one of 103 Squadron's top pilots, Squadron Leader J H Kennard DFC and for a short period of time we flew straight and level at about 3,000 feet over the Humber and up into the skies above Yorkshire.

Now, I did not know at the time, and never found out after, whether the worthy Squadron Leader decided to enjoy himself anyway, was convincing himself that his "kite" could, when necessary, really get him out of trouble, or was intent, together with his crew, on having a bit of fun – at my expense. And, judging by the grins on the faces of some of the crew afterwards, it would be no surprise if the latter motivation was the surer bet.

Anyway, it was only after I had crawled, by invitation, into the bomb-aimer's position, right in the nose of the aircraft – affording a superb panoramic view – that pilot Kennard began to go through a repertoire of "flying circus" manoeuvres that gave an altogether new dimension to the term "test flight".

We climbed at speed, just about vertically, then, suddenly, dived steeply, at even greater velocity, engines screaming – either in delight or protest – and with me wondering how far up I had left my stomach. Indeed, as the aerobatics continued, with cork-screwing tight banking, roaring down from height to low-level attack flying a hundred feet or so above the ground, my spinning head and protesting innards lost all sense of location within my body. Probably the whole thing lasted only a matter of minutes but it seemed to me like for ever; and in that space of time I had been shown two things. Firstly what it was like inside the Lanc. when on '"ops"' it was required to take extreme evasive action – or, at least, to have some indication of that; and secondly, that travel sickness was never going to be a problem for me, because in spite of it all, and the sudden unexpected assault upon my anatomy, I had not "thrown up". And when we returned to normal flight, I felt quite elated about that; quite chuffed with myself, in fact.

After we landed, the bomb-aimer asked me if I was OK. "Fine, thank you, sir." I told him and I think he was somewhat surprised and not a little disappointed! But he nevertheless patted me on the shoulder and I felt as if I had just been given my wings! Biggles – at last!

But that experience held me in good stead, for when, a few months later on a troopship about to negotiate the notorious Bay of Biscay, I felt no trepidation whatsoever!

Sadly, Squadron Leader Kennard and his crew were shot down on the 27th September 1943 – a couple of months after I had left Elsham.

~ ~ ~

The second incident could have dented my faith in the Avro Lancaster but as it occurred on a trip with my special "kite", "D" Donald Duck, I was prepared to give her the benefit of the doubt; and to apportion blame for the abberation – disquieting even though it was – to either a moment of capriciousness on "Duck's" part or, and more likely, to a squad of malevolent gremlins who had come along for the ride.

It had not been a long trip but as we returned to Elsham, I became aware of collective consternation among the crew and I asked my friend "Jock" Brechney what was happening.

"*We canna get the undercart down*," he told me. That was certainly not good news for me, for on this "scrounged" unofficial trip, I didn't have a parachute! I was aware of feverish activity in the area of the cockpit as we circled the drome and I sat on the bunk wondering if "Jock's" parachute could manage two bods!

It took a few circuits of the airfield before the undercarriage came to its senses – or the gremlins were shaken off – and it came down and, mercifully, locked. Faith restored. But I was a little hurt that old "Duck" had seen fit to put the wind up me in such a manner!

~ ~ ~

I imagine that there are not many people who can claim that they have been nearly run over by a Lancaster bomber; but I do have that dubious distinction. And the third episode in the trilogy of anecdotes relating to my "affair" with that aeroplane occurred, not even in the air, but on *terra-firma* with some emphasis on the *terra*, if spelt a little differently!

In Sid Finn's *Black Swan* (the history of 103 Squadron) the incident in which I was involved is recorded, although the manner of my involvement is not mentioned, simply because Sid would not have been aware of it. However, the background to my story is given in *Black Swan* and I quote...

> One day a Lancaster on air test was taking off using the runway parallel to a road leading to five cross-roads. Halfway along the runway the plane started to swing to port. The pilot put his undercarriage up and the Lanc. slid across the road and came to rest with its nose over the edge of the chalk pit.
>
> Right underneath the aircraft was a mechanical digger with men working around it (but not for long!). The air-crew walked out of the plane unharmed. Then a fire started in one of the engines and the bomber caught fire and eventually burned out.
>
> At the enquiry they came to the conclusion that the wireless operator's box of spare valves had become jammed between his feet and the rudder control. After that they made a special storage for the valve box.

Now you can see why I was so concerned when I left my inspection lamp on board the Walrus flying boat at the completion of my very first DI! (See Chapter 4)

How, then, did I crop up in the above scenario? As I remember it, I was a little put out on that morning because I should have been on a "day off" but, whereas, I should therefore, have had a "bit of a lie-in" and a casual, unhurried start to the day, other forces were deciding otherwise and I found myself ordered to make an a.m. appearance on the firing range. (The "powers that be" at Elsham insisted that we should keep our hands in on things military and periodically we were obliged to participate in activities such as assault courses, "defence of the airfield" exercises and sessions on the firing range.)

As I was "off" for the day, my best "oppo" Frank Wain, was assigned to cover for me on the D.I. on "E" Edward, but as he, too, was scheduled to be free in the afternoon, he and I had agreed to go into the town of Brigg for a brief respite in the civilian milieu; and to partake of a tea and a bun in a café, which is something we both liked to do from time to time.

I had called in at the Instrument Section prior to going to the firing range and there discovered that Frank was going up on an air test on "E" but would still meet me later on. And so, after my session on the range (where I had been sharply reprimanded for wearing shoes instead of boots!) I decided to take a short-cut across the drome and to the Section where I was to meet Frank.

I came up onto the road mentioned in Sid Finn's account of the incident and then started out across the ground between the road and the parallel runway. As I did so, I could see "E" Edward commencing her take-off run for the air test. I stopped to watch and at that moment "E" swung violently off the runway and came like an express train straight in my direction! For a moment of disbelief – it was well-known that the Lanc. had a tendency to pull to the left on take-off but this was ridiculous – I did not, however, dwell on my incredulity and ran like hell, the instinct for survival kicking in fast. Behind me I could hear the Lanc. crunching and screaming along the ground and as I looked over my shoulder I saw it slide across the road and then come to a juddery, sudden halt. Knowing that Frank was on board I instinctively turned and started to run towards the "kite" which I could now see was right down on its belly. And also, that the nose of the aircraft was right over the edge of the chalk quarry!

As Sid Finn wrote, the crew came out of the stricken "E" Edward and walked away (with my friend Frank among them). I ran over to him and he said he was OK. But when I pointed out to him where the Lanc. had stopped he said, "Bloody hell!"

And there is not much more that one could say at such a moment.

In the context of Sid's account he seems to place the above incident in December 1942 but I have it in my diary as occurring on 9 June 1943. And I am sure that I would have mentioned an event like that in my diary on the day that it happened! Also, I am not sure whether or not the plane burned out as Sid suggests. Certainly an engine did catch fire, but I seem to recall that the "fire boys" came out and got it under control and also that some of us went on board to salvage items of equipment that could be removed.

I do know that the "kite" was a write-off but I am not sure that fire was the main cause of its destruction. I must, however, hasten to add that I am not, here, being critical of Sid Finn. "Black Swan" is a superb book, full of extraordinary detail. It is just that my memory of the "runaway Lancaster" incident is at variance with Sid's account on two points. And Sid's recounting of the story was, to be fair to him, based on second-hand information.

~   ~   ~

Quite by chance I came across a rather quixotic sequel to the foregoing episode. And I must stress that this, too, is second-hand and anecdotal. But I cannot imagine any reason why there would be any need for anyone to invent it.

At a recent RAF Elsham Wolds Association Reunion, I met a man, Roy Smith, who, during the war, was a schoolboy in the Elsham area; and who still resides there. I was talking to him about the incident with "E" Edward and he then told me that, in addition to the men working at the bottom of the quarry, there were two others at the top and they had a dog with them. When those two heard the noise of the rapidly approaching Lanc. they took off with alacrity: and so, too, did the dog, literally because it ran straight over the edge of the quarry!

Hearing all the commotion up above, the men below looked up and one of them, seeing the dog in flight, rushed forward, judged the rate of descent and point of arrival to perfection and commendably caught the cur in his arms, whereupon the frightened and confused hound bit him!

There are many and varied casualties in a war!

The whole business of working on airfields was, by its very nature, hazardous: and I can only marvel that there were not more casualties than there were.

Flying accidents at and around air bases were common enough. Collisions, landing and take-off errors, faulty equipment, etc. caused many casualties, an aspect of the RAF's war effort which is not so well known. On the ground one had to be very alert and watchful, keeping eyes and ears open for things spinning, slipping, turning, catching fire and falling. The need for vigilance was instilled into us – especially on 'A' Flight with "Chiefy" Clacker in attendance.

In a hangar on one occasion, an "oppo" caught his foot when a pile of heavy oxygen cylinders shifted during unloading. I broke all weight-lifting records and risked an early hernia, so that the lad could remove his damaged foot. But, in doing so, I succeeded in causing an avalanche of cylinders that could have crushed us all, but miraculously didn't. My rescue mission, and the great Herculean effort, were immediately forgotten and I was on the receiving end of a tirade of, shall we say, uncomplimentary observations from my companions. No gratitude at all!

Fire vigilance was constant, especially in the vicinity of petrol, oil, bombs and ammunition; and you had to keep an eye to taxi-ing aircraft, swinging tail planes, and slip-streams.

It was just as well at Elsham that we were blessed with a Medical Officer who is remembered by all who were there with great affection. Flight Lieutenant "Doc" Henderson, a wonderful man: kind, understanding and possessing a lovely sense of humour. You knew about "Doc" even if you never required his services. He cared a great deal about the air-crew lads and was fully tuned into their fears and strains and their need to act wildly on occasion. He also flew on "ops" – some authorised, some not – and he flew sixteen in all, each time with a different crew.

I have mentioned, just in passing, that there were occasions when bombs fell out of the aircraft at the dispersals and it was quite a disconcerting experience. It happened in my presence twice but fortunately on both memorable occasions, the "cookies" did not explode. But I can assure the reader that when a 4,000lb blast bomb that looks like a boiler tank thuds suddenly onto the concrete somewhat adjacent to where you are standing, it does cause a sharp intake of breath and the holding of same for a record-breaking period of time! And a few minutes afterwards you grab hold of yourself to confirm that you are still alive! Sometimes at Elsham and at other bases, prematurely falling bombs did explode and in The

RAF Elsham Wolds' 50th Anniversary booklet ex-Flight Engineer Sandy Rowe reminded us all of the occasion when the bombs dropped from a Lanc. when at dispersal prior to take-off on operations.

> *On 23rd August 1943 (I was lucky once more for I had left Elsham in July and had I still been there, I could easily have been in the vicinity! Author) some bombs dropped out of an aircraft at dispersal when we were preparing to leave for Berlin, and when we were moving our aircraft, PM-H, out of the danger area, the whole lot blew up, including the aircraft from which they had dropped.*
>
> *Although the explosion was heard in Grimsby I never heard a thing – being so close. My wireless op. was killed, a local farmer, Mr Woods, was injured in a leg by a flying oxygen bottle, and PM-H was badly damaged.*
>
> *The fire engine crew were so pleased with us – PM-H had impeded their progress to the incident and had saved them from being blown up also!*
>
> *We survivors from PM-H walked across the field to camp and were having a beer in the Sergeants' Mess when "Doc" Henderson found us and gave us each a couple of tablets to take. By midnight I was ill. Presumably "Doc" thought we were going to bed – and failed to tell us that drink and his tablets didn't mix!!*

On the ground or in the air, there were no hiding places!

~ ~ ~

Undoubtedly, ex-personnel of all the bomber squadrons and on every airfield could relate claims to distinction. Stories about events, or people, or certain aeroplanes that marked them off as special; or, in some way, different. There were several such "claims to fame" at RAF Elsham Wolds but three are worthy of mention.

Firstly, 103 Squadron was the only unit in Bomber Command to operate with the succession of Wellingtons, Halifaxes and Lancasters, each make of aircraft replacing the other, in that order, between 1941 and 1945.

Secondly, at Elsham Wolds there was "stationed" the most durable, the greatest surviving Lancaster bomber in the whole of the Command. She was Lancaster PM ED 880 M – known to all as "Mike Squared" and later as "Mother of them all".

"M Squared" – so called because she operated with both 103 and 576 Squadrons out of Elsham and Fisherton, came through 140 sorties, carrying a variety of crews. And any individual member of air-crews in Bomber Command, in order to equal that truly remarkable record of survival, would have had to complete something like five tours of operations.

"Mother of them all" should have been preserved, proudly displaying her 140 symbols, including the DFC painted on her side, of service and stood at the main gate of some post-war RAF camp; or given a place of honour in an air museum. But like so many of her kind, she went to the scrap heap.

~ ~ ~

A special dispensation from the King was necessary to allow three brothers to fly as pilots on the same operation out of Elsham. These were the Henry brothers from New South Wales, Australia, and on that raid – on Cologne – John completed his tour of 30 "ops", David was on his 23rd and for Gavin, it was his very first. They all three returned safely and, remarkably, all survived the war.

And there is a connection too, with "Mike Squared" because John Henry was the pilot who was given the sad, funereal task of flying that veteran Lancaster to the scrap yard. John Henry was sentimental enough to believe that something at least should be salvaged for posterity and he brought back "M's" bomb release cable, which is now the property of the RAF Elsham Wolds Association.

~ ~ ~

Going On Leave

I went home on leave three times from Elsham: a 48- hour pass in March 1943 which I spent at the home of my girlfriend at Sidcup in Kent; seven days in May when Ethel managed to get a week off work and we spent the leave at my home in Witham, Essex. And then came the posting overseas, and in June I had fourteen days' embarkation leave, which I split between Church Stretton, Shropshire, Birmingham, Sidcup and Witham. I remember so much about those interludes away from the business of war at Elsham. It was good to visit relatives in those places and then to return to my home town.

That great feeling of release and anticipation as the journey home began. The clickerty-clack of the train's wheels as they sped you along the track. Then the slightly acrid smell of the Underground, the rumble of the Tube trains and their rocking progress through the maze of tunnels. Feeling good, sitting there looking up at the map of Underground stations on the other side of the carriage, confirming the route in my mind, even though I knew it well enough. *"Change at the Bank for Liverpool Street."* It is all etched in my mind and I can never travel on the Tube today without being transported mentally back to those times and to the many journeys on the London Underground network either on leave or on a posting. (And now, with the fading eyesight of old age, I can no longer read those diagrams of stations!)

I recall how Ethel and I clung to every enjoyable minute of the rationed time we spent together on those leaves and how quickly those precious days and hours sped by. I remember how both my mother, and Ethel's mum, also, did all they could to enhance our "brief encounter" and stretched the meagre civilian rations to ply us with the limited treats of war-time Britain.

How good it was to shed my uniform and, by donning "civvies", to peel away the military life-style that had become the "norm" of one's existence.

How good it was, too, with Ethel on my arm, to retrace my old haunts of childhood and youth around my dear old home town of Witham and to meet and to talk with so many friends and acquaintances, hearing again the delightful Essex dialect.

And then, one remembers also, the irrevocable march of time, each minute each hour and day biting into those supremely happy periods of leave; and the sad railway station farewells, trains pulling out and uniformed bodies leaning out of carriage windows exchanging poignant waves with tearful female figures, ever receding into distance on platforms as the trains pull out. And yet...

And yet, there was always something else pulling at your heart and mind in conflict with the heavy-heartedness of those partings. It was the need to rejoin and be with your "oppos" back at the base. To continue your part in what you were all doing together as a team and in the comforting embrace of comradeship. And if that now sounds trite I make no apology. It was the way it was and only those who have, or did, experience that great sense of interdependent warmth of comradeship will truly understand what I am writing here.

Even when, at the end of my embarkation leave, and the farewell to my mother and father (my mother, in particular, distraught) and to Ethel, brave in her sadness; and when the destination was unknown, the period of separation inestimable and the outcome always a lottery – I could not, in the midst of my own melancholy at the parting, dispel the curiosity, the "sense of adventure" that vied for attention.

But, in any case, an overseas posting was something I had volunteered for – so I could hardly complain!

~   ~   ~

Thoughts of Home

The fields and copses, the general rustic ambience which enclosed the airfield and camp at Elsham were constant reminders of my home town. Those root-crop fields evoked memories of my childhood when my pals and I stole turnips from a farmer's field, hid in a ditch and ate them raw. And we did that, not because we were desperately hungry but, like "scrumping" apples, because there was an element of "naughtiness" in it and a touch of the spice of risk. In any case, there was a more compelling motivation, which was that we just loved eating raw turnips!

~   ~   ~

Sometimes at Elsham, out on the Flights I would, during a lull in our activities – such as when the armourers were bombing up – I would sit on top of the dispersal bay bank, light a cigarette, and wallow in a bit of homesickness.

Not far away a farm worker would be hoeing between the rows of beet; a skylark would suddenly rise, doing its avion Indian rope trick and flocks of starlings did their version of "circuits and bumps". And I would wonder if the farm worker, when he took his break, would sit by a hedge, eat a thick cheese sandwich and drink from a bottle of sweet, cold tea as we used to do when we went pea picking back home.

All around this enclave, bristling with the machinery of war there existed the normality of a rural way of life that had, with few changes, been going on for centuries. What were those lines..?

What is this life if, full of care,
We have no time to stand and stare?

102

and I remember, once, when one of the riggers joined me and as we shared a light for our cigarette he said:

"It's worth havin' a go for, ain't it!"

Yes. It was.

~　~　~

Staying with the rural aspect of the RAF's presence in such strength and numbers in Lincolnshire, the following little anecdote is well worthy of inclusion in this chapter of "odds and ends". It is something I had forgotten about until long after the war. I read it in *Black Swan*. And I am indebted to Sid, once again, for jogging my memory. In fact, why not let Sid tell the story, as it was told to him...

As you may remember, there were a couple of dispersals at Elsham with haystacks at the side of them. In the spring of 1943 two pairs of sparrows decided to start nest building in one of the Lancs. One built in the flame damper on the starboard outer engine and the other in the flaps. This caused a great laugh with the ground crew. Can you imagine it, an operational Lancaster with two birds' nests sticking out of it!

Before the mechanics ran the engines up in the morning they pulled the nests out and, as soon as they had finished, the birds started building again. This went on for a few days. The only one who didn't see the funny side of it was the "Chiefy". He even asked us not to talk about it in case word got around. He really was a worried man.

The birds eventually gave up. I'll bet those lads hated having to destroy the nests but a much worse fate would have befallen the eventual chicks had the nests been allowed to stay.

Author's comment: I only wish that the above story had had a different, more appealing ending, i.e. that the Lanc. chosen as a prime site for building by the sparrows had been withdrawn from "ops" until the eggs were laid and hatched. Yes, well, we are all entitled to a bit of unrealistic fantasising at times!

~　~　~

A few years ago, quite by chance, I read a letter in a magazine from someone who had served at Elsham Wolds. He wrote that a slogan: *"YOU BEND 'EM, WE MEND 'EM"* was displayed in large letters over the great doors of the station's biggest hangar. Well, I guess if that is so, then it was done after I left Elsham for I have no recollection of it. But I must say that *"YOU BEND 'EM, WE MEND 'EM"* would be a most splendid and appropriate motto for all the aircraft servicing ground crews and for all time. And wouldn't it have a great ring to it if it was worded in Latin:

OMNIA FRACTA REPARAMUS... Well, why not?

You would have found all kinds of examples of ingenuity and "make do and mend" on an RAF Bomber Station in World War II. Here is a simple, but nonetheless effective, example: Bicycles were numerous at Elsham and were used for various purposes, either on or outside the camp and airfield. Consequently there was a lot of wear and tear on the tyres and punctures were frequent. Inevitably of course, there came a time when the inner-tube became irreparable. Or, even if not, puncture outfits and patches were somewhat hard to come by. So some of the lads – air and ground crew alike – stuffed the tyres of their cycles with grass! It did not make for a comfortable ride but it enabled a continuity of mobility; otherwise it meant long walks everywhere. And no one wanted that!

The Barnetby Archaeologists

During my seven month's service at RAF Elsham Wolds, I thought of Barnet-le-Wold only as the local railway terminus and the place where the WAAFS were billeted. Now, of course, it is the focal point for the RAF Elsham Wolds annual reunion; but it is also to me, the place of residence of Roy and Sheila Smith. As I mentioned earlier in this chapter, I first met Roy and Sheila a few years ago on a walkabout on the site of the old airfield and since then we, my wife and I and Roy and Sheila have become good friends and they have been very supportive to me in the writing of this book.

It must have been very exciting for Roy and his schoolmates living, during the war in close proximity to a very active bomber station but his interest did not decline after the war and when the airfield closed down.

He started his 'archaeological digs and foraging' for souvenirs and over the years, he has assembled a quite remarkable collection of memorabilia ranging from Brylcreem bottles to pieces of aircraft, from bullets to cutlery and even a truly astonishing find - aWorld War I bomb of the kind that was 'dropped by hand' from the cockpit of the flying machines of that time. (Elsham was also a RFC base in the First World War.)

Roy also has an impressive collection of books and documents and he and some other enthusiasts in the area have been and are still active supporters of our Association.

Just recently, whilst talking to Roy he has corrected the detail of the sequel of the story of the 'runaway Lancaster' which appears in this chapter. Apparently, one man only, a Mr. D. Wraith, was working at the top of the quarry when 'E' Edward screeched along the ground towards the quarry and he had such a narrow escape that he was taken to hospital with shock. (Hardly surprising!)

Roy says also, that no one has ever been sure whether the story of the 'falling dog' is entirely accurate or locally embellished. But whether it is authentic or local folk-lore, it is a damn good story!

However whatever the credibility of the anecdote, what follows here to complete this chapter is., not only absolutely authentic, but is also a fascinating, if also poignant story.

Roy and Sheila's son David caught on to his parents' enthusiasm for the search for artefacts and what he discovered one day proved to be of great significance to a family in Australia.

I must allow David to tell this story in his own words

THE LOST IDENTITY DISC

My name is David Smith and as a boy I spent many hours at the old airfield of Elsham Wolds. One-day not far from the sergeants mess on the farm belonging to Mr Dodds I unearthed a round disc,

 with the inscription M G Western RAAF. It was his identity disc. Had he lost it? Was it a spare had he survived? It was a complete mystery, which it remained for a few years, until a friend started work at the newly built Anglian Water works in the corner of the airfield, who told me about the Elsham Wolds Association for veterans. He knew of a Mrs Westrup who looked after some of the records. As she lived nearby, he arranged to visit and check the records, which he did that afternoon the 16th December.1996.

Flight Sergeant Western was the mid-upper turret gunner of Lancaster DV342 G2 which had taken off at 16:27 hours for Berlin. Sadly all were killed, the date 16th December, 1943, 53 years to the day! If possible I had hoped to trace any living relatives to return the disc.

Mrs Westrup thought we would have little success.

By chance, three years later my father was talking about the disc to Don Charlwood, the author of *No Moon Tonight* at the Elsham Wolds memorial service. He was most interested and said he would help if he could. True to his word Don got in touch with Mr Charles Hawes of Canberra, who in turn rang Peter Western in Marion, South Australia, inquiring if he was related to M G Western, which he was, if possible would he contact us in England and send any information he could about Malcolm?

Peter and his family had been deprived of information for years. It must have been quite a shock to receive a phone call from out of the blue, inquiring after Malcolm, after all these years.

Malcolm had a cousin Margaret Malcolm was her idol. He also had a sister who now lives in America.

Peter kindly sent a copy of Malcolm's obituary in the state paper and also a copy of the last letter he received from Malcolm. Sadly it was written on the day he died, his 20th birthday.

This together with Mr Hawes information and archive material from the Association have enabled us to piece together the story.

MALCOLM'S STORY

Malcolm (pictured right) and Peter were best friends sharing the same grandfather. Their family had emigrated from Devon England to Australia in 1848, buying land just outside Adelaide, growing grapes and other stone fruits and growing to a total of 200 acres by 1850.

Malcolm has a sister Alison who now lives in America, a cousin Margaret in Australia, both idolised him.

At 19 Peter joined the infantry to fight the Japanese, on leave he met Malcolm who said he had joined the Air force and would be trained as a gunner. It was the last time they met.

Malcolm arrived in England and eventually joined 576 Lancaster bomber squadron at Elsham. An extract from Malcolm's last letter shows that he was just settling down.

"I hope to settle down here for some time, there is a terrific amount of walking to do on this camp, as we live a long way from the main part of the camp. One thing it has given me a huge appetite, the food is good here at this place, good for England anyhow".

On the 16th December 1943,at 16:27 hours Malcolm's aircraft flown by F/O McAra took off for Berlin. The mission got off to a bad start. Just after takeoff in cloud Flight Sergeant Scott collided with another aircraft, crashing at Ulceby with no survivors. Another failed to take-off. Eight aircraft bombed this target, but Flight Officer McAra and crew failed to return. In 1947 investigations as to the fate of Lancaster DV342, confirmed it crashing over Lichenberg, then the Russian sector of Berlin. An eyewitness account by the German police chief said it was travelling west to east and over 10,000 ft when it exploded scattering wreckage over a wide area. Malcolm's body was not identified, but is thought to be interned in the British Military Cemetery at Heerstrasse, Berlin. He is remembered on the Runnymede Memorial London, Lincoln Cathedral and Elshams book of remembrance. Strangely in 1946 Malcolm's fountain pen was recovered from a German shop, and returned to Malcolm's mother by the British Army authorities in Europe. After Malcolm's farther died, he left a sum of money to the Westminster College near where he lived, as a memorial to Malcolm.

The money earns interest each year and is used to help the most promising agriculture student of the year.

The disc and all the information we have gathered has been forwarded to Peter, and is displayed at the college in Malcolm's memory. Now when most of Lincolnshires airfields have been returned to agriculture or made industrial estates, finding Malcolm's identity disc has highlighted the huge personal sacrifice made by many, for freedom for us all.

LANCASTER 1 DV342 G2

F/O R.S McAra	Sgt J.L Barratt	F/Sgt C.Chapman
F/O G.L Blackacre	F/Sgt E.Russon	F/Sgt M.G Western
	F/Sgt A.A Harris	

12. 'ERKESSES': A TRIBUTE TO THE WAAFS

There is a strength of quiet endurance as significant of courage as the most daring feats of prowess. (Tuckermaw)

I am unable to write at any great length about the WAAFS who served during World War II because I did not know them. That is to say, that although I met them – or some of them – talked with those with whom I was acquainted and saw various of them at their work, I did not know them in the same way that I knew my ground crew comrades – or even the air-crews. It was just not possible for any of us lads to share the same kind of intimacy (in the non-sexual sense) with the WAAFS as we did with each other. We who serviced the aircraft not only worked together but also lived together. We were very much aware of each other's characters, personalities and temperaments; each other's moods, opinions, interests, habits and foibles. We probably knew each other as well as most people in our lives did, or ever would. And in the familiarity of our male- bonding existence we did, in many ways, even lose the inhibitions that are an integral part of the "norms" of civilian life.

In no way, therefore, could we be on the same level of "together-ness" with the WAAFS as we airmen experienced with each other. Nor, undoubtedly, in reverse. The male and female personnel of active RAF bases such as Elsham Wolds did not so much "commune" as "co-exist".

We met, talked (even dated), were co-involved in some aspects of activity, experienced the same dramas on the drome and the various ambiences. We shared the essential purposes of the ground staff – a collective *raison d'être* – and enjoyed together some social events plus, unquestionably, that special sense of comradeship that was so much a remembered feature of Elsham.

And so, even if this chapter is relatively short, due to compara-tively limited intimacy, there are perfectly adequate grounds, and evidence, to support my retrospective personal tribute to those young women who served in RAF Bomber Command at Elsham Wolds. And this salute and acknowledgement of the WAAFS is, in fact, confined to my acquaintance with those at Elsham, since that was the only place in my six years' service that I encountered the women's branch of the Air Force in any meaningful way.

Prior to my arrival at Elsham the only contact I had experienced with the WAAFS was restricted to lining up for food service in cookhouses or on visits to admin. blocks, and to medical centres. Then, after Elsham, overseas, even though WAAFS did serve abroad, I, personally, cannot recall ever encountering any of them.

If readers have come this far into my book they will be well aware that this is not an empirical thesis, a dissertation or a statistical record. It is a narrative of remembered observations and impressions. And that being so, how could I ignore the presence and the invaluable in-put of our female contemporaries in the story of the combined efforts of everyone at Elsham? There would be an incomplete "impressionist picture" and a similar omission to that which, in part, motivated me to write the book in the first place – the paucity of material written about the role of the ground staff in post-war accounts of RAF exploits.

First of all, then, who and what were the "girls in blue"? As I remember them, they were, in the main and like us 'blokes', very young; which is why I tend to refer to them as girls.

Again, in similar fashion to us (us in this context being the male "erks") they had come into the RAF from all corners of the UK; and were, in the majority of cases, of working-class origins, with among them, some who could be described as "1930s lower middle class", having attended Girls' High Schools and the like. (I refer here, of course, to WAAFS of lower rank.)

It goes without saying that the girls were of all shapes and sizes, of varying personalities and that some were attractive and pretty, whilst others were less so. In a contingent of several hundred that would be inevitable just as we lads, too, were an assembly of "all sorts". But it was what the girls had in common, rather than any of the features which separated them, that is important and relevant.

The characteristic of the WAAFS that sticks most in my memory is their collective earnestness. They took their responsibilities very seriously and wanted so much to give of their best in whatever role they happened to play: and all the assignments and duties that were undertaken by the girls, far from being on the margins of the station's activities, were essential and integral to the whole scheme of things. Those of us "erks" who were aircraft servicing ground crews – at least in the time when I was at Elsham – could make our assessments and judgements about the worthiness of the WAAFS by passing observation of them at their work; or through conversations with them in off-duty situations such as in the NAAFI, or in their company at social events in the gym. (Or, in the case of some, when dating). But there were airmen who did work alongside the airwomen in some ground staff "trades", such as in the Transport Section, in Admin, Radio and Radar, the Photographic Unit, on the Catering side, with the Control and Intelligence Sections, in the Parachute Section and in various stores. From all of those areas of activity – and from others I have omitted to mention – came, with few exceptions, positive and complimentary comments from the males in those "trades" about the competence and conscientious-ness of the WAAF personnel; all of which confirmed the admiration we blokes in the ground crews – or most of us – held for the girls.

But there is no reason why it should have been any other way. The WAAFS, I am sure, did not set out to prove anything to us. Why should they? Just as we did, they wanted only to prove to themselves – and perhaps to each other – that they could apply themselves assiduously to their tasks, reach the required levels of competence and to achieve self-esteem. So, why should any of us males be surprised, anyway, that females can do all that? But yet we often were; and the respect we, eventually, accorded the young women who shared Elsham Wolds bomber base with us was, at least initially, somewhat grudging. And, in the case of some of the lads, never given at all. So, let us be honest here, because the truth is, and it explains the ambivalent attitude that many aircraftsmen had towards aircraftswomen, that we were, generally, male chauvinists. We were so because we were products of the male-dominated society in which we had grown up. A society in which male and female gender roles were defined and stereotyped.

At the family level, the man was the main – and often only – breadwinner and deemed to be head of household. In the wider world, positions of power and influence were occupied, in the great majority of cases, by males. Men were the leaders, the decision-makers and much of literature and films reinforced the concept of men as heroic figures to whom women must be seen as "weaker" and therefore destined to a supportive role in peace and in war. And it was a view of the "nature of things" that we all imbibed and internalised. And how extraordinary that situation was when one reflects on the fact that women had, in the First World War, clearly demonstrated their ability and adaptability to take on jobs and responsibilities that had hitherto been within the exclusive domain of men. Not forgetting, also, the enfranchisement of women in 1918 and extended in 1928.

110

So, yes, when the guys joined up to go to war in 1939 and after, the prejudices, the normative assumptions about the respective roles of males and females, enlisted with them.

Once again, then, women were having to break down the barriers and destroy the myths. But, there was one vital difference between the First and the Second World Wars... The 1939-45 version was much more a *people's war* and a total war. Civilians became legitimate targets and bombs did not discriminate between men and women, nor between adults and children. And whilst families waited for their serving loved ones to come home to them, the war came to them.

Courage, heroism and fortitude were qualities that could no longer be seen as gender monopolised in a war in which "everyone was in it together".

Perhaps, then, as that murderous conflict progressed, there developed a much greater awareness of total involvement, which predisposed a lessening of the "male superior syndrome". And that changing of ethos, coupled with the evidence of our own eyes as far as the WAAFS were concerned at Elsham, engendered a more accepting attitude among us "erks".

The term "erkesses" is my invention. I cannot ever remember hearing a WAAF referred to in that way; possibly in the lexicon of slang, if one were inclined to be pedantic, it could be argued that "erk" is of male gender. But in my book, the WAAF girls were "erks" in their own right.

Of course, like everyone else, and in the time-honoured tradition of the lesser ranks in HM Forces, the girls were not averse to having a "good old bind" about some grievance or other; but another remembered thing about them was their general cheerfulness.

Whatever the conditions and stresses of life on the station, the "lasses" ("Bud" Senior's affectionately chosen word) were ready with a smile, enjoyed a good laugh and often a song when gathered in groups. They also enjoyed banter and many could hold their own in repartee. It was inevitable, in the male-dominated *milieu* of a bomber base, that the "lasses" would have to "take a bit of stick" from the "lads". But, in the case of some of the WAAFS from tougher backgrounds, they could give back more than they received – expletives included!

"Come on gal, show us your passion killers!"

"One look at you is enough to kill the bloody passions in any girl. Sod off and play with your joy stick!".

("Passion killers" referred to the RAF-issue knickers, long and unfeminine, the WAAFS were required to wear.)

The more I think about it the more I realise the extent of the cultural shock it must have been for those girls who came into the Services from protected and more genteel families. (Hard enough for blokes in that situation.) The imposition of rigid discipline; the barrack-room accommodation and the rough edges of its way of life; the conditions and relative privations – and the aura of war, difficult to ignore on a bomber station. But such girls had ridden it out, adapted and had become part of it all. It had not been easy for them and I know the truth of that because I heard about it from some of the WAAFS who had been in that particular situation.

~ ~ ~

Some of the duties and functions of the WAAFS brought them into close contact with the air-crews and brought them right up to the sharp end of the realities of war.

Let us consider three such "trades" as examples...

Imagine yourself to be one of the girls whose job it was to drive the air-crews to and from their aircraft. You transport the flyers in your "tilly" truck out to the waiting Lancs, when they were going on "ops"; and you go out to pick them up when they return. Inevitably, you get to know the young crews, know them by name and joke with them. As you drive you listen to the conversations going on behind you and learn something about how individuals approach the ordeal that lies ahead of them. And then comes the morning when you go out to pick up a crew and the dispersal bay is empty. The Lanc. is not there and the crew has "gone for a Burton". You will never see Bill, Harry, "Ginger", Peter – whoever – again. And only last night these guys were laughing and joking in your "tilly", and they were due for a spot of leave.

It stabs at your heart and there are tears in your eyes but you have to push your sadness away because there are other crews to be picked up and taken to their de-briefing. They can do without your grief – they have enough of their own: and you will have to get used to this for it will happen again, and again. "Brylcreem boys!", "Glamour boys!". Reality is somewhat different.

What of the parachute packer and custodian? She, too, knows the flyers, issues the parachutes to them, takes them back in when the crew return. But some do not return and there are empty spaces in the racks – until the chutes are replaced for a new crew.

Then there were the girls in the radio and telegraphy 'business', who exchanged communication over the air-waves with the aircraft. On duty at your sets at the time of the E.T.A. (estimated time of arrival) of the bombers returning from "ops", you would know who was calling in – and who was not; and like your WAAF colleagues who ferried the crews and those who looked after the parachutes, you could put faces to crew members on various of the Lancs. But now you receive the always-dreaded "darky" – the radio message that tells you that a "kite" and its crew are in trouble...

"...*two engines out of action*", "...*tail plane shot up*", "...*undercart gone*", "...*dead and wounded on board*", "...*bomb stuck in bomb-bay!*"

You sit in the middle of mounting tension and acute anxiety but it is your duty to stay calm, to encourage, to pass on advice and instructions.

Battening down the emotions, sticking at the job was "par for the course" for any of those girls; and so too was the handling of that sense of loss which was a regular feature of life on a bomber station. It was something else, among many other experiences, which was shared by both WAAFS and RAF ground crews. And because of the difference between men and women – whether socially or genetically programmed – we and they handled our sadness also differently.

(It is somewhat difficult in these days of political correctness, for males to be complimentary to females without risking the accusation of being condescending and patronising. I can only say to the ladies who may read this book – and especially to those who are ex-WAAF – that my acknowledgement of the part played by the WAAFS in World War II is genuinely felt and honestly given.)

One of the slogans employed by the feminist movement in the 1970s was, *"Different therefore equal"*. I was never quite sure about the certainty of that equation, but whilst I am a firm supporter of equal rights for women, I do also believe that there are fundamental variations in the make-up of women as compared with men. I firmly believe, also, that that is how nature intended it to be and I echo wholeheartedly that wonderful phrase of the French *"Vive la différence"*. And that is why, also, that I retain another fond memory of the WAAFS at Elsham, for, in spite of everything that worked against it, most of the girls managed to retain that essential femininity. Quite an achievement under the circumstances.

~   ~   ~

Inevitably when men and women – especially young men and women – are thrown together in situations such as I have been describing there will be flirtations, liaisons and romances; and such was the case at Elsham.

Most, though, tended to be ephemeral, even if, in some instances passionate. And contrary to modern folk-lore, sex was not invented in the 1960s. It is a human drive and natural function which is not diminished by war, but rather, in many ways, stimulated by it.

The official line at Elsham was to discourage attachments between male and female personnel and the latter were billeted in the "Waffery", two and a half miles away from the camp, and just across the road from the railway station at Barnetby.

Of course, the behavioural preferences of the "powers that be" were never going to receive a cooperative response and the whole thing had a strong element of the "King Canutes" about it. Love – and lust – will always find a way, or two, and they did!

If I remember correctly, the ground staff lads were not a little miffed at what they saw as the WAAFS' tendency to gravitate towards the air-crews; and some obviously rejected aircraftsmen did use some rather derogatory phrases to express their disgust and disappointment. But the preference of some of the girls (it did not automatically apply to them all) was perfectly understandable. Well, it is now. It wasn't then!

At a personal level, and I must ask the readers and my wife, who was then my girlfriend, to accept my word for this, my relationship with the WAAFS was, without exception, purely platonic. I was well aware of some very attractive girls on the camp and there were "opportunities". But no entanglements ensued, even though there were "social occasions" in which they might have occurred, such as in the NAAFI or at the events put on in the camp gym.

I knew a number of the girls by name and others by sight. There were three in particular with whom I was very "matey", exchanging cheery – and sometimes cheeky – back-chat as we happened to meet or pass each other on the drome; or meet for longer conversations in the NAAFI. I can, just, recall their faces, but not, unfortunately, their names, although Betty rings a bell down there in the corridors of the mental archives; and so does Grace. One of the girls was a very lively lass from some part of the north of England, one a quieter but equally friendly young lady from somewhere in Kent; and the third a tough, down-to-earth "Brummie".

They were a driver, an R/T operator and a clerk. But I really cannot recall who was which. And I wish that I could, because they

114

were a delightful trio to share some moments of relaxation with; and with lads such as "Bud" Senior, Frank Wain and Harry Batty joining in, they were gatherings of "oppos", male and female, to be remembered with great warmth, even if lacking in detail.

~   ~   ~

I did, once whilst at Elsham, have a date with a WAAF. Yes, I must own up to it. I did it as a favour for an "oppo", one George Turner – about whom much more later – and it was a *blind date*.

It seems that George had met another member of the WAAF somewhere and had made a further date with her but with the proviso that it should be a *double date* as her friend wanted to come along. I was not enthusiastic and would, as I remember, have preferred a quiet night on the camp as I had had a couple of hectic days out on the Flight; but George, in that persuasive way that he had, assured me that it would be fine. *"We'll have a laugh and I reckon you'll be all right there mate..."* he said. Well, I was not sure that I wanted to be *"all right there"*. I didn't mind a bit of female company and a cheery sort of a night out, but that was the limit of my expectations.

The four of us met up in a pub in Scunthorpe but with no set plans for the evening. *"We'll play it by ear,"* said George, as we entered the pub. And when the girls came in a few minutes after us, I knew, immediately, which one was George's "date". She was tall, blonde, good-looking and her uniform did nothing to diminish the shape of her figure.

Now, here we had the classical set-up of the blind-double-date situation. The pretty gal brings along with her the... er... *less than pretty one* so that the contrast is emphasised. (The ploy is used by blokes as well, of course!)

Anyway, my "date" was a big girl, almost as tall as her friend but about the same measurement as her height in circumference. She was possessed of a rather chubby, plain face, but whatever she may have lacked in looks, she surely made up for in enthusiasm. To say that she was verbose would be an understatement. It was difficult to get a word in edgeways, or any other way. And she chortled a lot, telling jokes that even George felt less than comfortable with!

After a couple of drinks, George got up with his blonde and announced that they were "going on somewhere" (and to me – in an aside – he gave the pretext of leaving me and "five by five" alone, nudge, nudge, wink, wink!)

Eventually, my vociferous companion – after downing her third beer, one of which she paid for – suggested that we, too, should leave and go for a walk. I must have been mad to have acceded to that suggestion. In the vernacular of today, it would be said that she "came on strong!" Her passion was frightening; and I literally had to fight her off, which wasn't easy given her size! It took some time for her to conclude that I did not share her desires; and when, finally, she got the message, she turned very sulky and in angry frustration, refused my offer (courageous in the circumstances) to walk her to her bus. (She and George's blonde were from some other base. So I wondered how did George first meet the blonde?) Thus, the Amazon and I parted the worst of friends and I returned to Elsham exhausted and a little wiser!

I did not see George until the next day when he launched into a unrestrained account of his night of sheer pleasure. He listened, eventually, to my sad story and found it absolutely hilarious. *"Thanks for helping me out mate,"* he said. *"I'll stand you a pint in the NAAFI tonight. Anyway, it's just as well it turned out like that – it kept you on the straight and narrow!"*

I am sorry to have to relate this sorry story of my one and only date with a WAAF. It did not, I am pleased to say, have any adverse effect on my general opinion of the WAAFS. And I daresay that lass whom I met in Scunthorpe was just as keen and able in whatever job she did on her base. She did tell me what she did but I have now forgotten. Her name is no longer in the front of my mind either. Bertha would, though, have been appropriate!

That girl obviously fancied me but I couldn't reciprocate, a situation in matters of the heart which is a bit sad really. And that *"Hell has no fury like a woman scorned"* is another of life's truisms that I learned that night. Frightening!

~ ~ ~

I went out with George Turner, on our own (i.e. without the usual 'gang'), only twice. The above is an account of what happened the first time. The second excursion was eventful too – we ended up spending the night in a police cell! More later!

~ ~ ~

This, then, has been my personal salute to the WAAFS, those young women whom I have chosen to call the "girls in blue". I hope and trust that I have done them the justice that is, to my mind, unquestionably due to them.

Some people, on reading this book, might be persuaded to point out that, after all said and done, the WAAFS, whatever their role, just carried on that traditional female function of being supportive. And that is true. But then, you see, so, too, were all of us, men and women alike, who served in the RAF as ground staff. It was another of those things which we shared and had in common.

It is probably true to say that we who were the aircraft-servicing "erks" were closer to "the action", closer to the air-crews, than anyone else (although, as I have shown, some of the girls were not far behind in that relationship) but we were all there – aircraftsmen and aircraftswomen, to give maximum support to the guys who flew in the bombers. And that is what we did, together.

They were extraordinary times and the experience we all shared will stay in our memories forever.

NOTES:

(i) Possibly there is, somewhere, a definitive and comprehensive account of the part played by the WAAFS in the Second World War. But if there is, then I am afraid that I have been unable to find it. Quite probably, as in the case of RAF ground staff as a whole, it is an aspect of the exploits of the Royal Air Force that has been neglected.

There is, however, a gem of a little book passed on to me by a friend, which is a splendid cameo of the lives and experiences of the "girls in blue" and is, appropriately, set in the scenario of a bomber station very similar to Elsham Wolds.

The book is entitled, *A WAAF in Bomber Command*, written by Pip Beck and published by Goodall Publications Ltd. Pip Beck was an R/T operator and, apart from giving a lucid and graphic account of the training for, and the execution of that very responsible job, the book presents to the reader a realistic insight into many other aspects of the life of a young girl in the Services during the war.

It is an appealing read, not least of all because the author is so self-effacing and comes over as a really nice person. It is particularly gratifying to me because Pip Beck's story confirms most of the reasons I have chosen in my book to write so complimentarily about the WAAFS. And, in addition, she epitomises so clearly the observation I have made about the majority of these girls' admirable capacity to maintain, against the odds, their essential femininity. I heartily recommend the book to you.

(ii) There is one ex-WAAF whom I know and who was stationed at Elsham – albeit after I left – and I cannot consider this chapter as complete without giving her a mention.

She is Shirley Westrupp and she was one of the transport drivers to whom I have accorded a particular accolade. But, above all of that, Shirley was a driving force behind the idea and the formation of the RAF Elsham Wolds Association; and who, for some twenty years "kept it flying" with limited resources and with a great personal touch. In the end, but only recently, advancing years and less than robust health forced her to "retire".

Those of us who enjoy the pleasure of belonging to the Association – and the consequent continuation of our war-time comradeship – have a great deal to thank Shirley for. She lives at "Halltop", an old farmhouse that stands atop another one of north Lincolnshire's rare hills, with a panoramic view of the surrounding countryside. And within that scope of vision is the site of what was once Elsham Wolds aerodrome – a word I know she prefers to airfield. So the memories are close at hand for Shirley and within the very ambience of where she lives.

We will remember many things, Shirley, but perhaps, above all, those Saturday mornings when you opened "Halltop" to all, or any, of us members to "call in" for light refreshments and to "chat start" the Reunion weekend. Thank you.

~ ~ ~

(iii)   Why, I wonder, are men repeatedly taken by surprise when women show the qualities and capabilities to which I have referred in this chapter? Throughout history women have shown courage, fortitude and endurance in the face of all kinds of dangers, privations and discrimination. Dammit, they give birth in pain do they not? And run their homes and bring up their families employing a great variety of skills in that process. And in these modern times with females coming more and more into the professions and positions of responsibility and influence, we males – if we have any grasp of the social, economic, political and scientific scene at all – must surely now realise how much talent and ability have been lost and wasted over many preceding centuries.

Well, at least their efforts during the First World War earned women the vote. And the second great conflagration has brought to them many more opportunities.

But does there have to be a war in order to advance the rights of women?

~ ~ ~

In the book, *A WAAF in Bomber Command* by Pip Beck, there is this poem composed by her...

> *Through the static*
> *Loud in my earphones*
> *I heard your cry for aid.*
> *Your scared boy's voice conveyed*
> *Your fear and danger;*
> *Ether-borne, my voice*
> *Went out to you,*
> *As lost and in the dark you flew.*
> *We tried so hard to help you,*
> *In your crippled plane -*
> *I called again*
> *But you did not hear.*
> *You had crashed in flame*
> *At the runway's end*
> *With none to tend*
> *You in your dying.*

13. PERSONALITIES

In most respects my memory has served me well and that, together with the help of a reference or two to my diary, a 'jog' on occasion from ex-comrades, and consultation of other publications and documents, has enabled me to put this book together. It is, therefore, most regrettable and irritating that, in some instances, the names of people have been lost in the mists of time. And, unfortunately, my usually reliable sources have proved unhelpful, at least in this particular area of reminiscence.

In some cases I can recall both names and faces, whilst in others faces but not the names that go with them; and, extraordinarily, I seem to have the capacity for bringing up on the screen of my mind, the nicknames (and countenances) of some fellows but not their actual names.

There is less lapse of memory as far as my compatriots in the "instrument bashing" business are concerned, both in name or face; but that is, perhaps, not so surprising since it was they with whom I spent most time at Elsham. Yet, even so, there were many other ground crew lads with whom I was fairly well acquainted, especially out on 'A' Flight, but whose names simply will not come to mind. In fact, "Chiefy" Bob Clacker is the one and only name out of all those mechanics out on the 'A' Flight range whose moniker I have retained.

Yes, this particular withdrawal of labour on the part of certain brain cells is irritating but it need not detract from the purpose of this chapter, which is to say something about, and to give little pen portraits of, some of the inhabitants of RAF Elsham Wolds, circa 1943.

I will, as said, come on to my own particular buddies in due course, but first let us look at some of the other, remembered characters whose 'behaviour' is recalled even if their names are not.

Nicknames. Well, of course, the usual Jocks, Taffies, Scousers, Geordies, Cockneys *et al* and the "Timber Woods", the "Smudger Smiths", the "Chalky Whites" (or "Knocker Whites"), the "Johnny

Walkers" and so on. They were all par for the course. But some of those with nicknames are well-remembered, such as "Ginger", a tall, rawboned and red-haired (obviously) "Brummie" engine fitter on 'A' Flight.

In many respects, "Ginger" was another "Bert" described in Chapter 8, because he was so conscientious about his engines and a perfectionist. He, though, was so intense about it all, driven as if by some demon. He worked, not only because other people's survival was at stake but as if his life depended on it also! It was, however, the language that accompanied "Ginger's" fiercely concentrated efforts that one remembers. He had a fluency in oath-ridden invective, enhanced somehow by the "Brummagem" dialect, which was directed at the weather (he was at his best when rain was running down his neck), at the war, at "Gobbles" (i.e. Goebbels who, for some reason, "Ginger" chose to castigate rather than Hitler!) and even at his beloved engines, especially when "snags" did not respond – as he expected – to remedial treatment.

Few of us "erks" were prudes but even the most easily offended person could not have been unamused when "Ginger" went off into one of his harangues. The delivery, the way it flowed out was so funny and, as "Ginger" was usually totally oblivious of the make-up of his 'audience', visiting officers and senior NCOs were often seen to smile.

The thing about it was that "Ginger's" tirade was not just torrid, for all the 'effing and blinding' was interspersed with strange adjectives, all, it would appear, of his own invention. Expressions such as: *"Bible-bucked"*, *"Humpty Dumpty"*, *"Jumped up, never came down"*, *"Snotty-nosed"*, *"Barrel-bunged"*, and several other assorted fulminations.

It was really all about "Ginger's" commitment, and his string of mixed oaths, his tirades were his personal version of the 'hype-up'. But he was a damn good mechanic and a well liked guy. And, arguably, the living personification of the meaning of the word *vehement*!

~ ~ ~

Then there was "Beetle", a big, ungainly airframe fitter, whose nickname derived from the enormous size of his feet, ('beetle crushers') and it was said that his feet, encased in invasion barge-sized boots, arrived everywhere several minutes before he did! "Beetle" was one of those unfortunate souls who just cannot help being clumsy; and the harder they try to correct their awkwardness, the more unwieldy they seem to become. The big lad stumbled, bumped into things, and people, knocked things over, and trod on various objects with those monstrous feet. *"Yeow! That's my bloody fingers you've just stamped on, you clumsy great sod!"*

"Beetle" was a lovely lad, a gentle giant with a ready smile on his round face and when someone would shout, *"Look out lads, clear the decks, here comes 'Beetle'!"* he would just grin sheepishly and invariably walk into something or knock something over.

It was just as well that "Beetle" did not work on the same "kite" as the intensely driven "Ginger". That would have been a most interesting encounter!

In the Spring of 1943, my "oppos" and I were obliged to move out of our *des res* Nissen hut that had sat in the winter mud on the edge of the airfield and to join a whole multitude of other airmen in a new, massive-sized hut nearer to the centre of the camp. We dubbed it the "longhouse". It was a move that did not please us because, although the new billet was warmer, more weather-proofed and pristine – plus being more conveniently situated – it was too close to supervision; and we felt that we had lost that close-knit intimacy we had enjoyed in the 'outback'. But that was not all; because thanks to the arbitrary allocation of bed spaces, we found ourselves dispersed along the length of this huge barrack. And, just to add to our displeasure, we discovered that because of the admix of so many different "trades" among the hut's occupants, there was a constant coming and going of "bods" throughout every day and night.

Anyway, as you can imagine, in a billet of such proportions and capacity, it contained every possible kind of character and personality. There were 'old sweats' and new arrivals; quiet men and loud men; snorers galore and 'wind emitters'; 'line shooters' and phlegmatics; the garrulous and the reticent. They were *all* there.

Two lads in the "longhouse" were devout Christians who never swore, drank or smoked and who prayed before retiring to their beds. It takes a deal of moral courage to uphold and display one's religious beliefs in a *milieu* of profanity and 'laddish' behaviour and there was, in the hut, the inevitable mild ribbing. But, it must be said that, apart from one or two of the more moronically stupid elements in our midst, we all accorded those two young men (both of whom were pleasant and friendly) due respect. Neither of them attempted to preach or to convert and that, too, was appreciated. They just became a part of the daily scene and this *détente* between the more secular majority in a billet and the pious individual was something I encountered in other stations also.

Whether or not the lads would have shown the same tolerance towards someone exhibiting the rituals of other forms of religion I cannot say, for that was a situation that never arose in my experience of service life. Certainly, there was less forbearance towards anyone who exhibited any hint of homosexuality or even the suggestion of an effeminate demeanour. In general – again, as in the case of male chauvinism – the attitude towards "poufters" was culturally-driven and was inclined towards ribald ridicule and/or contempt.

It was much less easy for a homosexual to "come out" in those days than it is now – and even today, it still requires courage.

(At the time I was at Elsham, I was twenty-two and had been in the RAF for about three years, but I was still somewhat naive and ill-informed about the nature of diverse sexual inclinations; all I really knew was the 'folk-lore' about it and the prejudice – a state of mind which will be demonstrated in a later chapter.

I did know a fair bit about 'what went on' in the homosexual behavioral sense, mainly as a results of my meeting with Danny, a torpedoed American merchant navy sailor in a hospital in Greenock, Scotland. Danny was a most extraordinary character, larger than life and full of hair-raising anecdotes which he relayed to me in the ward at night when sleep did not come easily. If you think of the character McMurphy in the book, and film, *One Flew Over the Cuckoo's Nest*, you will also have a mental picture of Danny. But, although that tough seaman from the US of A, imparted a deal of description and incident to me, there was no analysis there; no attempt to *understand*. And so I continued to retain the popular 'sniggering' attitude towards the 'sexually different' for quite some time to come. It was, for many years, a most uncomfortable concept for me to handle.)

~ ~ ~

The "Wee Jock" was the personification of a cartoon kind of Glaswegian Scot. Not a 'typical' Scotsman, for they are as varied and individual as are any other nationality, but he was the product of the pre-war Gorbals or some other tough area of Glasgow; and it showed.

"Jock", resided in the "longhouse" and was difficult to ignore, even in a billet as copious as that was. He was diminutive, about five feet four, of slim but wiry build, and was loud and garrulous; and even though he held strong opinions on everything – usually anti everything – it was not always possible to follow his drift for his accent was Rab C Nesbitt plus! Even for those of us who had been in the service for some time and whose ears had become tuned into dialects, much of the "Wee Jock's" diatribes was lost on us. But for all his gritty outpourings, he was a very friendly and good-natured little man and generally well liked. Pity, then, about the booze! Drink created a disturbing metamorphosis. It was like Dr Jekyll taking the potion that turned him into Mr Hyde. It seemed that the *alter ego* of the usually affable – and it must be said funny – "Jock" was, when into his cups, a ferocious Jimmy Cagney! Drinking and fighting were synonymous activities in "Jock's" psyche. And apparently, fierce altercations became such a regular feature of the 'wee laddie's' nights out that he became a social loner, erstwhile companions preferring not to become so frequently involved in 'punch-ups'.

It was unusual for "Jock" not to return to the hut unscathed after a trip to Scunthorpe or some such place, and one had to wonder what his adversaries looked like. (It was easy enough to become involved in fights during the war – in pubs, at dances, wherever, but apart from guys like the "Wee Jock", who seemed to thrive on brawls, most of us preferred to avoid such situations (wherever possible) and we just went out to enjoy ourselves. Mind you, "Jock" and his ilk tended to regard fist-fighting as enjoyment!)

When "Jock" returned to the hut after his inebriated excursions, it was best to leave him alone for he was by that time somewhat morose and then, in turn, embarrassingly maudlin. And he eventually made it into his bed, growling curses at the RAF, Hitler, the Army and Navy and *all Sassenachs*.

What always puzzled me was how our resident Glaswegian managed to make his way back to camp, contrived to arrive by the 'witching hour' (23.59 hours) and, in his dishevelled and oft-damaged state, escaped the attention of the SPs.

Another strange thing about '"Jock"' was that when he drank in the NAAFI, his bellicose nature seemed to desert him and instead he was always most amiable, tending only to burst into song. *"Ae belong ta Glasgae"* was rendered with irritating frequency. And even when some of the lads told him to *"put a sock in it"* and suggested that he could do everybody a favour by going back to Glasgow, he just laughed and took no offence.

There were theories about "Jocks's" less combative behaviour in the NAAFI. One was that he knew he was among friends – even if the majority of them were Sassenachs! Another explanation was that he knew well enough that if he cut up rough in the NAAFI, the SPs would be on him like a ton of bricks. (I was never convinced of that theory.)

Thirdly, and I would give more credence to this one, it was mooted that NAAFI beer was so weak that it failed to make him even irritable, never mind bellicose!

If I ever knew, I have certainly forgotten now the nature of "Wee Jock's" trade in the RAF. Perhaps he should have been an air-gunner; but then, who would have understood his communications on the intercom!

~ ~ ~

As far as I am aware, Leslie Howard the quintessential English actor ("*The Scarlet Pimpernel*", "*Pimpernel Smith*", "*Gone With the Wind*", etc. etc.) did not serve at Elsham Wolds; but his double most certainly did. Tall, fair-haired, slim, he was an LAC who had as far as I was concerned, just a walking-on part in the big production that was 103 Squadron. I have no idea what his name was but we actually referred to him as "Leslie Howard"; and not only did he resemble the actor but also spoke with that same languid, 'upper crust' accent.

"Leslie" was employed in admin. in some capacity and I encountered him just in passing but more particularly in the cookhouse when our presence there happened to coincide. But it was in that 'eating place' that "Leslie" endeared himself to all who witnessed his 'act' and put a wide smile on all their faces. He would get in line for his meals and when, say, some kind of stew was slopped onto his plate by a serving WAAF, he would turn to the "erk" next in line and say, in that 'posh' drawl of his, "*I say, bloody caviar again, old chap. Utterly tedious, don't you think? I really will have to speak to the management.*"

Or, he would say to the bored girl dispensing the victuals, "Excuse me my dear," ("Leslie" was somewhat older than most of us) "Do you think that we might, just occasionally, see the menu? Oh yes, and the wine list if it might be arranged?"

Initially, the cookhouse personnel were not a little bemused by this approach, being accustomed to more ribald comments. But once the penny of irony dropped, they too would smile and respond in kind. "*Sorry, your lordship, but there's a war on and caviar is all we can get!*"

At the long table, after "Leslie" had finished his meal, he would emit a little burp, apologise, give his chest a slight bang with the heel of his hand and say, "*It's these damned radishes y'know. Must ask cook to be more selective with these salads!*"

125

He made great play with the tea in his mug, sipping it, rolling it around his tongue and then commenting on the lines of "Ceylonese. One can always tell. It has that certain exotic bouquet, that richness of aroma and little tingle on the tongue that comes from the exquisite tea plant born of wedlock twixt the blessed soil of Ceylon and a climate bequeathed by the Gods!"

When in the NAAFI, "Leslie" would lean back in his canteen furniture chair, puff on his Woodbine cigarette and say to everyone at large, "Excellent club for one to belong to this, isn't it? Graceful surroundings, tranquil, first-class service. One can sprawl in one's leather armchair, draw on a fine Havana cigar, read 'The Times' with a G and T in one's hand. Parfait as they would say across the Channel. Oh, la Belle France. Poor, poor, Paris. That damned Schiklegruber – awful type. Riff-raff. Never be a member!"

I did not record "Leslie's" observations, but the above was the general tenor of them and typical of content.

He was not with us for long and, I guess, given his obvious background, he probably went off for officer training. One has to wonder, however, why – and how – he had escaped so far from the old boys' network. He might, of course, have been a maverick of his class – as some were, such as Peter Ustinov for example – who opted to at least start their military experience in the lower ranks.

"Leslie" was a lovely man and very much at ease in the company of the 'lads' and they with him.

It was an interesting speculation as to what the conversation might have been between "Leslie" and the Duty Officer when the latter came to the ORs' Mess to ask if there were any complaints. Possibly such an encounter did not occur, for I am certain we would have heard about it. Pity really, because it would have provided us all with great entertainment. And, I'll wager that if that 'meeting of minds' had occurred, you would have been able to hear the proverbial pin drop in the 'eating house' at that moment. "Leslie" was another of the many "ships that passed in the night" during one's service life and as so many of them did, he passed from my mind. But on a certain day in 1944, whilst I was serving in Italy, the memory of that suave, but a so likable man, came suddenly back to me. It was the day that the news of the liberation of Paris came through. And I thought how joyful he would have been.

~ ~ ~

We had our own entertainers at Elsham. Natural and very funny comedians, who were brilliant tellers of jokes and who could also create laughter out of almost any situation. Any one of them could have done well in "show biz" after the war. (We did, also of course, have our fair share of those blokes who think they are comedians but are not! And they can be, can they not, the most embarrassing people to have around!)

There were a couple of "erks" on 'B' Flight who were great impersonators – of well known entertainers and of certain persons on the station, and who, in *falsetto* voice, did a more than passable and hilarious impression of the Andrews Sisters singing *"I'll be with you in apple-blossom time."*

There were some really good singers and among them (not surprisingly) a Welsh lad – I think in the Motor Pool – who could render opera and church music in a rich tenor voice that would have been well appreciated among the discerning folk of the valleys of South Wales, as well as giving great pleasure to us when we heard it in the Lincolnshire Wolds.

Another lad, a tall dark-haired Londoner, would have been a hit on the Karaoke scene had that been around in those days, singing the Al Bowley songs of that generation.

To my knowledge, there were three piano players among us, two of whom were the "bar room ivory ticklers", who played joyfully by ear and were good for a sing-song in pub or NAAFI.

There was, however, a corporal who really could play and could read music. His playing, whether of 'light' or classical music was well-appreciated but I recall one night – although I am not now sure whether it was in the NAAFI or in a pub – when he was playing and an inattentive, noisily chattering audience caused me to risk my neck by yelling at them to be quiet.

The "corp" was performing Chopin and then, by natural progression, into the *"Warsaw Concerto"* theme from the very popular film *"Dangerous Moonlight"*. I liked both Chopin and the concerto, being very moved by its haunting, tragic but yet defiant resonances, and I wanted to listen to it.

Fortunately, the gathering subsided into silence – or near silence – and the "corp" gave me a smile and a nod of appreciation and I felt a brief moment of unaccustomed power!

~ ~ ~

I have no wish to 'knock' ENSA shows. There were some really good acts among the many who had volunteered their services to the cause of "entertaining the troops" and it could not have been easy for any of them, travelling all over the world and often living rough. But I have to say that casts of ENSA's touring shows would have benefited from the presence among them of some really talented people in the ranks of H M Services.

Surely some of those singers, musicians and entertainers I saw and heard at various RAF stations must have "gone on the boards" after the war? They may not have reached the heights of others who came out of the Services and into eventual fame, such as Spike Milligan, Harry Secombe, Peter Sellers, Max Bygraves *et al*, but the talent was certainly there.

~ ~ ~

There were many characters and personalities about whom one could write but before switching the focus of my memory to those I knew most of all – my fellow "instrument bashers" – there is one other young airman I must mention.

Maxie, a tough-looking, muscular Cockney to whom I found myself living next door (i.e. in the next bed-space) in the "longhouse", was one of those guys who look as if they were not born but quarried! And even though, in those days, I could take care of myself, I regarded this bloke with some apprehension, but I very quickly discovered that my fears were unfounded because Maxie was not at all overtly aggressive or pugnacious. He was, if anything, laid back and quite diffident. Yet, even so, you just knew that this character was not one to cross.

He was a General Duties 'bod' and an AC2, a rank above which he had no ambition whatsoever to rise. He reminded me of a drill-sergeant at Bridgnorth who once told us that we were all AC2s only because, *"There ain't any bloody AC3s!"* Maxie, if there had been an AC3 rank, would have been in it! And I am sure that at whatever point in time his military 'career' ended, he would have been still exactly where he started.

I doubt – assuming him to be still alive – whether Maxie would ever be a member of the Elsham Wolds Association, for he was never all that keen on the RAF at *that* time, never mind in retrospect. It could be said that Maxie and the RAF were incompatible. They never really 'got on'! It was nothing personal against the RAF. It was just authority – no matter how it was dressed – that the Cockney had found irksome, for he was the epitome of the 'free soul'.

Maxie tended to absent himself a lot – without permission. When feeling 'cheesed' (fed up) he just went. He was also inclined toward an unfortunate attitude which RAF authority construed as insubordination. I became, within a short space of time, his 'China'

(Cockney rhyming slang 'china plate' – mate!) He was on 'jankers' (punishment) when his decision was made to make a 'China' of me. I sneaked a sausage sandwich into him in the guardroom one evening. That was all, but you would think I had given him an *official* leave pass for a whole year! And soon after he completed that particular 'sentence' he found an opportunity to demonstrate his friendship.

I had come into the hut one night after an extended duty and had flaked out on my bed, absolutely whacked. Some of the lads had been out on a binge and had crashed back into the hut tipping up the lines of beds, occupied or not. When one of the crew reached my bed he bent down to lift it but found his wrist clamped in a vice-like grip.

"I wouldn't do that mate," said Maxie. *"Move on!"* The airman hesitated, looked up at Maxie and wisdom penetrated his intoxicated mind. He moved on. And, of course, none of the other inebriated lads even considered tipping over Maxie's bed!

He was a loner really. He told me that his great ambition was to go to Australia and to build bridges. "Why Australia? Why bridges?" I asked him.

"Just fancy it, that's all," he replied. "Nothing much to stay in this country for after this lot's over."

I wonder if he ever made it to Australia; and did he ever help to construct a bridge or two? Or did he find the discipline required in that situation too irksome for him and perhaps quit the job a quarter done? But I liked Maxie. He had no pretences and, in his own way, he was honest. He was one of life's genuine mavericks and with such people there is little anyone can do. Nor, perhaps, should we even try.

~ ~ ~

(The incident when the inebriated "erks" came back to the hut and were tipping up the beds, was just one example of the turmoil that went on in that place. Because of the great variety of 'tradesmen' resident in the hut and the diversity of duty rostas, the traffic in and out of the hut was constant day and night. And in addition to that, there was that intrusion into and interruption of sleep when various groups of "bods" (and individuals) returned to the hut in boisterous mood, (something most of us were guilty of from time to time!).

But in the May, when better weather enhanced the frequency of "ops", the work had piled up and the hours on duty increased.

129

Consequently, one or two of us "bashers" unilaterally – and without official sanction – moved out of that 'railway terminus billet' and bedded down in the Instrument Section.

"Chiefy" Willmott had no objections, thinking, perhaps, that in this way he would always guarantee to have one or two of his 'lads' on immediate hand if needed. But when superior ranks discovered our absence from the hut, we were ordered back again. Everything must be in its place, you see. But just for a brief spell we 'refugees' literally 'slept on the job'.

~ ~ ~

My "oppos", the "instrument bashers". I have referred to some of them here and there in the book, just in passing, but they are worthy of a closer look. There are three to mention first of all because they were not with us for long, even though they were fellow residents of the original Nissen hut.

First, Harry the Geordie, with whom I arrived at Elsham together with Don Boast. Harry was an ever-cheerful, optimistic, Tynesider with a great sense of humour enhanced by that delightful north-east dialect. Had he stayed, he would have been an asset to the Section and a valued "oppo", but he had earlier volunteered for training as air gunner and was posted to gunnery training school within a few weeks of our arrival. We did not keep in touch, but I hope my Geordie friend survived the awful casualty rate that was so much a feature of the air-gunners' lot.

"Paddy" (I think Ryan, but my memory might be faulty in his case) was another like Maxie, tough as teak but not overtly combative. He was of medium height, stocky and compact and a quietly spoken Southern Irishman. I once asked him why, as a citizen of the Irish Republic, a neutral country whose history was one of antipathy towards Britain, he should be serving in the RAF? He told me that whilst he was not particularly enamoured of English governments (not the *people* he insisted) he was, above all, anti-Fascist. He said he had fought in the International Brigade in the Spanish Civil War, and I am sure that was genuine, judging by the authentic sounding stories he recounted to me about it. And he had seen the civil war in Spain as a prelude to this larger conflict.

"Paddy" left Elsham some weeks before the move to the "longhouse" and if I remember correctly, he too was heading for air-crew training of some kind. Yet another ship – and a very interesting one – that passed in the night. The RAF in war-time was like that – a constant movement of personnel resulting in brief encounters.

130

~ ~ ~

Don Boast was the chunky little Londoner with whom I had not only met again on arrival at Elsham but had been through all the training months at Bridgnorth and Melksham. Why, after but a few weeks at Elsham – and after having been posted there following his release to industry – Don was then sent on to another heavy-bomber station (Downham Market, Norfolk) I do not understand. But "ours was never to reason why" and so the reunion between Don and me – and our anticipation of serving at Elsham together – was short-lived.

I did visit Don, very briefly, down at Downham Market some time later but that was to be our last contact. That same familiar story, transient friendship. But transient though they were, those friendships were highly valued and never forgotten.

~ ~ ~

I hold such fond memories of Dougie "Pop" Tyler. He was a really lovely little man from Leicester and called "Pop" because he was somewhat older than the rest of us -not quite old enough to be the father of any one of us, but not far off. He certainly looked to us to be 'ancient' and he had about him an *air* of maturity that enhanced that impression. A very senior figure in our youthful midst. Oh he was still young enough – mid to late thirties I guess – to enjoy a pint or two and to dress up, very dapper, in his 'best blue' and to go dancing. But he, unlike some of us, did understand the parameters of acceptable behaviour and thus, in that sense, kept a 'fatherly eye' on us. Indeed, he was not slow to admonish any of us 'young lads' if he considered our behaviour, or even our attitudes, out of order. Dougie and I got along very well but even so, I was not excluded from his reprimands if he thought that I was misbehaving at any time.

Just as I learned a lot about servicing Lancaster bombers from Ron Grantham, so Dougie was also of invaluable help to me. He was another of those men from the Midlands who seem to be genetically fitted with technical know-how. I took many cues from Dougie, not only about the job itself but also about approaches and attitudes.

I find it very sad to reflect that had I been aware of the existence of the RAF Elsham Wolds Association just one year earlier I might well have met up with my old friend and confidant just once more, after so many years. Dougie "Pop" Tyler died just before my fist visit to the annual reunion. After he died, his son kindly passed on to another ex-comrade of ours, Bas Lowe, some of Dougie's memorabilia, including one of his note-books from the Instrument Training School at Melksham. The notes and diagrams relating to the theory of aircraft instrumentation are comprehensive and, as one would expect of "Pop" Tyler, impeccably kept and precisely detailed.

All I can say is that some of the material in that note-book must have gone right over my head – or straight through it – because I have no recollection of all that in my note-book!

Yes, Dougie was a fine man and I feel privileged to have known him.

~ ~ ~

Frank Wain, my closest "oppo" at Elsham, was a Yorkshireman, from Sheffield, of medium height and of stocky build. In his mid-twenties, he was very level-headed and realistic. He and I became friends almost immediately after I joined the 'gang' in the Nissen hut and he did a great deal to show me around and to help me to settle in. Frank was also another of my mentors in the Lancaster-servicing routines and it was always good and reassuring for me to know he was around, out on the 'A' Flight range.

You always knew where you stood with Frank Wain and he was as straight as a die – as one would expect from a Yorkshire lad. And one thing I will always remember when I think of him was that he epitomised, absolutely, the essential civilian on loan to the military. Not in a hundred years would they have turned Frank into an unquestioning, military robot. He went through the motions of pander, saluting "yes sir, no sir, three bags full sir" and all that; but he tended to regard it as meaningless 'bull' and an irritation. Just as well, then, that his war-time role was in the RAF and given a priority to use his undoubted technical skills to service aircraft. There was no other function in which Frank could have served his country to greater effect.

Frank was quite determined to emphasise his civilian identity – he was the only one among us who had white linen sheets on his bed! He was, unlike most of us, married and his wife was the provider of the linen and the laundry service. And although Sheffield was not too far away from Elsham, Frank did not go home that often, so I guess there must have been a regular parcel post between Mr and Mrs Wain.

Of course, it was a great joke among the lads that any "erk" should have sheets from home on the bed; but Frank was impervious to any of the derision and said something to the effect that *"wearing hair shirts was a form of self-punishment in which he did not propose unnecessarily to indulge."*

What was the official view of this piece of creature comfort non-conformity? I honestly do not remember whether Frank hid the sheets (how could he have done that!) or whether the 'powers that were' simply ignored it, which was more likely at Elsham than it would have been at many other stations.

Frank and I spent a lot of time in each other's company and talked of many things. He had various interests, from sport to engineering and from social and political issues to railways. A really good mate and a conscientious mechanic, scrupulous and with little patience for anyone who was less than aware of his responsibilities. A man like that could be forgiven his antipathy towards military 'bull' – and the comfort of linen sheets on his bed!

~ ~ ~

Alan Dilks was a very wound-up, energetic lad from Nottingham. If Dougie Tyler epitomised the more mature and sensible element among us, then Alan personified callow youth. Voluble, opinionated, scatty and volatile. He would switch from amiable good humour to petulance or outrage (rather like modern footballers!) in an instant without changing gear. And, naturally, that being his nature, the lads would goad him and 'wind him up' just for the hell of it. Something on the following lines for instance...

> *"Hey Dilky, what have you done with my boot brush?"*
> *"I haven't seen your bloody boot brush."*
> *"Come on, hand it over. We know they're all Robin Hoods in Nottingham!"*
> *"WHAT D'YER MEAN BY THAT? ARE YOU ACCUSIN' ME OF THIEVING, YOU BASTARD?"*

And then someone else would call out something designed to fuel the flames of Alan's indignation and as he whirled round to retaliate, the first tormentor would, behind Alan's back, throw his boot brush onto the irate young man's bed, saying, *"There it is. I knew you had it, Dilky."* And in the midst of the ensuing laughter Alan would realise he was being 'wound up' and that would enrage him even further. But, just as quickly, his temper would dissipate and he would mumble something about "rotten sods", throw the brush at the lad who had 'accused' him and grin sheepishly.

It was amazing, though, how easy it was to set him off and it was some time before he began to cotton on. I understand that, after I had left Elsham, Alan did calm down and 'grow up', probably under the influence of Dougie Tyler, who did always keep a 'fatherly' eye on him.

Possibly the proof of Alan's eventual conversion to a more level-headed approach to life was his allocation to the responsible task of 'oxygen king', driving the cylinders out to the "kites" and replenishing the bottles stowed aboard the Lancs. Or, perhaps, it was the *decision* to give Alan that particular role that calmed him down. That old psychological ploy.

He was, in any case, a likeable enough guy, very open and generous. And, in any case, he was, after all, a *youth*, just as most of us were – and we were all inclined to be a bit scatty at times!

~   ~   ~

Bas Lowe was a very tall, good-looking lad from Leicester, but originally from Chester. It was in the March of 1943 when Bas joined us in the Instrument Section at Elsham, and because of his easy and affable manner very soon became 'one of us' and part of the team. In fact, Bas brought yet another asset to "Chiefy" Willmott's 'gang', for he, too, was damn good at the job and tenacious in finding the causes of "snags" and in remedying them.

Bas was a non-smoker and non-drinker and he did not join us 'cowboys' on jaunts into town or village. But he was not, by any means, a straight-laced guy; and his disinclination to join the 'revellers' was never resented by anyone. In fact, I think that one of the features of Bas's personality was his great sense of humour and his laughter, a characteristic he has retained to this day, for yes, Bas and I were reunited at the Elsham Reunion in 1991 and we are now very close friends.

I never saw Bas play but he was, by all accounts, a very good soccer player. I say, *'by all accounts'*, because football was not organised whilst I was at Elsham but it did become quite a feature of the camp's social activity after I left.

Everyone tells me what a fine centre-half he was; and that, naturally, would have enhanced Bas's popularity both as a key member of the Instrument Section team and of the station side.

Bas Lowe has been extremely helpful to me in the writing of this book, filling in gaps in my memory and making, in the next chapter, a contribution of his own. He served at Elsham until the end of hostilities in Europe and was then posted overseas to India as the war in the Far East continued.

Bas and his wife Beryl and my wife Ethel and I now go to the RAF Elsham Wolds Reunion as a foursome, where, until recently, we were joined by Ron Grantham and his wife, Doreen, who married him while she served in the NAAFI at Elsham. Poor health has now prevented Ron and Doreen from coming to the reunion and we sorely miss their company. But this passing reference to Ron Grantham now leads into a word or two more about him.

Ron was just great to have around. He had a kind of status because he was a 103 'old boy' and everyone recognised his prowess as an "instrument basher". He always enjoyed the 'gatherings' in the Section, listening to the jokes and the banter that rolled around that companionable workshop.

"These are a grand bunch of lads here kid," he would tell you in his unmistakable Yorkshire (Bradford) accent. And he was right. They were.

None of us would ever go far wrong if, when we had a problem on the job, we turned to Ron for advice. He shared his 'know how' willingly and generously.

He served right through to the end of the war at Elsham and reached the dizzy heights of corporal. He nearly went overseas when the European war ended. Apparently, he got as far as dockside, awaiting embarkation when someone discovered the absence of his name "on the list". So he didn't go. And that was as it should be for Ron had 103 Squadron and Elsham Wolds printed into his body like Brighton rock. You could almost say that Ron Grantham was RAF ground crew Elsham Wolds.

~ ~ ~

I remember our immediate 'boss', "Chiefy" Willmott, as an astute supervisor for not only placing individual members of his team in positions appropriate to their abilities and temperaments, but also in balancing tolerance – of high-spirited young men – and firmness when it was required. He was also protective of his 'team' and considerate of their needs.

Both of our corporals, Clifford and Simpson, were respected and liked because they never pulled rank on us but did pull their weight when the chips were down and extra hands – and experience – were needed.

I am sure that our trio of NCOs was an essential ingredient in the making of the comradeship of the Instrument Section 'crew'.

135

~ ~ ~

Wally "Bud" Senior and Harry Batty had several things in common. Easy-going, friendly guys; both good at their job. They were accomplished dancers and liked the company of the opposite sex, and both were successful in their quests in that direction. Yet, in that context, Wally and Harry were quite different. In fact they were proof of the theory that there is more to sexual attraction than mere physical appearance.

Harry was a strikingly handsome young man, and well built. Wally, on the other hand, could hardly be described in the terms of a matinee idol. He had one of those faces that looked as if it needed 'ironing'; and his build was all points and angles.

But in terms of 'pulling the birds' our two estimable "oppos" were up there with the best.

The secret with Wally was the sheer warmth of his character. He was an outgoing Mancunian. A lovely man whom I remember with great affection, and he was another of the "instrument bashers" at Elsham who contributed considerably to my own growing confidence in the "trade", and one of the first to welcome me into the Nissen hut when I arrived there.

Others in our 'crew' were: the gentle giant, "Lofty" Bartlett, a most genial and easy-going heavyweight with extraordinary grace for a man of his size.

Freddy Lloyd, an ex-'brat' (RAF apprentice) who later reached senior NCO rank at another base.

Edwin "Kenny" Kennington, who I recall was a very serious young "instrument basher", somewhat more mature for his age than the majority of us were. And he, too, is a member of the Elsham Wolds Association with whom I was delighted to be reunited at one of the reunions in the 1990s.

"Organ Stops" (or Eddie Cantar as I called him) whom I mentioned earlier in the book, is remembered by Bas Lowe, Ron Grantham, "Kenny" Kennington and myself certainly as the "lad with the staring eyes" who seemed to be perpetually astounded and worried. The strange thing is, though, that none of us have any recollection whatsoever of his actual name. And it should be staring us in the face!

~ ~ ~

No. I had not overlooked George Turner. Whoever could! But I thought it appropriate, in a review of my ex-comrades in the "instrument-bashing brigade" at Elsham, to leave a pen portrait of the redoubtable and indefatigable GT until last.

I was never sure about George's home territory but wherever it was – somewhere in southern England – it must have been a locality in which it was an advantage to be 'streetwise'. Big George could irritate and aggravate you to breaking point; and then turn away your anger in an instant by turning on the charm and making you laugh at yourself. He was voluble, energetic and, at times, argumentative. But above all, the thing that we remember most about him was his cheek – and his prowess as a 'scrounger'.

Every group of military personnel throughout history has had its opportunist gleaners – and many of them thankful to possess such types in their midst. And GT was one such.

He established his own brand of *entente cordiale* with cookhouse staff, especially the female ones; and somehow managed to obtain "late duty meals" – both when he had, and when he hadn't, been on such assignments! Whilst we were in the 'musical box' (i.e. the Nissen hut where the "instruments" resided) George very rarely came in, from wherever he had been, without some item of sustenance (some bread for toasting, a couple of sausages, a piece of cheese, whatever) or without something to burn in the stove (a chunk of railway sleeper once – God knows where that came from!). *"The Lord helps them as look after themselves,"* he used to say with that infuriating but beguiling grin of his.

GT was quite prepared to converse, perfectly at ease with anyone, irrespective of rank or status. I am sure that had he been in a line-up for inspection by King George, he would have found some chat-up line with which to address H.M.

I recall an incident in the cookhouse one day and it went something like this: The Duty Officer was on his rounds and remarked on the rather dirty drinking mug from which GT was sipping his tea.

"Disgustin' isn't it sir," said George. "Not mine though, belongs to someone else."

"Who is the someone else?" asked the officer.

"Don't know his name sir. One of the 'bods' on the Flight."

"I thought perhaps you wouldn't," observed the officer, with a wry smile.

"I hope you don't intend to drink from that mug. What is your name?"

"Turner, sir."

"I'll remember you Turner."

"Thank you, sir. You too, sir!"

That is the way George was and a mixture of cheek and charm enabled him to get away with things that others never would.

But you could not help but like him. He was, indeed, the epitome of the 'likeable rogue' because he could also be so kind and generous. I wonder whatever happened to him? I hope he survived the war and that he still lives. I can well imagine that he would have done well for himself in the Army Surplus and scrap-metal business after the war. Or, possibly, he might have married and settled down to a mundane, routine and respectable way of life. But I must say that that image does not somehow sit comfortably in the mind.

I just wonder why it is that when I read T S Eliot's *"Macavity the Mystery Cat"*, I am reminded of GT. And, not surprisingly, he does crop up again in this book.

(Perhaps not surprisingly also, whenever I used to watch *"Sgt Bilko"* on TV, I would think of George Turner.)

~ ~ ~

As one would expect the air-crews abounded with characters and personalities and some were decidedly charismatic. Even the Lancs were regarded as having individual characteristics and personalities, of which the legendry 'M Squared' was a shining example.

Ground crews had their own perspective for 'humanising' the aircraft.

"No problems with her today. She's in a really good mood this morning!"

"There's always some bloody thing wrong with this 'kite'. She should go into the sick bay and have a thorough medical!"

"She's a tough old bird. Always getting knocked about but she comes home every time!"

Similarly the air-crews would express their views on the aviatorial idiosyncrasies of their "kites".

"She really doesn't like it up there in the cold. I'm sure she shivers at 15,000 feet!"

"This one really does pull to the left. I'm sure she has a mind of her own and doesn't want to go where we're going. And who could blame her!"

"I think she feels pregnant when she's got the bomb load in her belly!"

"She's a lovely old 'kite'. She'll always get you back – or die in the attempt!"

Inevitably, some pilots were more notable than others and more talked about. In some cases it was because they were more flamboyant or were seen to be more skilful, or tenacious or because they were extraordinary survivors in spite of being 'knocked about' on "ops".

And some of them were famous for possessing all of those attributes such as the legendary Flt Lt Van Rollegan ("the mad Belgian"), DFC DSO AFC who completed two tours of operations, i.e. 50 "ops", and then volunteered for a third.

Such pilots were regarded by the ground crews with a certain amount of awe but others who were, perhaps, less of the 'super star' kind, but were, nevertheless steady, reliable 'drivers' also received the respect due to them.

There were instances when ground crew would, whilst respecting the exploits of a particular pilot, not hold him in high regard on a personal level because the man was 'snotty' or a 'rank puller'. (Few pilots, in my experience at Elsham and elsewhere, were in that mould – and even less so if they were NCOs. But they did exist. On reflection, however, when the flyers were distant, tetchy, even apparently pompous, isn't it just possible that it was *their* personal way of handling their responsibilities, fears and concerns? Again, in that situation, as in all others, it was a matter of character and personality.

Crew members, as well as the pilots, abounded with characters of every kind, from the quiet and withdrawn to the comedians, and right through the gamut of personalities to the 'crazy bastards'. There were some guys in air-crew who were "designed by their very natures" to be there. The kind of blokes who would have ridden the 'Wall of Death' at big shows in civvy street; who would actually enjoy a bar-room brawl and, if it had been in vogue at that time, would have been among the first to do the bungie-jump!

And, as Don Charlwood mentioned in one of his books, the bravery of air-crew members such as wireless operators, was never sufficiently recognised.

It is a strange experience at the RAF Elsham Wolds Association reunions when I meet some of the air-crew veterans who were there at the same time as I was – even on 'A' Flight – and yet, as far as I remember, did not 'meet' at the time. I must have seen them quite frequently and may even have been on nodding terms with them.

Don Charlwood is a good example, flying out of 'A' Flight in "B" Beer. (If only I had known he was going to be a successful writer; or to even be aware of what a really nice and decent man he is.)

It is one of the good feelings one experiences at the Elsham Wolds reunions to meet and become acquainted with people who were contemporaries up there, even if we were unaware of it.

Finally I must mention two ex-gunners, Alex Gamble, a diminutive and interesting academic from London and Frank Sharples, a 'chirpy' lad from Lancashire, who has become a most encouraging supporter in my ambition to write this book.

Frank was the mid-upper gunner on another of 'A' Flights' "Bs" – "B" Bertie – and as with Don Charlwood, I must have seen him on numerous occasions at the dispersals. Frank did, in fact, complete his tour of 30 "ops" at about the same time as I left Elsham to go overseas. I would certainly have known Frank had I been a regular member of "B" Bertie's ground crews for he is, even today, an extremely gregarious and friendly northerner whom it would be difficult to ignore. But he has told me a rather sad story concerning 'B' Bertie's crew which I will relate in a later chapter.

~ ~ ~

Whether remembered or forgotten in the mists of time; whether they were among my closer comrades in the ground crews, or other ground staff; whether they were WAAFS or the men who flew in the Lancs., the knowledge and awareness that I was among such fine people who served at Elsham – such characters and personalities – is so much a part of my warm nostalgia for those times and that place.

Footnote

It is somewhat surprising, and disappointing, that on the several attendances that I have made at the RAF Elsham Wolds Reunion, I have not, yet, found any ex-ground crew men – other than the "instrument bashers" who worked on 'A' Flight coincidentally with me. Or, if there are any, there is now no mutual recognition. Most 'veterans' to whom I speak appear to have gone to Elsham after my departure from there or worked in the hangars or on other Flights. But then, perhaps it is not so surprising for, after all, out of all of the "instrument bashers" who were my comrades up there, I have been reunited with three only – Ron Grantham, Bas Lowe and "Kenny" Kennington.

We do sometimes forget just how old we all are; and how many years have passed by since those days.

14. Rapport & Discipline

This chapter sets out to focus on two important aspects of the way things were in the 'family life' of the RAF base at Elsham Wolds. And although I have paid some regard to both in other parts of the book, there is a need, I believe, to emphasise both their nature and their significance.

Firstly, then, two *personal* experiences which illustrate quite emphatically that rapport, that close regard that air and ground crews held for each other.

Standing in one day for one of our 'team' who was on leave, I carried out a D.I. on one of the "kites" which was scheduled for "ops" that night. The next day I was astounded when Flight Sergeant Willmott called me into his office and told me I was to be charged with negligence! Apparently the crew of the Lanc. had reported on their return that the flexible hose at an oxygen point in the aircraft had leaked as a result of a tear in the material. This was serious and, as the airman responsible for the inspection the previous day, I was to be held accountable. (Incidentally, this also underlines what I have been saying about the exacting nature of the job.)

I was sick to my stomach but I could not feel guilty because I was so sure I would not miss something as obvious as that. The oxygen supply was something about which we were always being urged to be particularly vigilant. Also, I had, on several occasions, complained in the Instrument Section about the positioning of that hose. It was adjacent to a bulkhead in a narrow part of the fuselage interior and was subject to abrasions in that position as people continually brushed past it – especially the air-crew in their bulky flying gear. I was prepared to swear on a stack of Bibles – or RAF manuals – that when I made my morning inspection I had detected no tear at that point. That, in fact, is what I stated, quite emphatically, when, after a few days of 'sweating it out', I came up on the charge.

My Flight Sergeant, Willmott, spoke up for me, confirming my previous observations on the positioning of the oxygen hose; and commending me as a conscientious airman. For that I was extremely grateful. But, something even more gratifying than that was revealed to me later, which was that "Jock" Brechney had, on behalf of "D" Donald's crew, put in a good word for me. It was a gesture of support spontaneously given and totally unsolicited. Is it any wonder that I held that crew in such high regard?

The outcome of the 'trial' was an admonishment, which in one sense was saying – "We can't just dismiss the charge – be extra careful in future." In another, it was accepting the references of those who had reason to know something of my attitude to the job. So in the end, it was congrats all round from our three NCOs and from all my "oppos". And later in the day, "Jock" took the trouble to come and find me and to shake my hand.

It was gratifying also, that some adjustment was eventually made to that particular oxygen point – although I cannot now remember whether it was moved to another position or protected in some way; but something, I know, was done.

~ ~ ~

The second example of air and ground crew rapport – and in this instance, it also demonstrates the almost tribal nature of squadron membership – occurred on a trip down to Downham Market aerodrome in Norfolk. I had heard that one of our Lancs. – not one of 'mine'- was going down there for some reason, and knowing that my old "oppo" Don Boast was now stationed on that base, I cadged, and was readily given, a place on board.

Like Elsham, Downham Market was vast but I eventually found the Instrument Section and sought out my old friend. We had a convivial reunion, reminisced and made comparisons over a mug of cocoa. But soon, Don had to get back to work and so we parted company and that – as it turned out – was the last we saw of each other. I had left the Instrument Section and was strolling leisurely across the drome towards where the Lanc. – which was standing, so it seemed, with an air of superiority among Downham Market's Stirlings – when a strident voice called upon me to "halt!" I turned to see a very spruce and ram-rod Flight Sergeant striding purposefully in my direction. This, I guessed, must be the station's Disciplinary Senior NCO, a conclusion which came as something of a surprise because, although we did have such a person as that at Elsham, he tended not to be obtrusive, or intrusive, in the vicinity of workaday activity on the airfield. (He came into his own on parades [except pay parades as we will see] and various military-like exercises that might occur from time-to-time.)

Of course, I did not record the ensuing proceedings of this totally unexpected encounter with the Downham Market "Chiefy Discip." but the following is very close to the gist of it. The Flight Sergeant looked me up and down with obvious distaste. I was wearing my rather crumpled working-blue uniform, less than pristine working boots, my forage-cap was tucked into my belt and my hair – unquestionably longer than regulation length – was wind-blown.

"You are a disgrace to the RAF!" roared the NCO. "What are you?"

I offered no response, mainly because I did not agree with his assessment.

"I said, WHAT ARE YOU?" he repeated, but louder. The problem I had was whether to make some reply to indicate my disagreement, and risk the charge of 'insubordination'; or to remain silent and thus stand accused of that most resented and snide of all military charges, 'dumb insolence'. (Yes, there are many *"Catch 22's"* in HM Forces.) I remember, though, how perplexed I was because I had seen, as I walked around the airfield, the "erks" working on the "kites" or scurrying about on foot or cycle, attired in the usual mixed apparel of overalls, leather jerkins, shirt-sleeves in some cases, and hatless in others. No different to the normal scene at Elsham, as far as I could see. Was it simply because I did not appear to be walking to any purpose?

(Perhaps I should have followed the old dictum "...if you are not actually working then carry with you a piece of paper which will make it look as if you have a purpose. And if someone should stop you and question your mission, you just say you are on your way to the toilet!")

As it happened, I was not obliged to make the responsive choice because two of the Sergeants from the Lanc. – the wireless operator and the mid-upper gunner – strolled up at that point.

"What's going on?" the latter asked.

The Downham Market Flight Sergeant continued to glare at me. He seemed almost demonic. "Not that it's any of your business," he said, "but I'm drawing the attention of this so-called airman to his scruffy appearance. He is a disgrace. And I'm having him!"

One of the sergeants took my arm and pulled me away. "Go and get aboard the Lanc." he told me.

"Stand still," roared the Flight Sergeant, now apoplectic. "I haven't finished with you."

"Oh yes you have, mate," said the Wireless Op. "He's one of ours and if he needs disciplining, *we'll* do it."

"Don't call me 'mate'," snorted the very irate NCO. "I shall see this is reported to your Station Commanding Officer. I want that airman's name." He, like a football referee, had taken a note-book from his top pocket. But I was obeying *my* Sergeant's instructions and was walking away.

The Disciplinary Flight Sergeant was now uncertain about his next move, having discovered that I belonged elsewhere and not to Downham; and also he was dealing with two air-crews' NCOs. *"I want his name!"* he demanded.

"We don't know his name," the Sergeants told him, which was true, they didn't. Then they turned on their heels and left the "Chiefy" standing there.

When the two Sergeants caught up with me, I said, "Thank you for that."

"That's OK," smiled the Wireless Op. "You disgraceful airman."

"Yes," said the Mid Upper, "And get your bloody hair cut!"

It was then that I realised the somewhat dishevelled appearance of my two companions. They looked worse than I did!

Some twenty minutes later we took off from Downham Market and flew back to Elsham. I don't know to this day if the Flight Sergeant ever did send a report of the incident, but if he did it must have got buried somewhere for I never heard another word about it. My fervent hope was, though, that I would not follow Don Boast and be posted to Downham Market!

~ ~ ~

The essence of the bonding link between the air-crews and those who served them on the ground is well illustrated in one incident recorded in Molly Burkett's *Once Upon a Wartime III*.

The distinguished Squadron Leader Ken Butler[5] recalling in Molly Burkett's book, his arrival at Elsham and his consequent introduction to his allocated Lancaster "I" Item:

---

[5] Squadron Leader Ken Butler, who is mentioned earlier in this book, was a leading figure in the planning and implementation of *Operation Manna* – a rarely mentioned, humanitarian action by the RAF Bomber Command in World War II when as the Germans pulled out of Holland, falling back from the Allied advance, they left no food, no fuel for warmth, no medical supplies, nothing whatsoever for the Dutch people in areas of the country.

As we drew up to it, the Flight Sergeant lined the ground crew up and stood them to attention. Then he put out his hand and as you always do in that situation, I went to shake it but he put his other hand over mine, looked up into my face and said, 'She's a good bus, sir. If you look after her she will always look after you and bring you home safely.'

Respect for the Squadron Leader certainly. But also strongly implicit in that gesture by the "Chiefy" was that feeling of pride, so often unspoken among the ground crews.

"She's a good bus, sir." Yes, and we have made it so, me and my lads. That is what he was saying.

You who fly and we who tend to your aircraft – we are in the same team.

DISCIPLINE

Military organisations are not democratic institutions, nor are they debating societies. By their very nature, they proceed on the basis of orders and instant obedience. That is the 'nature of the beast' and it all functions on the basis of authority invested in the echelons of rank.

There are, however, variations on the theme in cases where situations and circumstances demand a modified approach; and I have already outlined, in Chapter 5, the manner in which RAF Bomber Command, perforce of its operational nature, developed its own, possibly unique, and diverse patterns of discipline, viz...

(i) Discipline of air-crews on operations by mutual understanding of role expectation; and authority of command invested in the pilot, the "Skipper", even if he were of lower rank than other members of the crew.

(ii) 'Spit and polish-type bull', inappropriate in the case of air-crews and generally resented by them.

(iii) The exacting responsibility of the aircraft-servicing ground crews, conceived by them to be *their* disciplinary priority. And 'bull' seen as an irritating intrusion and of minor importance.

Herewith, then, a sample of anecdotes that give further emphasis to the ethos of 'law and order' at Elsham Wolds.

~ ~ ~

The first story relates to the sartorial expectations of both the ground crews and the hierarchy of command, which situation I referred to in earlier chapters and to which I gave some focus in the incident at Downham Market related at the beginning of this chapter.

Ground crews dressed appropriately for the weather and for working situations; and if the apparel had individual diversity – and, in some cases, appeared to be a trifle 'scruffy' – that seemed not to cause any undue concern to the 'management'. There was, in fact, that mutuality of interest and of priory between upper and lower ranks, which was to *"keep 'em flying"*.

Anyway, let me hand over to my good friend and ex-comrade at Elsham, Bas Lowe, to tell the story of something that occurred on the station after I had moved on.

The general public conception of the 1939-45 wartime airman was one of Brylcreemed hair, immaculate blue uniform, shining buttons and equally shining footwear. That was because RAF personnel did present themselves in that smart fashion outside the camp; and, indeed, it was most unlikely that an airman, or airwoman, would have been allowed to go amongst the public in anything less than an immaculate appearance.

However, if the airman was one of those who not only stayed on the ground but also spent his working life on a typical heavy-bomber station on the eastern side of England, he would be clambering in and out, and all over those bombers as a mechanic servicing the various pieces of equipment that made up the aircraft – engines, electrics, wireless, radar, instruments, airframe, armour etc.

Out on the Flights, it was permissible for the mechanics to dress according to the season. In the heat of summer they might wear just underpants under their overalls, whilst in the bitter cold of winter various extra clothing would be allowed, such as woolly hats, scarves, pullovers, gloves (or mittens) and leather jerkins (sleeveless jackets), the latter over their overalls and together with wellies with the tops turned down and inside were worn thick sea-boot stockings. The enemy was that freezing-cold north-east wind that came straight from Siberia.

Except for the overalls – and even that was overlooked on occasion – this garb was accepted around the camp, even in the Naafi and the cookhouse.

146

The exceptions were the CO's parade, held monthly, church parades and other special occasions. Forage-caps, though, were expected to be worn at all times around the camp. (This because airman and NCOs were not permitted to salute officers when hatless.) Most improper! (Such a complexity of rules and regulations you see! Author)

As might be expected, there were some officers and NCOs who severely frowned on this cavalier attitude of airmen but they were, reluctantly, forced to acknowledge that the airmen who were mechanics were doing a job of work similar to a mechanic in civilian life, but often under much more difficult and unpleasant circumstances.

One such NCO, a Disciplinary Flight Sergeant (he didn't come from Downham Market, did he, Bas? Author) decided that this cavalier attitude to dress must be curbed and chose a Pay Parade as being the most opportune time to bring his authority to bear on the maximum number of airmen in the minimum amount of time. Not for him the 'odd bod' to be put on a charge for being improperly dressed. This must be in the grand manner.

To fully appreciate the circumstances of their situation it must be explained that a Pay Parade for ground staff airmen was held immediately after breakfast and not in the relative comfort of a heated building such as the Accounts Department or camp gymnasium, but just inside the open doors of a hangar where two folding tables were set up together with their accompanying folding chairs. At the table would sit the Paying Officer with his entourage of Pay Accounts NCOs. The first NCO would call out the last three digits of an airman's service number and his surname. Each airman lined up on parade, would, when his name and number was called, wait for another NCO, skilled in the art of figures, to read out the amount to be paid, and then step forward to pick up his 'wages', after, that is, a third NCO had counted the money out from the piles of notes on the table for the Paying Officer to push forward.

The airmen would then gratefully salute and move smartly away and check to make sure that the Accounts NCO's sums agreed with his own estimates and that no mistakes had been made (Deductions were made from the fortnightly pay for various misdemeanours such as arriving late back at camp from leave, [or from other forms of 'release' from duty]; the loss of personal equipment, and other 'minor' offences.)

After receiving his pay, the airman would report to whatever was his appropriate Section and, in the case of an aircraft-servicing ground crew "erk", he would very soon be 'on his bike' and on his way out to the Flights where the bombers awaited his particular attention.

In other words, the day's work, on the day of Pay Parade, whether it be out on the Flights, in the hangars, in the armoury, wherever, began after the receipt of one's 'wages'.

On the particular morning when the Discip. Flight Sergeant made the momentous decision to impose his authority on the matter of dress, the weather was cold and wet and, more importantly for the aspect of the day's work ahead on the Flights, "ops" had been on the previous night. And, as usual, on the morning after "ops", there would be 'bags of work' to be done out there; and, as usual, the various mechanics were attired in their customary winter working garb.

On this day, however, the jubilant Discip. "Chiefy" standing by the hangar doors stopped the "erks" on their way to Pay Parade and ordered them to go back to their billets to get dressed properly for a parade. No "buts" or "whys" were accepted. It was a case of "go back to the billets and change or go on a charge". So, consequently, time passed and out on the Flights the various "Chiefies" were looking at their watches and wondering what the hell was happening. Then the lads began to arrive – and having, remember, been obliged to change dress twice – naturally, explained their tardiness. Well, this to the Flight "Chiefies" was like a 'red rag to a bull'. No SHQ Flight Sergeant was going to push around their Squadron blokes!

(SHQ and Squadrons were not always in the same Air Force.) "I'll soon sort 'im out," and straight on the phone to the Squadron Engineering Officer to tell him what had happened. He, the SEO, immediately phoned the Adjutant.

No one knew what conversations passed at top levels but at the next Pay Parade, a Sergeant was detailed to carry out the duty. And incidentally, this duty was rather like the policeman who stands outside No. 10 Downing Street. He is there 'just in case'.

One wonders what it was like in the Sergeants' Mess that night. Was Bomber Harris ever told about the affair?

You can imagine a "Daily Express" headline: "SHINY BOOTS BEFORE BOMBS".

After the incident, the Discip. Flight Sergeant was much less conspicuous and was obliged to confine most of his function to the kind of parades where 'proper dress' was required.

~   ~   ~

Officers on RAF bomber stations during the war who were in positions of command were required to make judgments on matters of discipline somewhat akin to those of Solomon.

Where should protocol always prevail? In which circumstances should the rules be insisted on and in which could they be bent? When should there be strict scrutiny and when could blind eyes be turned?

The whole thing was complicated and complex in a situation where (a) the bombers must be maintained as airworthy and at readiness and (b) the morale of air-crews must be sustained and their sometimes wild behaviour accommodated.

Sometimes it was only a fine line between offences regarded as serious and those less so, whilst some were more obvious then others. Some 'crimes' could be absorbed within the culture of a particular station, others were beyond local custom and practice.

Given the wild shenanigans of off-duty air-crews, both on and off the station – and in which it was not entirely unknown for quite senior officers to be involved – one can understand the dilemma that faced COs and Adjutants, especially since they understood only too well the need of the flyers to let off steam; and they, too, would have, at some time, participated in such 'parties' themselves. And because the ground crews had their own kind of pressures, they too could act in a wayward manner, on occasions when let off the leash. So fine judgements needed to be made in their case also, when they came up on a resultant 'fizzer' (charge).

There are three books with which I am acquainted, each of them recounting stories of behavioural abrogations at Elsham Wolds and of the official lines taken as a result of them. From the three books, Sid Finn's history of 103 Squadron, *Black Swan,* and Don Charlwood's *Journeys Into Night* and *No Moon Tonight,* are the following examples of the kind of thing I mean.

How could a CO deal with a situation whereby a bunch of his air-crew went out on the town and, in order to dispense with distinctions of rank, all turned their uniforms inside out?

Or, on another occasion related to Sid Finn by ex-gunner Sergeant Alex Gamble, when another crowd of flyers (or possibly the same bunch?) mounted a parade in the town of Brigg and performed rifle drill with brooms acquired from God knows where and marched up and down the street. When the local constabulary arrived on the scene, the airmen 'arrested' them, took them to the police station and locked them up! After which the cell key was lost! And to further complicate the issue for the CO, the order to 'arrest' the policemen was given by a Wing Commander who was in the thick of all that roistering!

In the event, it was the Adjutant who was called upon the next day to deal with the miscreants and they were 'severely reprimanded' and advised that in future they should spread such exuberant activities much further afield. (But, quite possibly, there might well not have been a future for some of those flyers.)

~ ~ ~

One has to feel for Adjutants. They were the 'see to it' officers, delegated by COs to deal with a great deal of routine administration but also with disciplinary matters, especially with minor misdemeanours – and, far too frequently on a bomber station, being required to write those so difficult letters of condolence to next-of-kin when a member of air-crew was lost on operations. Adjutants were, in many ways, unsung heroes who smoothed the many tangled paths of life, and death, in the hectic world of the war-time bomber base.

Most offences for which one could find oneself 'on a fizzer' were minor and routine, such as those I have mentioned previously – arriving late back on camp; loss of some item of personal issue; insubordination and the like. But those charges relating to dereliction of duty or negligence (such as the charge on which I found myself) were regarded much more seriously and punished more severely if a guilty verdict was given.

The usual punishments for routine offences were the docking of a certain amount of pay, or 'jankers', which consisted of reporting to the guardroom three times a day in best blue and sometimes in full pack, plus being put on some menial task, such as peeling spuds, washing up dishes and baking tins, etc., or cleaning up around the camp. The duration of this punishment was seven to fourteen days, depending on the seriousness of the offence. But, again, the operational priorities of the squadron had to be considered and mechanics were wanted in the hangars and out on the Flights and not 'potato bashing' or 'bloody road-sweeping'.

~ ~ ~

The case of the missing geese, which is also featured in Sid Finn's *Black Swan* demonstrates at once both the audacity and the stupidity of some characters in HM Services.

Christmas was approaching and the CO had acquired a brace of geese which were kept, for security reasons, in the back of the guardroom, a place inhabited by the 'snoops' (Service Police) and therefore of maximum security, one would assume. But on Christmas Eve an airman was stopped at the main gate by the 'snoops' and hidden about his person was found one of the two fat geese.

Therefore the CO still enjoyed his Christmas feast whereas the airman in question did not go on Yuletide leave but spent the time instead on 'jankers' after some fast-track punishment. Given that the owner of the birds was the CO – although the thief was possibly not aware of this – the sentence was relatively light, the CO undoubtedly invoking the spirit of Christmas; even so, I would hazard a guess that at some stations (e.g. Calshot) the culprit might well have been 'shot at dawn!'

And here is another pressing thought on the above incident. Could the goose thief have been George Turner? NO WAY! For a start, if GT were going to perform such a felony, both birds would have gone! And they would never have been found on his person! George would have been somewhat contemptuous of such incompetence. In any case, he would have been much more discerning about the identity of the owner of the property.

~ ~ ~

There was pilfering and then there was real thieving, and the latter was never countenanced either by the hierarchy or by the rank and file. There were four airmen involved in the following caper, two sergeants and two aircraftsmen. The two NCOs had stolen rations from their mess and sold them to civilians. The two aircraftsmen had rifled clothes in the camp gym cloakroom and then attempted to sell their loot – cigarette lighters and crested combs – to the "erks" in the billets, in all probability, therefore, endeavouring to sell, in some cases, such items back to their owners! Such stupidity is incomprehensible. Deciding whether it was day-time or night would have caused such blokes extreme cerebral agony!

It is amazing, too, that pain of another kind was not inflicted upon them, when I think of some of the lads at Elsham. (The likes of the "Wee Jock", "Paddy" and Maxie, for instance). Anyway, the four were detected, charged and found guilty, and on a wet and windy

Elsham day the whole Squadron was assembled on the parade ground to witness the removal of stripes and insignia from the uniforms of the four disgraced airmen and they were discharged from the Royal Air Force. A week later the four came up before the 'beak' in Brigg and received prison sentences. There would have been little sympathy for the four among the lads. There was no love for 'Robbin bastards' of that particular ilk.

~ ~ ~

Yes, there were lines drawn between acceptable (almost expected) misbehaviour and the unacceptable kind.

When I was doing my Instrument Training Course at Melksham I was one of a small group of our Intake who lived in London or reasonably near to it, who occasionally 'escaped' from camp and stole a few weekend hours at home. It wasn't as if we were abrogating our duties, for the weekends were, usually, free. Even so, we were officially AWOL and we took a chance on spot checks and roll calls. Indeed, the whole thing was very chancy, a minefield of possible disasters.

There was the leaving of camp, the unpredictability of hitch-hiking (and the risk of thumbing the wrong kind of vehicle), crossing London in the Blitz (there were some 'dodgy' moments in that respect!), avoiding the Military Police on the Underground, negotiating the platform strewn with Londoners sheltering from the bombing – and, eventually, usually very late on the Saturday night or off the early-morning milk train, reaching home. And then leaving home on the Sunday afternoon to get back to Melksham by whatever means by 23.59 hours on that night.

Was it worth it just for a few hours at home and hearth? We certainly thought so; and there was a taste of risk and adventure about it. Had we been caught, we would, most certainly, have been put on a serious charge. But yet, should not the 'brass' have had a sneaking regard for our nerve, audacity and initiative? After all, had we become prisoners of war we would have been selected for the escape committee straight away! Oh, no, of course we would not – only officers were expected to show initiative and escape, and not the 'other ranks'.

So, yes, we broke the rules. But no one suffered as a result of it. No crime in my book, anyway.

~ ~ ~

I am not sure if the following anecdote is RAF apocryphal or not, but knowing RAF Bomber Command as I did, I can well believe it.

Some of the lads went into a town near their base, visited a few hostelries, consumed a pint or two and then found themselves involved in a bit of an altercation with another group of servicemen of some kind. The Military Police intervened and hauled the lads off to the MPs' HQ.

In due course, the "fighting erks" came up in front of their CO, who had already heard about the fracas. He gave the lads a severe talking to and seven days' 'jankers' each, not so much because they had been fighting but *because his information was that they had lost*!

15. WAR GAMES

In 1943, with the Germans now up to their necks in Russian snow and mud, and with the main might of their war machine engaged in that savage campaign, it was most unlikely that the Wermacht was about to invade Britain, let alone attack Elsham Wolds airfield. The decision makers of the RAF, it would appear, were unconvinced of such an improbability; or, were persuaded that military exercises were good for our souls, for, every so often, we were called upon to play terrestrial war games.

There were two versions, the first of which involved various elements of the ground staff in sorts of 'commando courses'. And the second was 'defence of the airfield' exercises, which, when possible, included members of the aircrews who were not on "ops". (Possibly in their case the idea was to keep them busy and out of mischief!)

Funny old things, explosives…

The news of these exercises was never greeted with wild enthusiasm and we shared some trepidation when we were informed that the organiser in charge of those military gymnastics was to be an ex-Black Watch Sergeant by the name of Thompson. He had been, we learnt, wounded in action at some point in the war and was now seconded to the RAF as a Flight Sergeant responsible for combat-training. Well, everyone said he was ex-Black Watch, and the first time I saw him, I was more than ready to believe it. How did he get wounded I wondered? He looked to me as if he could function as a human obstacle against Tiger tanks!

Anyway, the scheme got under way and we found ourselves running, shooting, bayoneting, climbing ropes up the north face of the Eiger (quarry), swinging on other ropes across water, and crawling under barbed-wire while Thompson's minions fired shots to encourage us to keep our heads – and bums – down. We had lectures on weapons and stripped and reassembled Bren guns, (one actually, I think it was shared!)

154

During the process of it, all we discovered our various levels of fitness, which, for those of us in reasonably good nick, was not too burdensome; exhausting for others.

I feel sure, though, that "Jock" Thompson was not very impressed with our general military air – or lack of it – but give him his due, he did try. By God, did poor "Jock" try, but I think his pride had been somewhat dented by having to leave his elite regiment. And I know he looked askance at the relative familiarity between ranks in the RAF on that bomber station. To him it was alien and incomprehensible and, given his background, his attitude was absolutely understandable.

One incident I do recall in particular about that brief association with 'soldiering'. The 'lesson of the day' was HAND GRENADES and the instructor was one of Flight Sergeant Thompson's Sergeants. (I cannot, now, recall his name, although I most certainly should, given the circumstances of the incident.)

We were being instructed, up on the edge of a quarry, on *"pulling the pin, counting and throwing"*, and, also, firing those black 'pineapples' from the barrel of a Lee-Enfield rifle. But that was not all. Having accomplished the first part, not without a hint of nervousness, we were then introduced to *priming* the grenades, before hurling them at the unseen enemy in the valley below.

"You have to be very careful," said the Sergeant, "not to overheat the primer with your fingers as you insert it into position. Got it?"

Oh yes, we got it. Apart from Dentist Parade, I think that was the first time I had ever seen "erks" jostling to be last in a queue!

Many of us viewed this exercise with some distrust, even though we were in almost daily contact with those 4,000-pound bombs. But, there is something very personal about the menace of a hand grenade!

We were moving inexorably towards the sand-bagged pit when an airman with banana-sized fingers, sweating profusely on a cold day (sweaty... hot fingers...) managed somehow to lay in the fuse, and close up the grenade. He then pulled out the pin threw back his arm – and dropped the bloody thing!

Some of us collided as we dived for cover. After a moment or two there was a distinct thump of an explosion. Cautiously we raised our heads. The Sergeant stood in splendid isolation. *"Right lads,"* he said, *"who's next?"*

He had simply picked up the grenade and thrown it away. And as we sheepishly gathered around him, he said, *"Now you see what I mean about treating these things with great care. Funny old things is explosives!"*

There were no recriminations against the lad who had dropped the grenade. It was as if it were an everyday occurrence in the Sergeant's life – and perhaps to some extent it was – hence his extraordinary aplomb. Perhaps, too, it had happened to him often enough for him not even to comment on it, for "Jock" Thompson never mentioned it. I guess the Sergeant had put up with enough comparisons with the Scottish army as it was, and was not prepared to give "Jock" further cause for derision. The truth is, though, that 'banana fingers' had not, in fact, succeeded in drawing the pin when he dropped it. But we didn't know that at the time. The Sergeant had been making a point. Good bloke that Sergeant.

War Games II

I have often wondered, over the years, what would have happened if Britain had been invaded in the early part of the Second World War. If any of the exercises I experienced are any guide as to the possible outcome, one can only conclude that the enemy would have made considerable advances. On the other hand, you can never tell with the Brits. Like explosives, the *"Brits is funny old things!"* Different when it's for real.

We had a big 'defence of the airfield' exercise at Elsham one day in the winter of 1943, and we prepared to defend 'our patch' to the death... or something. The Army was to be given some practice at attacking an airfield and although we had always assumed it was the RAF Regiment's job to defend it, it seems they needed our help. The fact that that was probably galling to them, made us really 'chuffed' for there was no love lost between 'them' and 'us'!

Frank Wain, George Turner and I were allocated a strong-point defence position in a ditch on the outer environs of the airfield and facing across an open landscape. If the 'enemy' came we would see them miles off! We were to man a Bren gun, (the Bren gun?) which would either be in position or we would receive it after our arrival. What if the Army attacked before we got it? That was against the rules! Right!

It was a raw, cold day as we set off in the half-lit early morning and snow and ice-covered puddles lay white upon the frozen ground. On the way to our 'strong point' I tripped in a rabbit hole and twisted my ankle. That slowed us down a bit but we did eventually find the ditch and our 'marker' post. The Bren was not there.

"We'll be able to see 'em coming..." observed Frank, scanning the terrain.

"And nothin' to shoot 'em with!" complained George, smoking his umpteenth cigarette that morning.

"We'll go, 'bang, bang' you're dead'," I suggested.

We had frozen in the ditch for about an hour, slapping our arms and stamping our feet – one foot in my case, the other ankle swollen and painful – when two officers wearing armbands appeared from nowhere. (Just as well they weren't the 'enemy' because we hadn't heard them approach!)

"Where is your Bren, airmen?" one asked, thinking perhaps that the 'enemy' had taken it.

"Never seen it, sir," said George – and never one to miss an opportunity – "Is there any point in us staying here without it?"

"Yes airman, there is," one of the officers told him. "Stay at your post. We will make enquiries and see that the gun gets to you." And with that they departed.

Another hour. Hour and a half. No Bren. No enemy. Icicles had by then replaced flesh and bone and my ankle was killing me. I wanted the Army to come and capture me and rush me off to the warmth of a hospital. No one could have accused us of disloyalty.

We stood our ground, frozen to it, and although the ditch continued to be bereft of a Bren Gun, it was filling up with fag ends! A weak apologetic sun had appeared ineffectively in the sky when we agreed that no 'enemy' was coming our way, and that in any case, one of us was 'wounded' and needed attention. We made our way slowly, excruciatingly slowly, back to the drome and on arrival found it occupied by numerous heavily armed 'brown jobs' sitting and sprawling at ease all over the place. How did they get in? We had never seen a sign of them!

No one seemed to be able to agree as to the outcome of the exercise. The Army apparently claimed to have taken the airfield, whilst the RAF Regiment insisted that Elsham Wolds was *"safe in their hands!"*

It was the 'other lot' (that's us) who had let in the troops. Members of the air-crew – it appears – who had been on "ops" the previous night and had been disturbed from their well earned slumbers, had shown their irritation by firing flares into the sky; and thus confusing everyone because is wasn't in the script! We sat chatting with some soldiers in comradely fashion, passing round the fags, when an RAF Sergeant came up and said, half jokingly (I think), *"You should not fraternise with the 'enemy'."*

"Just respectin' the Geneva Convention," said George. The soldiers enjoyed that.

My swollen ankle gave me a few days 'excused duties', which I considered just reward for stoicism in the face of the ditch, if not the enemy. The big question was, what happened to the Bren Gun? Where did it go? Was it stolen? Maybe the Lincolnshire Poacher had grabbed it with an eye to a rapid increase in productivity after the war. Mind you, if he hadn't been with us that morning, it is quite possible that the other poacher, George Turner, may have had designs on the weapon. You never could tell with him!

May life have been kind to you George old friend. You were quite a character.

~ ~ ~

I love the story of one particular occasion when the air-crews were ordered to participate in one of these 'defence of the aerodrome' exercises – a story recounted by Austen Magor, who was at that time Squadron Navigation Officer, and recorded in *Black Swan"*. The following is my summary of that anecdote's preamble.

The air-crew were acting as the enemy – in their usual collective role in these capers – and, in practice, were to be transported to various places outside the camp and airfield, and be armed with wooden rifles and to have allotted to them the task of 'taking the Elsham Wolds RAF station', which was defended by the ground crews. (This story relates to a period later in the year of 1943, when I had left. I wonder, therefore, if (a) the RAF Regiment contingent were no longer there, as they are not mentioned, and (b) the Army was deployed as the 'attack force' only that once, in early 1943, in the episode related by me previously?)

Anyway, it appears that the air-crew 'invaders' were never successful in their 'assaults' on the perimeters of the airfield, mainly because there was no cover in those wide open spaces. (So, one has to ask, how did these 'squaddies' get into the camp in such large numbers on the day of my experience of the exercise? And Frank, George and I never even saw a sign of them until we 'returned to base' only to find them all there! But we'll let that pass – an appropriate comment!) But then came the day when the air-crews applied a bit of lateral thinking.

Here, then, is how Austen Magor completes the story...

I was in charge of a group of twelve men dumped six miles from the airfield at Brocklesby Station. The only instruction I had was to get my men as near as possible to the airfield without being observed. Much to the surprise of waiting train passengers, I commandeered the station waiting-room to discuss tactics. The following plan was worked out.

We would catch a train to Barnetby, which was only a mile or so from the airfield (perimeter), and then find some means of getting into the airfield through the main gate. We only had ten minutes for the next steam train. A quiet word with the guard and we all piled into the guard's van. Arriving at Barnetby, we all managed to get into the station waiting-room unobserved.

Luck was on our side. An aircrew bus had just arrived in the station yard to pick up a bunch of new airmen being posted into the Squadron. I had had several dates and many dances with the pretty WAAF driver, so it did not take long to persuade her to transport our party to the airfield, especially as the train she was meeting was not due for another fifteen minutes.

We boarded the bus and set out for the airfield. At the main gate, the guard, believing we were new aircrew, waved us through without challenge. Once inside I instructed the driver to take us to the Defence Headquarters where, to the astonishment of the Army Officer-in-charge, we took the six occupants 'prisoner' and claimed victory. Needless to say I enjoyed drinking the Army officer's beer that evening.

So, there you are. Is it not surprising what can be done with a little initiative, which often, as in this case, makes its own elements of luck!

I would, though, still like to know what had happened to those RAF Regiment boys, who never tired of telling us "erks" how bloody good they were at defending airfields!

16. THE SOCIAL WHIRL

We dined out quite a lot. Well 'in' actually, since our habitual eating house was the camp NAAFI! Egon Ronay might not have been impressed but they did a most acceptable sausage and chips in there – and sometimes a morale boosting fish and chips (and why not, since we were so close to Grimsby?) at a price (one and sixpence, i.e. about .08p) realistically related to an RAF ranker's unprincely income. And the beer wasn't too bad either, even though some of the more discerning airmen among us did describe it in somewhat ribald terms; something to do with gnats as I recall!

Above all, though, the NAAFI was a good bolthole in which to relax. It was warm and pleasant to just sit around a table with your "oppos", talking, having a laugh or playing cards. Pontoon and Brag were the favoured games and, as gambling in the NAAFI was *verboten*, we usually played for matchsticks each of which represented a halfpenny to be 'cashed in' later!

The ladies who served in the NAAFI were, generally, amicable, enjoyed repartee with the clientele and somehow provided a tenuous reminder of home.

Ron Grantham did, in fact, get on so well with one of the NAAFI girls, Doreen, that he married her. So I guess the grub and the ale could not have been that bad! Mind you, after they married, Doreen was posted to another station, as it was policy not to have husbands and wives on the same base.

~ ~ ~

The gym was the venue for all kinds of 'troop entertainment' and the impression I gained during my time at Elsham was that it was used more often for film shows, occasional live entertainment and dances than it was for P.E. – or P.T. (Physical Training as it was then called.) I doubt if many P.T.Is. (Physical Training Instructors) were kept consistently busy in RAF Elsham Wolds gym.

Audience participation was very much in vogue both at the film and the 'live' shows. Officer characters in films were often greeted with obligatory boos; and false heroics – especially in American films – received dutiful whistled derision, whilst love scenes were

160

urged to be more specific. And if the projector broke down, a not uncommon event, the lads would whistle, stamp their feet and sing *"Why are we waiting..?"* It was all very enjoyable in a chaotic kind of way. But it is ironic really when I reflect on all that, because in the cinema ever since then I am very annoyed if conversations among the audience disrupts concentration and the film!

Service audiences during the war were harsh critics but warm and generous towards entertainers who satisfied their tastes which ranged from bawdy comedians to pianists with a classical repertoire. One did, though, have to feel sorry for performers who did not meet with the approval of such fickle customers.

Another form of interruption during a show would result from messages on the Tannoy requesting both air-crew members and ground crew individuals to report to some place or other. Or, on some occasions, for the audience to be noisily swelled during a performance, by both air and ground crews coming in as a result of a sudden scrubbing of "ops".

Dances were held in the gym from time-to-time but some of us "erks" were more inclined to get out of camp and seek civilian-run 'hops' in local towns or villages. It was more of an 'escape' in such places and the local 'civvy gals' more plentiful, more 'available' (for the "likes of us") and they wore dresses! Well, "Bud" Senior was very convincing on that subject!

~ ~ ~

There were various places in the area to visit, the two biggest being the steel town of Scunthorpe to the west and the fishing port of Grimsby to the east. And then there was the smaller town of Barton-on-Humber to the north which was much visited by servicemen of various kinds. And, during my time at Elsham, Barton was placed out of bounds, partly because of the frequency of altercations between rival groups of service personnel; and/or – so it was rumoured – as the consequence of an outbreak of cases of venereal disease. I never discovered whether or not that rumour was true but Barton-on-Humber did most certainly take on the semblance of a 'frontier town'; and it could be a bit wild there on occasions.

In Brigg and Barnetby there were servicemen's canteens, and pubs were plentiful. But certain hostelries became more patronised than others, a preference determined by the degree of welcome accorded to HM Forces – and to the RAF in particular – since the Junior Service was so well-represented in the area.

Pubs were popular for having the right 'atmosphere' and where a lusty singsong could be enjoyed by airmen and locals alike. A train, 'the Barnetby Flyer' ran between Barnetby and Scunthorpe and was particularly well used by air-crews, many of whom were on their way to their favoured pub, "The Oswald". Many a night of carousing was held in "The Oswald".

Anther much-visited inn was "The White Horse" in Brigg and in the same town was "The Angel" and, also, the aptly-named, "The Dying Gladiator", renamed by the air-crew patrons, 'The Dying Navigator'.

However, my "oppos" and I discovered a hostelry called "The Fox", situated in the little village of Ulceby and that became our preferred 'watering hole'. We had some great singsongs in "The Fox" and, with local customers joining in, the songs were really belted out. Tonsils well lubricated we went through a wide repertoire of musical scores: *"It's a long way to Tipperary"* and *"Keep the Home Fires Burning"* from the First World War; *"Old Man River"* and *"Swanee"*. We travelled in song to the four corners of Britain and Ireland. *"Bonnie Banks of Loch Lomond"*, *"I belong to Glasgow"* (the "Wee Jock's" favourite 'hymn'), *"Mountains of Mourne"*, *"Danny Boy"* and *"I'll take you home again Kathleen"* (not a dry eye in the house – alcoholic tears!), *"Saucepan Bach"*, *"Cwm Rhondda"* and Cockney favourites, *"The Old Bull and Bush"*, *"My Old Man"* and *"Any Old Iron"*. We sang the 'pop' songs of the day; *"Blue Birds Over the White Cliffs of Dover"*, *"We'll Meet Again"*, *"Don't Get Around Much Any More"*, *"I'll be seeing you"*, and others. And of course, the war-time tunes popular with the Services and civilians alike: *"Roll out the barrel"*, *"Quartermaster's Stores*, *"Hang out the washing on the Siegfried Line"*.

We also did solos and my speciality was a rendering of the Ink Spots' *"Whispering Grass"* a choice of song not unrelated to the fact that it was one of the few songs of which I could remember all the words! The singing in "The Fox" must have been heard all over north Lincolnshire except, perhaps, in Grimsby and Hull where other, air-raid, noises prevailed.

At Ulceby we also discovered – or, in the case of some of us, rediscovered – the 'village hop' which was a great success there. By 9 o'clock packed to the doors. Little room to demonstrate dancing skills but consequently you were enjoyably pressed up close to your partner. Whatever the tempo, most of the dances became slow fox-trots! Chalk dust rose in a white haze from the floorboards on which it had been sprinkled to facilitate smoother movement. The three-piece (or was it a four-piece?) band – piano, drums, accordion and sax I think it was – could never do justice to the tunes associated with Glenn Miller, Harry James, the Dorseys, Artie Shaw and the like, but could not be faulted for their timing; absolutely impeccable. Pity about the lack of space!

But, you see, that was the charm of it all. Delightfully amateurish and no pretence to be otherwise. The 'village hop' was epitomised there in Ulceby, Lincolnshire – raffle tickets, a long queue for the toilet and all!

As far as I know there was never any 'bother' there. And the locals who ran the dances were lovely folk. So too, were the girls – full of fun and great company. It was so good for a brief while to get away from the grim realities of war, just a short cycle ride down the road.

In *The Lincolnshire Poacher* (the prototype magazine article that was the forerunner of this book) I did pay a long-delayed tribute to the good folk of Ulceby and wrote a retrospective 'thank you' to them for their warm hospitality but I must reiterate that acknowledgment now in this, the 'proper' book. It is their due.

~ ~ ~

We cycled everywhere, distance no object and that, together with the pedalling we did out on the airfield, kept us very fit. And it was just as well that the bikes were durable 'no-nonsense steeds' because one way and another they were ill as well as well- used! Those bikes had another splendid function also; they could be leaned on when one had imbibed a pint too many in a pub. They were, too, seemingly possessed of homing instincts (or radar) since they somehow always got us back to base!

It is quite extraordinary really that when I drove up to Elsham to attend my first RAF Reunion weekend, I experienced a strong feeling of disorientation and could not find my bearings. Yet, up there in 1943, with no signposts and in the blackout, neither I nor any of my "oppos" were ever unable to find our way around.

~ ~ ~

Twice only did I go off camp with George Turner as a twosome. The first of these occasions I have described in the chapter dedicated to the WAAFs in which GT 'dropped me right in it' with the formidable 'Bertha'.

On the second of these 'hazardous missions' we ended up sleeping in a cell in the police station in Brigg! My memories of that whole night are very blurred but I recall: (a) a desperate search for a lost haversack which GT had 'borrowed' and which contained something he was loath for anyone else to find. (b) A bit of a skirmish with some soldiers and then trying to cadge a night's 'kip' in their camp because we had missed all possible transport back to our place. And (c) trying to sleep on the floor of the guardroom of the Army camp but then turfed out by a very irate Sergeant Major. And then, subsequently, seeking accommodation in the Brigg 'nick'!

It has always been a relief to me that GT did not accompany me overseas. I just know we would have entered the Casbahs at either Algiers or Tunis and would never have been seen again! Mind you, there were some other 'crazy bastards' among our Squadron's personnel 'over there', but that is another story.

~ ~ ~

Grimsby. There I bought my first ever record of Glenn Miller – *"Moonlight Serenade"*, *"Chattanooga Choo Choo"*, *"I know why"*, and *"Little brown jug"*. All of those great tunes. That '78' is still around among my possessions somewhere. Wonderful, wonderful music.

Grimsby – a town in which I was 'inconvenienced'! I had somehow become separated from the other lads and, in the blackout, desperate for a pee, I stumbled across a public toilet. I knew I had made a mistake, directly I got in there – even in the blue-lamp dimness. There were cubicles but no upright porcelain! I thought – well I'm in here and there's no one about and I am desperate – so I entered a cubicle. Just then, I heard two girls coming chattily into the building and I froze, holding everything; There was a scream. "Look! There's a man in there. I can see his feet!" shouted one of the young ladies. Then two screams and the girls ran out. I quickly followed but when I reached the pavement, they had gone from sight. Breathing a sigh of relief, I started to move away when, round the corner, came the two girls, this time with a rather more mature lady in tow. There are times when you can think on your feet and this was one of them.

"A sailor has just come out of there!" I told the irate trio. Well, I was not about to incriminate the RAFF!

"Dirty peeping Tom!" said the older lady.

"Jack," I corrected her facetiously.

"Tom, Jack or Harry," shouted the woman, "You're all the bloody same!" With that she dived into the toilet building to check it out. I bade the two girls "goodnight" turned around and walked straight into a lamppost which gave me a black eye! I've never been to Grimsby since and, on that night, I thought it well named!

NOTES

(i) It was in "The Fox" at Ulceby that my farewell party was held when I was posted overseas. It was quite a night and a memorable one – or not, as the case may be. But, in any case, I will impart what I do remember of that 'assembly' at Ulceby circa July of 1943 in the next and final chapters.

(ii) In the course of this chapter I feel that I might be giving two erroneous impressions both of which need to be corrected.

The first is that life up there in north Lincolnshire in '43 was one big round of pleasure. Well, yes, we were young and lusty and ready to grasp whatever life had to offer. And we did, whenever possible, enjoy ourselves. But it was not constant enjoyment and it was a matter of grabbing a bit of fun and games in the interludes between the demands and the responsibilities that were placed upon us. On average we probably managed one night off camp a week. And in terms of leave and 48-hour passes, I estimate that in total – in the seven months I spent at Elsham – I had, excluding my embarkation leave, about twenty days furlough, only ten of which were at home. (Mind you, that seems excessive compared to the nearly three years abroad when I did not get home at all!)

The second correction concerns myself in the matter of alcohol consumption. I was never a great consumer of booze mainly because drink always tended to render me either silly or sophorific (or both) and it rarely took much more than a couple of pints to establish the beginnings of tipsiness, inhibitions swept aside, introversion replaced by uncharacteristic extroversion. (Singing solo in public for example!)

Which was the real me? Alcohol induced schizophrenic? I can only hope that I was never objectionable when 'into my cup'. And I know I was not, thankfully, aggressive or pugnacious; not, for example, like the "Wee Jock" and others like him I have had the misfortune to encounter from time-to-time.

17. A Tale of Three Cities

Frank Wain took me to his home in Sheffield when we once managed to get a 48-hour pass together. Frank's wife Joan, a lovely lady, made me very welcome in true Yorkshire fashion and it was a most appreciated break. The highlight of the weekend was the visit to Brammal Lane to see United and Wednesday in a war-time Sheffield local derby. It was Joan who was the keenest to go! A rabid football fan, unusual among women in those days.

A couple of tram journeys took us to the ground and we then found ourselves packed into a massive, heaving crowd high up on the terraces. We stood in a sea of cloth caps and neckerchiefs, worn like uniforms by the tough steel workers of the City of Sheffield. It was also my first introduction to the sight and sound of men urinating where they stood at the back of a football ground. And I remember becoming increasingly concerned about the bladder control of those fans standing immediately behind me!

The match had been on just a few minutes when I heard a male voice say, "Hey-up. There's a lass theer," (Frank's wife the solitary, single representative of the female gender, as far as I could see, in the whole crowd!)

"Bloody wimmin at football matches," came the rejoinder from his mate. "Shouldn't bloody be 'ere!" Male chauvinism very much alive and well in South Yorkshire.

Joan didn't seem to mind. She just laughed and continued to cheer the players on. Frank told me she just loved the game and had seen and heard all this ribaldry and anti-women stuff before. "How about the peeing?" I asked. "Doesn't seem to bother her," said Frank.

We all three were bursting 'to go' by the time the game was over. (I think the result was a predictable local derby draw) and sought public toilets before catching the tram for the journey home.

There were obviously some blokes up on those terraces who simply refused to suffer such discomforts! Whenever bladders come up in conversation, as they do when one gets older, I tend to think of Sheffield. So I do when either United or Wednesday appear on television; and it's nice to know that there is a toilet just down the hall!

~ ~ ~

Another 48-hour pass, this time to Birmingham.

In theory I was to spend the whole of it with my auntie, uncle and cousin at Streetly on the edges of the city, but that is not quite how it worked out. The journey proved to be eventful and during the course of it I added another new experience on that other journey called "life's highway".

I managed to get away from camp on the Friday afternoon and decided to hitch-hike to Birmingham, not for a moment anticipating any difficulty in that regard. It turned out, however, to be the most negative hitch-hiking experience for me in the whole of my Service life.

I walked miles and got nothing and, in fact, for incredulously long periods of time, I saw nothing on the roads. Eventually, an open-backed builder's truck stopped but, as there were three men in the cab, I was obliged to climb up on to the back where I sat among cement bags, sand and bricks. By the time the truck dropped me off I was frozen stiff and covered in a great variety of dust. I was, I gathered, somewhere between Bawtry and Rotherham. There was another long and lonely walk before an Army 13-cwt picked me up and eventually delivered me to Chesterfield.

It was now about 8 o'clock at night (or 20.00 hours if you so prefer!) and Chesterfield, like the roads of Lincolnshire and Yorkshire, had been that afternoon, was bereft of all signs of life. I began to feel that everyone had given up on the war and left Britain! I tramped around in the blackout gloom, my footsteps resounding in the eerie silence and, at last, discovered the railway station. No more hitch-hiking. Get on a train! Birmingham was still a long way off.

I found a waiting-room in which there was no fire and a blue-painted bulb gave light for six inches around its contours. There was a time-table on the wall but the matches I struck to illuminate it kept blowing out in the strong draught that blew down the platform. Apart from getting to Birmingham there was another problem...

I had told my aunt and uncle that I would be at Birmingham, New Street Station, in the early evening so that Uncle Reg could pick me up there in his car. (He was the only member of our entire family who had a car, although even that was not his own. It was a company car belonging to Lucas's one of Birmingham's biggest manufacturers, very involved in war work and Reg was one of their official drivers). By now it was around 9pm. I found a 'phone box and luckily had some small change. Just one little snag. I didn't know the number! Directory Inquiries said it wasn't listed so it must have been ex-directory because I knew they were on the 'phone – another singular possession in the family.

In the midst of all this an ageing porter appeared from nowhere like a scene from *"The Ghost Train"*. Not everyone had left Britain then! From him I learned the disastrous news that I wouldn't now get a train in the *direction* of Birmingham until the early hours of the morning! Visions of a fuming uncle filled my mind. He was a kindly man but always on a short fuse of patience. Had he checked the train arrival times? And if so from where, for he was not aware that I was hitch-hiking.

My theory had been that my 'lifts' would get me to Birmingham; that it would be easy enough to reach New Street Station in the evening and that I would find my uncle at the entrance. Oh the naievety of youth! But there is more...

How long had Uncle Reg waited? Was he still there? Had he made more than one journey between Streetly and New Street Station? Then came the brainwave. I couldn't 'phone Reg, but I *could* ring New Street Station and ask the London and Midland Railway to make an announcement – in case Reg was still there.

I got the New Street station number from the porter, put some more coins in the box and eventually got through. The response to my request was classic. The drawing in of breath and slow exhalation. "Oh no," said a Brummy voice. "We can't geeve personal messages loik!"

I explained, further, the situation and inserted my last coins. Another Brummy voice was on the line – higher authority no doubt.

"This will start something will this if we do what you are askin'. We'll be passin' on bloody personal messages all day an' night. Loik a bloody Forces Network on the bloody woirless!"

I then said something unbelievably stupid. "Come on," I pleaded. "Just this once. Nobody will know!" Well I was desperate!

Before I could pursue the matter further, the pips went and I rapidly shouted the essence of my message. "Mr Taylor, LAC Mawdsley, arriving New Street between 8 and 9 tomorrow morning!"

There was nothing more to be done. I was tired, grubby, hungry, thirsty and suffering from the three 'fs' which all ex-Service readers will instantly recognise. The porter had disappeared, so I returned to the cold waiting-room curled up on a bench with my haversack for a pillow and was dozing off when a voice said, "Hello airman!"

Later in my life that intonation of voice would have been recognised. I was then, however, not so informed and worldly-wise. I looked up and saw a tall civilian, smartly dressed and who immediately put me in mind of the actor George Sanders. He sat down on the bench, and chatted away in a most friendly manner and was most solicitous about my plight. When he discovered that I came from Witham in Essex he told me had relatives there. And they, as it turned out, were the sisters who owned the corner shop at the end of our road.

"George Sanders" clapped his hands with glee. To find an unexpected connection with home on a deserted railway station in Derbyshire, lifted my morale no end as well. When I told "George" that my train was not due until 6 o'clock the next morning he raised his hands in horror. (I was getting a lot of signals but I wasn't decoding them correctly!)

"Oh dear boy," he said, "You mustn't spend the night on this cold station. Come home with me. You can have a bite to eat and a drink and get a few hours comfortable sleep."

Oh sweet innocence...

I was profuse in my appreciation and we conversed easily as we walked to his house – a very respectable looking semi-detached about a mile from the station. Inside the house there was a fire burning in the grate and it was all very cosy and homely. I had, by then, even stopped worrying about Uncle Reg!

"George" called up the stairs. "Mother, mother, it's only me. We have the Air Force here tonight."

That ought to have pushed a note of caution through the letter box of my mind. But as I say, I was still very wet behind the ears (in spite of everything Danny the torpedoed American sailor in Greenock had told me).

My host gave me some bread and cheese and a mug of cocoa. "I'm afraid we only have two bedrooms," he told me. "So I hope you won't mind sharing my bed just for a few hours."

No warning light! No alarm bells!

I said that I could just curl up in a chair but he wouldn't hear of it. (Of course he wouldn't would he!) And he insisted kindly and firmly. "You lads don't often have the comforts of home," he said. "Sleep in a nice soft bed whenever you can old chap."

I was tired.

"George" was already in bed when I emerged from the bathroom.

"Call out goodnight to mother," he said and I duly obliged, but there was no reply. No sound of any kind from the next bedroom. (I

169

might well have been worried if, at that time, I had seen the film *"Psycho"*!)

I put out the bedside light, got down to my RAF issue underwear and slid gingerly into bed. Gingerly, I say, because although I was unsuspecting there was something instinctively inhibiting about sharing a bed with another male, albeit one old enough to be my father.

"I've put the alarm on for 5 o'clock," said "George", "so you'll be OK."

My alarm should have been ringing loudly but it wasn't and I quickly dropped off to sleep.

I must now be delicate, and I must refrain from detail, disappointing as that might be for *some* readers. What followed is, and probably was then, something of a blur. Whatever was happening brought me out of the haze of sleep and had me leaping out of bed, falling over a bedside chair in the process.

"George" was pleading for me to come back to bed. Not for a gold watch as big as a frying pan would I have returned to that bed! I had another fall, going down the stairs whilst trying to get my trousers on at the same time.

"George" was still pleading with me to return to bed.

I finished dressing in a state of confusion not sure whether to hit him, or to do and say nothing.

Still no sound from mother's room!

My host, this stranger in the night, now in a dressing-gown, insisted on making a cup of tea and switched to mundane conversation as if nothing had happened. Well, nothing had happened, really, but it was a close run thing.

I drank the tea and then quit the house, striding purposefully back to the discomfort but relative sanctuary of the rail station. On the way I passed a policeman. "Everything alright, airman?" he asked.

"Fine," I told him. "On my way to the station."

Arriving at the terminus I returned to the bench in the waiting-room, lit a cigarette and wondered if this 48-hour pass was really worth having.

About a half hour later, "George" appeared again and this time I was belligerent. He thrust a packet of cigarettes into my hand and apologised profusely. "I was terribly mistaken," he said. "I just thought you were willing."

God, I thought, I'll have to do something about that! Surely I don't look willing!

"George" left after a few minutes and eventually I boarded a wheezing train on my delayed way to Birmingham.

Uncle Reg had twice come from Streetly to New Street and luckily, on the second visit, he had waited around and had heard the message which the staff had, after all, made over the Tannoy system. He was waiting for me when I arrived on the Saturday morning. He was not a happy man and I was lectured about 'responsible behaviour' and 'petrol rationing' all the way to Streetly. Anyway, the rest of the weekend was pleasant enough and when Uncle Reg returned me to New Street on the Sunday evening, he gave me a half crown and suggested that next time I visit them I come by train.

"Yes, I will," I said, but not via Chesterfield!" I did not explain to him the reason for that remark.

When I got back to Elsham and related my experience to the lads it was greeted with predictable hilarity. For a while I was hailed as the 'Chesterfield Spire' but that soon wore off.

Today, I like to think that I am more knowledgeable, more understanding and tolerant. The story of Quentin Crisp, *The Naked Civil Servant*, touched me immensely and crystallised some of the confusion in my mind. Yet, I cannot be sure that if something like the Chesterfield incident happened again now, I would know quite how to handle it.

There seems to me to be no certainties in life, no absolute truths. All there are, are complexities which we do what we can to unravel. I can look back now and realise that "George Sanders", who had so scared and confused me at that time, was undoubtedly a very lonely and sad man.

So there we have a couple of 'spin offs' from the main account of my time at Elsham. And, after all, we do have to remember that it was during our lives in the Services, during the war, that most of us were growing up, and there were many lessons to be learned.

Now, however, back to Elsham and the concluding chapter.

171

18. Farewell to Elsham

When the Second World War began my dad, a wounded veteran of the 1914-18 conflagration, said to me, "Don't ever volunteer for anything." So I promptly volunteered to join the RAF, an act not of teenage defiance (the generation gap was not so pronounced in those days nor had it become obligatory) but taken rather because "adventure called".

Once in the 'RAFF' I continued to ignore paternal advice and volunteered twice, for air-crew, but was turned down; offered my name to go on a list of airmen in Coastal Command to form a unit in Archangel (Russia) to help establish a flying boat base there to assist in the protection of the Arctic convoys (a totally inexplicable piece of volunteering on my part given my aversion to the cold!) which thankfully never came to anything, at least as far as I was concerned; and then, later, I did ask the RAF to consider me for service overseas. And I must add that I never told my dad a word about all of that crazy volunteering.

Anyway, someone in the Air Ministry must have decided to take a chance on me for service in foreign parts for in June 1943, the notice of my overseas' posting arrived at Elsham. It came quite out of the blue really because I had more or less forgotten that I had volunteered.

The notification produced in me a conflict of emotions. A certain sadness and regret that I would be leaving Elsham; a pang of sorrow in the knowledge of what could be a long and distant separation from family and girlfriend and a pulse of excitement and anticipation at the prospect of "seeing something of the world" (I had, at that time, never been abroad, as was the case with the vast majority of the plebian population in the 1940s).

Where would I be going? Africa? The Middle-East, the Far East – exotic images! Surely not a delayed posting to Archangel! I had long since become disenchanted with that kind of destination.

The lads, of course, all had their predictions, some quite bizarre such as California to help train US "instrument bashers"; some gruesome and sadistic like on an airstrip behind Japanese lines in Burma. "Bud" Senior suggested a sort of lottery draw, the winner to

172

be the bloke whose prediction was geographically nearest to where I eventually ended up. I never did hear if the draw took place and if so, who won!

I was given a variety of 'jabs' by the M.O. and as he applied the needles, "Doc" Henderson, God bless his memory... wished me well and advised me not to drink too much of the 'local brew'.

Then came fourteen days embarkation leave and, as I have written earlier, the parting at the end of it from my parents and from my girlfriend, Ethel, was somewhat painful. And, as it turned out, our separation was one of nearly three year's duration; but how could I in all honesty complain about that! I had volunteered for this, hadn't I?

At the end of the fourteen days, I returned to Elsham where I resumed normal duties whilst all the paper work – clearance documents, travel warrants etc etc – were processed. And during that week, I carried out several D.Is. including my very last one on "D" Donald Duck. Two Lancs failed to return from "ops" in that week.

On the Wednesday, 7th July, we – as many "instrument bashers" as were 'available' and "Jock" and "Tiny" from "D's" crew – rode out on our bikes like a group of cowboys to "The Fox" at Ulceby for my farewell 'binge'. It was quite a night.

The ale flowed copiously and the singing was even louder than usual. Some of the locals on discovering the reason for the celebration, bought pints for me that began to line up on the table; but I know I failed to reach the end of that row of pint mugs!

The cycle ride back to camp was, apparently, quite hilarious. I say apparently because I recall little about it. According to what I was told the next day I had ridden my bike at great speed down an incline and straight into a closed farm gate and I had sailed over the gate landing on the grass on the other side, where I lay singing, *"He flies through the air with the greatest of ease, that daring young man on the flying trapeze..."*

"Pop" Tyler told me all this – and other things besides about that farewell party – the next morning. He shook his head as if in remonstration but there was a wide grin on his face. I spent most of that day nursing a slow-to-heal sore head, going around to say goodbye to many of the people I had got to know at Elsham, as well as collecting all the documents I would require and handing in certain items of gear, tools etc.

I left the bike until last, so that I could ride around the drome for the very last time, including a nostalgic ride from the Section out to

'A' Flight on that familiar route I had taken for the last six months or so.

With great good fortune, as I was chatting with various ground crew lads at "D's" Dispersal, her air-crew arrived, going on a cross-country or a 'circuits and bumps', or something, so I was able to shake hands and exchange mutual wishes of good luck with them.

They all thanked me, too, which was nice. "Jock" grasped my hand and told me that he reckoned the cycle ride back from Ulceby the previous night was more hazardous than an "op" over Berlin! He was, of course, joking – *wasn't* he?

I wanted on that day to lock up in my memory as much as I could of the sights, sounds and ambiences of that place that was to mean so much to me in retrospection in later years. I left Elsham Wolds on the 10th July to go to the embarkation 'clearing house' at West Kirby near Liverpool, on overseas draft number 7817.

Dougie "Pop" Tyler shook my hand and said, "Goodbye son, and good luck. We will miss you here."

"I will miss you too Dougie," I told him and meant it very much indeed. I was never to see that wise man again.

Frank Wain caught up with me at the camp gate as I was about to grab a lift on a truck down to Barnetby rail station. As we grasped hands he said, "Let us know what it's like over there. If it's OK, we might all volunteer to come over to join you!"

"Right," I replied as I climbed aboard the truck. "And if it's no bloody good I'll ask if I can come back here!"

"Take care old lad," said Frank.

"Look after "D" Duck," I called as the truck pulled out of the gates.

Frank and I did correspond for a while after I arrived in North Africa but for all the reasons these things happened during the war, we just, sadly, lost touch. And in spite of efforts to locate him in recent years, I have been unsuccessful. But the memory of a fine man and one of the best "oppos" I ever had the privilege to know in the RAF, sits most pleasurably in my mind. Just as Elsham does.

In a letter to Ethel at that time I wrote...

It's funny how you can get to be sentimental about a place like Elsham Wolds. Yesterday morning on the C.O.'s parade I looked around, seeing all the faces I knew, the familiar buildings and, in the distance, the Lancs at their dispersals, and I felt a lump in my throat when the band struck up and we all marched off.

I am not a lover of service life, nor of military trappings but here at Elsham on 103 Squadron, I have experienced a sense of purpose, of which I felt a part, and friendships with some great 'oppos' whom I will never forget.

Don Charlwood in Journeys Into Night put it this way:

When I was drawn back to Elsham in 1957 it was deserted and empty and overwhelmingly lonely.

It was a blessing over twenty years on when the Elsham Wolds' Association was formed.

Although our surroundings were much altered from the place we had once known, there could be no denying our deep attachment to the Elsham earth for it was the last place walked upon by many a comrade from many a country all bound by the RAF."

In one sense, the 103 Squadron motto, *Nole me tangere* was totally inappropriate because those of us who served with the Squadron at Elsham were touched lastingly by being a part of it. And being a part of whatever it was, made it *what* it was.

~ ~ ~

Just in passing...

Whilst stationed in Scotland and at a factory in Luton, I had been stricken from time-to-time with severe stomach pains and had been treated for colic, gastritis and God know what else, but the pains kept returning.

In the seven months I was at Elsham, in spite of receiving unwelcome floods of beer and such potentially harmful victuals as fried sausage and chips, my stomach accepted it all with benign cooperation.

Once overseas, however, the pains struck again eventually laying me low when combined with a severe attack of yellow jaundice. Obviously my innards had been just biding their time, laying in wait, ready to restart the rebellion. But, doing nothing at Elsham!

You see... there was something special about that place!

~ ~ ~

On the night after I left Elsham the Squadron took part in an operation over Cologne. All aircraft returned safely, but many more were to be lost in the next two years.

19. REFLECTIONS

Looking back through the pages of this book I realise the emphasis I have placed on the 'good guys' among my compatriots at Elsham which, of course, begs the question, "Where were all the 'bad guys'? Were there no objectionable characters in the midst?"

Oh, yes, there were; just as there are in all communities although sometimes it is a matter, simply, of chemistry, of individual likes and dislikes. But, yes, I can recall, rank-conscious officers; overbearing NCOs, and some snide, nasty, 'mouthy' and sneaky airmen with whom one came into contact from time-to-time. But it is my preference to push such characters into the far recesses of my mind and to "accentuate the positive".

Selective memory? Well, if you like; but you see, the "positive" dominated at Elsham.

~ ~ ~

Possibly it had something to do with the influence of some of the people I encountered at Elsham, but it was there that I began to widen my horizons of curiosity – about literature, music, social and political issues; about life I guess. And, perhaps, one does see life in a wider perspective when death is so constantly in attendance and mortality so frequently nudged into one's consciousness.

It was not that any of us brooded on death or declined into dark depression. In fact, as I have shown in the pages of this book, the death of others in the kind of situations I have been describing, induces a great lust for life and a desire to grasp all that it has to offer.

In my own case I began to crave for knowledge, realising with sudden acute awareness that there were huge gaps, chasms in my fields of education. I became an insatiable reader, and listened, an imbibing process which was to continue in the years I spent overseas, but it began at Elsham – where else!

~ ~ ~

When the bombers took off to go on their hazardous missions I often stood and watched with two emotions vying for priority in my mind. One, a strange kind of guilt that I was not going with them wondering if I had accepted, too readily, those two rejections of my application for air-crew on the grounds of colour blindness. Should I not have tried harder and pressed each of the M.O.'s. in question to have turned their blind eyes? I don't know, neither then nor now.

But then, pushing against that contemplative reverie was, perhaps, the more practical (sensible?) thought, "Rather them than me!" Most of us ground crew lads used to say that as we attended the high drama of 'take-off' on operation nights. We said it but how many of the others, like me, felt that we ought to be going over there with the flyers?

I have often wondered, also, how I would have coped with all that strain, stress and the demands had I become an air-crew member. I will never know the answer to that. I certainly like to think that I would have tried not to let anyone, or myself, down. But in a situation of that fearsome nature, one could only discover if one had the requisite qualities by actually taking part.

One thing is for sure, there would have been some incredible role models to attempt to emulate.

~ ~ ~

In a football match one often sees a situation whereby one of the teams are apparently fated to lose because they hit their opponent's crossbar and goal-post uprights several times, miss a penalty and have a key player carried off injured. And the other team grow in confidence sharing a collective belief that the game is there for the taking. But it doesn't always work out that way for life is more perverse than that; much less predictable, much less certain.

Similarly then, although in a very different and much more serious context (and in spite of Bill Shankley's famous dictum that football is much more important a matter than life and death!) is the matter of air-crew survival. Optimistic predictions for the future survival of a flyer based on earlier miraculous escapes or serious injuries, or on the number of operations completed, could never be made. It was a fact of life (and death) which has often occupied my retrospective thoughts.

Here are two examples...

Although we did not, as far as I remember, actually meet at Elsham, Frank Sharples and I must have been in close proximity at various times out on 'A' Flight. Frank, the chirpy lad from Lancashire whom I mentioned earlier in this book, and is now a fellow member of RAF Elsham Wolds Association, related the following story to me:

Frank was the mid-upper gunner on "B" Bertie and at the conclusion of their "ops" 'stint' at Elsham, the crew were posted to a Conversion Unit at Lindholme, Faldenworth and Sandtoft, separated after flying together as a good team. But now going to less hazardous duties.

However, Flight Sergeant Austin, the rear-gunner who was a South African, opted to stay with 103 Squadron and joined the new crew of "B" Bertie. On the night of 22nd/23rd August 1943, "B" Bertie was shot down by a night fighter whilst on a raid over Leverku.

It was that Russian roulette business again, with one bullet only in the chamber of the revolver. The hammer can click on empty chambers many times but push your luck too far and ... .!

I have often contemplated on the perversity of it all.

Similarly in *Journeys Into Night* Don Charlwood relates another example of the sad capriciousness of fate; and it was something the ground crews were only too well aware of and caused many a head to be shaken in dismay.

In the course of a raid on Esburg, "B" Beer (strangely enough, the other "B" on 'A' Flight) was hit by shrapnel and the wireless operator Sgt Burchell was hit in the face near the base of his throat, in the chest and on the back of his hand. His arm, also, was badly injured and the muscles were protruding in various places. Several times on the return journey Sgt Burchell, in spite of his wounds, crawled around the aircraft and over the main spar attempting to repair his damaged radio. The Lanc. got back home and Sgt Burchell went into hospital.

But yet, even after all that, he wanted to get back on "ops" (They only did it because they had to... Oh yes, says who?) However, by the time he was fit enough to do so, he was too late to rejoin the crew of "B" Beer and was posted to 460 Squadron at Binbrook, to join a fellow Aussie crew. (In fact two of the crew on "B" Beer were also Aussies – "Skipper" Sgt Geoff Madden, and the navigator, Don Charlwood.

Sgt Max Burchell was later killed when on "ops" over Hamburg.

One could so readily surmise that a flyer who could survive such horrific injuries must bear a charmed life. Well, once again, we can see that "it ain't necessarily so..." not by a long chalk.

How could one ever forget that one was there to serve such men as those and to feel a long-lasting pride in having done so.

~ ~ ~

I can hope that none who read this book will be disappointed that the narrative is not studded with descriptions of gore; with details of the mayhem of war. I have not felt the need to pander to voyeurism or to titillation. There are ample numbers of such records – some essential in the text, other simply gratuitous.

Aeroplane crashes, especially those which involved fire, are not pretty. Nor are dead, dying and injured air-crew members taken from stricken aircraft. Ground crews, especially those whose 'hands on' duties placed them at the horrendous front of such 'work', would never forget it; but are loathe to talk about it. Only if you saw it, or something like it – or even worse – would you understand that kind of reticence.

My experience is that those survivors of war who saw or experienced the worst scenarios of conflict are the least inclined to convey those horrors to others. They might talk about what they were 'in'; where they went; sights (some) seen; comradeship; fun and 'laughter'; the jobs they had to do. And civilians, also, if they had grim experiences in the Blitz, in most cases have to be coerced to retell their stories.

In this book I have given due attention to stress, fear, bravery, dedication, responsibility, grit and comradeship. The gory details I leave to others.

I want to conclude the chapters of *An Erk's Eye View* with a note of honesty.

In the process of writing the book I have outlined some of the reasons why, after so very many years, I came to 'put this thing together'. To recount an experience; as a tribute to lost and still living comrades; as a salute to bravery and to skill etc etc. But there was something else in there too, and it is that those years of war – in spite of their horrors, stresses, discomforts, restrictions, episodes of boredom and separation from home and hearth – contained a certain edge, excitement if you like, that few of us would ever experience again in peace time.

I am, as I have said, no war-lover nor a militarist; but I have often wondered – had the war not occurred as and when it did, would such an 'adventure', such travels into places (then untouched by tourism) and such a honing of the sense – all of that – ever have become a part of my life on which to look back and shake my head in both wonder and disbelief.

RAF Elsham Wolds was a major part of that experience to be followed by service in 'foreign parts'. And that story may also, one day, be told.

Postscript

It was never my intention that *An Erk's Eye View* should contain pretentious "messages", either overt or covert. I have, I hope, made it abundantly clear in the book that it does not set out to glorify war, especially one of such a scale of savagery as the conflict of 1939 to 1945 was. And I did not feel it necessary to preach an anti-war theme since, apart from the psychopaths and the otherwise disturbed, most people are surely "against" war, aren't they?

My book is the story of an experience, no more, no less; an assembly of remembered impressions and events which occurred in one corner of a vast stage on which was enacted the most gigantic war in the history of mankind.

The addition of this postscript was a decision made only after long deliberation and a deal of heart searching. But in the end the need to "exorcise some ghosts that have haunted the corridors of my mind" proved to be too strong, too compelling, to resist.

There are things I feel the need to get off my chest, or, more appositely, off the end of my pen.

PART I – THE OMISSION

It was, I think, the distinguished American broadcaster and writer, Ed Murrow, who said of Sir Winston Churchill that he had *"mobilised the English language and sent it into war".*

It was a wonderfully succinct tribute to the many inspiring speeches delivered by the war-time PM. And among those memorable orations was the famous salute to "the few" who fought and won the Battle of Britain. Never, in fact, had so much been owed to so few; and in gratitude and recognition of that effort and victory a Battle of Britain medal was awarded to the young men who flew the Spitfires and Hurricanes against the Luftwaffe armada.

No one has any quarrel with the award of that medal – but now let us consider another, less-known, less-often quoted piece of Churchillian valedictory oratory, in this case uttered at the end of the Second World War. It was a tribute to RAF Bomber Command via its Supreme Commander, Air Chief Marshal Sir Arthur Harris:

"All your operations were planned with great care and skill. They were executed in the face of desperate opposition and appalling hazards. They made a decisive contribution to Germany's final defeat. The conduct of those operations demonstrated the fiery gallant spirit which animated your air-crews and the high sense of duty of all ranks under your command.

I believe that the massive achievements of Bomber Command will long be remembered as an example of duty nobly done."

A fine tribute indeed to the personnel of RAF Bomber Command. But it then immediately poses a question. Why in view of such an accolade as that, was a campaign medal, in its own right, never awarded, at least to the air-crews of Bomber Command?

There were, after all, a whole range of campaign medals: Burma Star, Africa Star, Italy Star, Atlantic Star, Normandy Star etc. etc.; and, of course, the Battle of Britain medal.

So if the efforts of RAF Bomber Command did have such a vital role in the defeat of Nazi Germany, why was that achievement – especially in view of the horrendous casualty rate that was incurred – such a vital contribution, not recognised in a tangible form of decoration? Remembering, also, that Bomber Command was the only arm of Britain's Forces that took the war to the enemy in his territory, from 1940 until June 1944.

It is not that the veterans of Bomber Command are "glory seekers" or "gong hunters". Those that I know are too self-effacing and modest for that. Nor do I have any personal axe to grind. What it is, is a question of recognition of the terrible demands that were made upon those air-crews; of the guts it took to make those extremely hazardous *"journeys into night"*. A fitting tribute, also, to the 55,000 comrades who *"did not return"*.

Something very significant in relation to this matter emerged from the publication in a truly remarkable book, published in 1990 by Production Consultants plc. It was entitled *The Few* and within its pages twenty-five ex-pilots who flew and fought the Battle of Britain tell their individual stories of their experiences in that *"finest hour"*. But here is the interesting aspect of the book which connects so forcibly with the contents of this postscript. Each and everyone of those ex-fighter pilots made an earnest appeal to the publishers to produce a companion volume, an anthology of the reminiscences of ex-air-crew members of Bomber Command. The collective opinion of the authors of *The Few* was that:

> *"For sheer determination, courage and dreadful conditions of cold, fatigue and constant mortal danger, nothing could surpass the example of their brothers in arms in Bomber Command."*

That is one hell of a tribute from those Battle of Britain pilots. And they, too, must find it perplexing that a Bomber Command medal was never authorised.

(In response to the appeal of the twenty-five ex-fighter pilots, Production Consultants did publish the companion volume and it was, most appropriately, entitled, *The Many*.)

Who was it who made the decision not to award the Bomber Command medal? And at what level? It is inconceivable that somewhere along the line the same people in high authority who decided to launch the strategic bombing campaign; who organised it, resourced it, and ordered its execution and escalation should then, it would seem, back away from rewarding those whom Churchill so warmly praised, with a symbolic decoration of gratitude.

Perhaps, also, Stalin should have given a Russian "gong" to the air-crews of Bomber Command, for it was Bomber Command, together with the USAAF, that kept up the assault against the Third Reich until the logistics were in place to launch the Second Front for which the Soviet leader had been clamouring since the German invasion in 1941. The same bomber forces which had diverted German men and guns from the Russian front and hampered supply lines.

Quite apart from the strategic bombing campaign role of Bomber Command in World War II, it also attacked shipping, harbours and speciality targets. And, carried out the highly dangerous business of laying mines.

Nor should it be forgotten that Bomber Command even played a significant part in the Battle of Britain for, together with units of the Fleet Air Arm, it attacked the German invasion barges assembled at the Channel ports and suffered heavy losses.

The only conclusion that one can come to about the omission of a Bomber Command medal is that the sustained bombing of Germany, and then the bombing of Dresden, in the end, proved to be too controversial.

Well, whether or not that incident (the raid on Dresden) was unjustified or not; or whether the strategy itself was militarily inappropriate, or morally wrong, is open to debate – and has been ever since the end of the war – that should not, in my opinion, have detracted from the courage and durability of the men who flew those gut-wrenching missions and who believed they were putting their lives on the line in order to destroy one of the most evil regimes ever to foul the earth.

It is, it seems to me, as if the absence of the Bomber Command medal somehow passes the buck of recrimination to them – the RAF air-crews. It is something of a sorry story and it leaves a somewhat bitter taste in the mouths of many of those who flew the bombers – and of those who gave their unstinting support and conscientious service on the ground.

Some people will, I know, say, *"...all that happened a long time ago, so why not just forget it?"* That, I suggest, is an easy cop out. An injustice that is not redressed is not diminished by time.

PART II – THE CONTROVERSY

First we were heroes and then some people branded us as 'war criminals'.

Those words epitomise the bitter reaction of the men who flew with RAF Bomber Command in World War II to the opprobrium heaped upon them by a diverse assortment of critics since the end of the war. Words, too, that could be carved onto the gravestones of the thousands of those airmen who made the supreme sacrifice.

What, then, is this controversy all about? Of what offence do the veterans of RAF Bomber Command stand accused?

Towards the end of the war, in February 1945, there was something of an outcry over the RAF raid on the city of Dresden in east Germany. It was a city full of refugees, fleeing before the advancing Russians. To this day, no one is sure who ordered the raid to take place but it was not Air Chief Marshal Sir Arthur Harris, for he was, in fact, opposed to it.

But then, at various times since the war, the whole strategic bombing campaign – and by implication the RAF and the USAAF, although much more the former than the latter for some reason – has come under critical attack. And the main thrust of the attack has been on moral grounds because of the consequent civilian casualties.

The condemnation has emerged from various quarters – writers, academics (including revisionist historians) pacifists, representatives of both extreme wings of the political spectrum and from certain sections of the media. All, of course, are entitled to their opinions for, after all, freedom of expression was one of the fundamental principles for which the Second World War was fought. And there would have been precious little of it had the Nazis prevailed: a thought, perhaps, worth keeping in mind.

It will, naturally, given the content of my book, and my expressions of admiration for my erstwhile comrades in RAF Bomber Command, that I feel the need to throw my hat into the ring and to stand up in defence of those men and women with whom I served. However, I do recognise this issue as a moral and ethical area for debate; but then, so too is the subject of war itself.

I wish that I could write what I have to say on the issue in just a few words; but there are just too many aspects, too many impinging events and developments to allow for succinct comment. So I do ask the reader to bear with me as I "make my case".

Where to start? It is advisable and necessary I think to begin at the personal level and to reiterate some of the things I have said about myself in the book. It is necessary because I do not wish to be misunderstood, or have my words misconstrued.

This book, has not been written by a war-lover nor by a jingoistic anti-German (anti-Nazi, yes, but not anti-German per se). I am, by nature, non-aggressive and far from bellicose. Since the war I have supported various peace movements and human rights organisations.

I have great admiration for those people of infinite patience and vision who strive to bring about peace in such seemingly intransigent situations as those in Northern Ireland, the Middle-East, areas of Africa, in Korea or wherever. In his later years, Sir Winston Churchill famously said that, *"Jaw, jaw, jaw was better than war, war, war"*. Absolutely right. (And, coming from him, even more compelling.)

I do not, however, believe in peace at any price; and that is where I, regretfully, must be at variance with the pacifist viewpoint.

An absence of war is not necessarily peace; ask the survivors of Nazi-occupied Europe. What I cannot comprehend is how anyone could be a pacifist in the face of something such as Hitler and the Nazis. I respect and admire the principles of passive resistance but how long would Mahatma Gandhi and his followers have lasted to make their case for Indian Independence had the occupying power been Nazi Germany?

184

After the fall of France in June 1940, there was in Britain support in some quarters for making a "deal" with Hitler. Among them were Nazi sympathisers, including some in high positions; but there were good and decent people who recoiled from the prospect of a continued war and saw a settlement with Hitler as a preferred option. Apparently there was something on offer from the Fuhrer which, put simply, was that Britain and her Empire would be left alone, whilst Hitler retained possession of the conquered nations of Europe. (There was more, including the question mark over the future of the Royal Navy, but we won't go into that.)

What I find incomprehensible about that proposal is that some folk were actually ready to accept Hitler at his word. It is inconceivable that the Nazis would have "left Britain alone". How long would it have been before, for example, Hitler would have demanded the handing over of British Jews? And the rounding up of others deemed to be sub-human in the twisted racial creed of National Socialism? Or before the Germans marched in, in the same way as they did into Vichy France? Professor Michael Burleigh, author of *The Third Reich, a New History*, has said, *"...had the Nazis won the war and conquered most of the world they would have found somewhere else to perpetrate war. They believed that peace was weakness."*

It has always seemed to me that the trust some people were prepared to place in the future intentions of Adolph Schiklegruber, was the worst case of collective naivety since the good citizens of Troy dragged that ridiculously-sized white horse into their doomed city! And, since we are to discuss morality, where would have been the morality in the abandonment of the peoples of Europe – and, later, including Russia – to the brutal suppression of Nazi occupation?

Yes, I am aware that there are those who would say that even a "peace" of that kind would have been better than the horrors of the war that ensured from the rejection of Hitler's "terms". And that fighting the war achieved nothing anyway. Well, as to the former proposition, whilst no one can deny the terrible nature of the Second World War, had it not been fought how many millions more people would have gone to their horrible deaths in the "camps" or been taken into slave labour to serve the needs of a system so depraved and evil it defies description and belief.

How could we make peace with something as manically gruesome as that? And as to the second suggestion that fighting the war achieved nothing, well, I think that is a terrible distortion. First of all it defeated Nazism. Then it established the longest period of peace among the countries of France, Germany, Belgium, Holland etc, etc (yes and Britain) in all their histories. It brought in a new concept of trade and cooperation and established in Germany, a fine democracy and an abandonment of its traditional Teutonic lust for war.

Yes, problems have arisen since the war, some but not all attributable to events in the war, such as the ambitions of the Soviet Union, the obsession of America with safeguarding the sanctity of capitalism; areas of contention in the Balkans, the Middle and the Far East. But the Cold War never actually became "hot" due in some measure to the existence of nuclear weapons yes, but also because in the end cooler heads came to the ascendancy. But, in any case, is anyone really suggesting that a world ruled by

Nazi Germany and Imperial Japan would have been a viable alternative to contesting both of those powers, whatever the post-war consequences may have been?

World domination by Fascism was the problem for our generation then, in the third and fourth decades of the 20th Century. What would happen in the world after dealing with that problem was not on our immediate agenda.

On the subject of the controversy over the bombing of Germany itself, again I set out my personal stall:

1. I have never condoned the bombing of Dresden. It was, I believe, unnecessary, strategically of no value, and was probably ordered as some kind of sop to Stalin.

2. Whilst I understand the rationale for the bombing campaign in general – which I will outline in due course, and can see, in a total war, why it had to happen – it is something that has never sat comfortably in my mind. And I have sometimes felt that it became a matter of "overkill" in its latter stages: although, again, that was undoubtedly another grim manifestation of the momentum which a total war gathers about itself.

I visited Germany not long after the war and saw for myself the terrible devastation wrought by the Allied bombing. In Cologne I saw a scene of rows and rows of skeletal buildings and mountainous piles of rubble; and I saw the battered Gothic cathedral standing against that stark backdrop like a hand raised in remonstration. It was a scene that gave me no satisfaction, no sense of triumphant joy. What I did feel was a sadness that it had had to come to this. But it was not RAF Bomber Command who was the target for the anger that accompanied my sadness. (Nothing could ever divert me from the admiration for the courage of the RAF air-crews who had this terrible job to do. For the cities of Germany were not – like Guernica, Warsaw, Rotterdam et al, undefended, as the Bomber Command casualty rate confirms; and they were fearsome battles that were fought in the skies over Germany.) It was the Nazis who brought this devastating nemesis upon the German people and as far as I am concerned the "buck stops right there" with that bunch of psychopaths who took over Germany in 1933 and embarked on the irrevocable road to disaster.

I have written above, that it saddened me that it – the ruins of Germany cities – had to come to this. What I saw in Cologne was the terrible and terrifying outcome – the chilling logical result – of total war.

I think it has to be seen this way. Three times in the course of 69 years, the Germans (Prussians in 1870) launched attacks on neighbouring countries and the third of those, in 1939, was pursued with consequent savagery beyond anything seen previously. It would seem therefore, that the Allies response was not simply to defeat Germany, but to crush her for once and for all. The RAF and USAAF became instruments in the pursuit of that policy.

Nevertheless, the terrible price paid by the aircrews cannot, and should not, be ignored. The German cities were heavily and ferociously defended and that is why, whatever people may feel the 'rights' and 'wrongs' of the policy may have been, the courage of those aircrews has to be recognised.

It is, I am given to understand the practice in French courts of justice to, first of all, before deciding guilt or innocence, ascertain exactly what occurred. It is, apparently, thus less gladiatorial than the procedures are in England. It is an approach I propose to invoke in my "defence" of the branch of the Royal Air Force in which I modestly served.

How and why did that bombing strategy formulate and then was exacted? Out of what context did the policy emerge? What were the conditions and circumstances that set it all in motion?

These are, I contend, areas of consideration seemingly ignored by the "critics".

If the bombing of Germany had been a perverse act, at variance with the general character of the war, I could not find it possible to try to explain it away or to excuse it. But it was not like that; and my bone of contention, with those who have occupied the high ground of moral judgement, is that they have selected out one aspect of a war of attrition on which to focus their attentions, disregarding every other horrendous thing that was going on. They have dipped their ladles into a cauldron of a boiling brew of cruelty and barbarism and sought to find one single ingredient.

It is as if, say, in the case of a woman on trial for stabbing her husband to death, the judge directs the jury to disregard any reference to the mental and physical brutality of the murdered man which went on and on and eventually led to the act of desperate violence.

That eminent Welsh politician, Aneurin Bevan was fond of prefixing a discussion by saying, *"You tell me your truth and I will tell you mine."* In other words, what is your perception of the matter under discussion, what is your premise for taking that viewpoint? Tell me that and I will tell you how I perceive it.

The following is my perception of how and why the bombing campaign against Germany occurred. And if other people's assessment is different to mine, then that is their prerogative.

In order to make my case I have to go over some ground of familiar history but it will be in outline only.

When Britain and France declared war on Germany on 3 September 1939, after the Nazis had invaded Poland, the US President, Franklyn D Roosevelt appealed to all combatants to refrain from bombing civilians. All, including Hitler, indicated their adherence to that restraint. The Luftwaffe, nevertheless, bombed the virtually undefended city of Warsaw. (An act which should have come as no surprise since the Condor Legion – the Luftwaffe at practice – had already bombed undefended cities in the Spanish Civil War.)

Britain, however, ever intent upon playing by the "rules" (I am not trying to portray Britain as "whiter than white". Our history is not unstained by any means, but this is the situation as it was in this particular instance), with a policy strictly adhered to, of attacking, from the air, military – and particularly naval – targets only. This approach to the war was epitomised by an exchange, which I paraphrase, in the House of Commons during the period which came to be known as the "phoney war".

Julian Amery MP asked if, as part of the policy of economic warfare against Germany, the RAF might bomb the Black Forest (I have no idea why. Author) The Air Minister, Sir Kingsley Wood was aghast, asking the Hon Member if he was aware that that (the Black

Forest) was private property? *"He will be asking us to bomb Essen next!"* (My italics. Author.)

What happened, then, to change all that and to transform Britain's attitude and response?

April 1940, the Nazis invade Denmark and Norway and, in spite of some courageous efforts by British Forces, especially by the Royal Navy, it is something of a debacle and the Nazis march in!

May 1940, the Nazis invade Luxembourg and the Low Countries, bomb Rotterdam, and then smash through into France, by-passing the "impregnable" Maginot Line. The French and the British Expeditionary Force are driven back by the awesome German war machine and refugees on the clogged roads of France are bombed and strafed by the Luftwaffe. (*Total war is giving* out its calling card.)

In the end the BEF and remnants of the French Army are, literally, driven into the sea but are rescued in their thousands by the "miracle" of Dunkirk whilst a small number of British and French troops tenaciously hold back the advancing Germans.

Now I have to ask readers who were not around at that time, to try to transport themselves in their imagination to the period between June and December 1940. To try to place themselves in the situation that Britain found herself in during that period. First, it had been a psychological blow; the people of these Isles are not used to seeing their army defeated.

Second, the mighty and efficient Germany war machine is encamped just a few miles across the English Channel, champing at the bit to launch an invasion.

Third, the Nazis now have at their disposal, numerous airfields and ports and harbours, all over Europe.

Fourth, the enemy occupies a 16,000 miles coastlines from Norway down to the French-Spanish border.

Fifth, Britain stands alone to face their awesome menace.

Sixth, no good news, either, from the Middle East or from the Mediterranean.

Seventh, the desperate Battle of Britain is fought and won, but it is a close run thing. The Luftwaffe turns its attention on bombing London and other targets.

Then, the Blitz – London, Bristol, Southampton, Plymouth, Swansea, Merseyside, Birmingham et al. The war is no longer in some foreign land. It is in your neighbourhood, down your street, in your backyard! Your world, the one in which you have grown up, explodes and burns around you. This is total war. No man, woman or child is exempt or excluded. And private property is no longer sacrosanct!

Whilst you seek shelter wherever you can find it, Hitler's wolf-pack U-boats and surface raiders operating out of newly acquired bases in South-West France and Norway, are sinking more and more tonnage of shipping on its way to Britain with life-line supplies of food, equipment, oil and raw materials.

There is rationing and acute shortages of just about everything. If you work in the factories, the docks, the offices, wherever, you work long hours and your sleep, uneasily, in a troglodyte existence, is restless and broken. You live in a blacked out world and you are virtually surrounded by the deadly Nazi enemy. The bombers keep coming and it seems that nothing can stop them and so ease the pain of it all. (I recall, when crossing London by underground when on a posting or on a pass, negotiating a way through the hundreds of Cockney families bedding down for the night on the Tube platforms and voices calling out, *"Oi, Raff, why ain't you up there shootin' them bastard Jerries dahn? When are you gonna start givin' them buggers some of wot we're gettin'?"*)

An excerpt from the splendid book, Finest Hour by Tim Clayton and Phillip Craig, and published by Hodder and Stoughton, sums up succinctly the mood of the time. "Terrified, confused, sullen and depressed, more and more people trudged out of London. Oxford took in twenty-thousand refugees bringing with them rumours that the capital was largely in ruins. But the Ministry of Information morale report brought comforting news to the government. There was anger, plenty of it – at the Germans and also at the local authorities – but there was no serious desire for peace and little bad feeling directed at the government. What most people seemed to want was revenge."

Fear apprehension, discomfort, anger and a burning desire to hit back. So, ask yourselves this question, as you visualise that desperate, fearful situation in Britain in 1940 – What do you suppose the overwhelming answer would have been had a referendum been held on the question, "Are you in favour of a bombing offensive against Germany?

And if the question had also been put, "The Nazis have sown the wind, they will now reap the whirlwind." Do you agree with that proposition? Again, what would you calculate the response would have been? It is not a question of whether or not it was "right". It is how it was. That was the reality of the time and moral niceties were not very high on most people's agendas.

Hitting back? The war-time PM, Winston Churchill, was not one to just sit and take it. This is what he told Lord Beaverbrook in July 1940, even before the blitz, or the Battle of Britain.

> *"When we look around to see how we can win this war, I see that there is only one sure path. We have no continental army which can defeat the German military power. The blockade is broken and Hitler has Asia and probably Africa to draw from. Should he be repulsed here, or not try invasion, he will recoil eastward and we have nothing to stop him. But there is one thing that will bring him back and bring him down and that is an absolutely devastating, exterminating attack by very heavy bombers from this country upon the Nazi homeland! We must be able to overwhelm them by this means, without which I do not see a way through."*

But, as it happened, an effective bombing offensive did not prove viable until February 1942 because the aircraft, navigational and the technology etc. were not adequate to carry it out. Although, even so, it was good for the morale of the British people when the Whitleys, the Hampdens and the Wellingtons flew valiantly but far too often, ineffectually to Germany.

There, then, is the first part of the context in which the bombing of Germany has to be seen. The first rationale behind it – from out of fear, anger, frustration and desperation. And then the war was to escalate, turning into a brutal, unremitting, total war of attrition. A war which seemed to take on a savage momentum all of its own, an atavistic roundabout from which no one could alight until it ground to a shuddering halt.

And the cause of that lurch into such an apocalypse? The Japanese attack on Pearl Harbour, turning the war into a global conflict, and bringing the USA with its enormous potential into the conflict. But, before that, an event which was to provide the second rationale behind the strategic bombing campaign against Germany – the Nazi invasion of Russia in June 1941.

As the Nazi war machine drove further and further into the Soviet Union, and approached Leningrad, Moscow and Stalingrad, Stalin, called on Britain to open a Second Front, to pull some of the might of the Nazi forces away from the Soviet Union.

Churchill had to tell Stalin that an invasion of Fortress Europe was not a feasible option at that time (the USA was not then in the frame) and the logistics for such a military venture were just not in place. But – that until such time as a Second Front could be opened, a massive relentless day and night bombing offensive against the industrial heartland of the Third Reich would be mounted. And that offensive was launched in February 1942 when the heavy bombers – the Stirlings, Halifaxes and Lancasters – became available to the RAF, plus improved navigational aids and other sophisticated technology. The Americans, now based in Britain, would send their Mitchells and Flying Fortresses over to Germany by day.

The German campaign in Russia was one of the greatest savagery and that, plus the equally brutal conquests of the Japanese in the Far East, established the general nature and pattern of the war, the earlier "softly, softly" approach lay abandoned and rendered futile. It is in the light of all that, that the bombing campaign over Germany must be seen.

The air attacks on German cities were not, essentially, attacks upon civilians but were aimed and intended to destroy the Nazi industrial heartland and their supply lines. But civilians, as in all wars – especially in modern conflicts – become victims. Civilians work and live in industrial areas. It is the story of total war with its chilling logic.

Civilian sailors on merchant ships are legitimate targets because the ships they sail on carry the sustenance of the enemy's war machine. Thus, also, the civilians who manufacture or transport the materials of war are legitimate targets. Otherwise remove them from the area under attack. It was on that kind of logic that the battle lines were drawn in World War II and the strategic bombing campaign became an integral part of it.

But, what was the alternative, given the circumstances and conditions I have outlined here? How else, until June 1944, could the war be taken to the Nazi enemy? Of course it was not pretty. None of it was, but it was how it was. Brutality tends to beget brutality.

There were specific targets, requiring precision bombing from very hazardous low altitudes; but it was not possible to apply such exacting requirements to the raids on concentrated industrial areas. Unrealistic to single out each individual factory or depot, whatever, especially at night. Also the bombing had to be carried out at high altitude, otherwise the losses among the air-crews would have been even more horrendous than they were.

How did those of us who served on the bomber bases feel about it all? For the most part, the service personnel below a certain high rank level are seldom privy to big plans and strategies; especially among the lower ranks who know only their corner of whatever is going on. I would say that the general situation was that we knew we were involved in a war. And in that war the enemy bombed us and we bombed them. People shooting at each other is what war is all about. The question of ethics did not really arise; and I would think that a question on the subject would have been received with great puzzlement. Some of the lads would have lost relatives and friends in the Blitz. My own girlfriend and her family had been bombed out of their dockside home. I had my own personal experiences of the Blitz in London, Southampton, Swansea and on Clydeside. They are not pleasant memories. (Those who have been so critical of the RAF, seem to overlook all that and conveniently forget to mention that thousands of civilians in Britain were killed in the Luftwaffe bombing of London, Coventry, Birmingham, etc.)

But, it was not a matter of callous indifference to the suffering of people in Germany. Many of the air-crews were acutely aware of the havoc they wrought and some have said so in the books they have written since the war. In *Journeys Into Night*, Don Charlwood refers to an entry in his diary where he expresses his repugnance at having to kill women and children. But this was the great dilemma, the paradox and dichotomy of it all. To ensure the defeat of Nazi Germany, terrible things had to be done. It was not glorious, war isn't. But it took a hell of a lot of guts and durability on the part of "ordinary" people to defeat the Nazis; and among all the emotions I carry with me relating to those times, there is a large part of me that is proud to have been a part of the struggle against Nazism.

The killing of civilians

In Germany, the war against civilians began in 1933 when gangs of brown-shirted thugs took to the streets and beat up, humiliated and smashed the properties of thousands of civilians. They were called Jews. Then the Jewish civilians together with thousands of others deemed to be the *untermenchen* by the Nazis, were pushed into the trains "going east". In the "camps" they were starved, beaten, obscenely medically operated on, shot and gassed to death.

Six million civilians of the Jewish race were mass-murdered together with countless thousands of other civilians – socialists, trade unionists, gypsies, Slavs and anti-Nazi Germans.

Thousands more civilians died in the forced labour camps and in the cellars of hundreds of Gestapo headquarters.

Can you read about the Jewish ghetto in Warsaw, or see the film, *"Schindler's List"*; or watch the BBC series on the Nazis; or take in, just for two examples, what happened at Lidice in Czechoslovakia and at Oradour-sur-Glan in France – can you contemplate all of that and much more, such as the high percentage of the 20 million Russian dead in that war who were civilians, many of them murdered by special extermination squads, and still isolate the strategic bombing campaign against Germany for exclusive moral scrutiny?

Acts of war are not to be compared with acts of genocide or cold, calculated bureaucratically organised torture and annihilation.

In recent years, whilst in hospital I met a man who had fought in the People's Army – Resistance – in Poland. When I mentioned the controversy over the bombing campaign he said:

> *"If you had seen some of the things I saw in Poland you would never have felt the need to raise the question."*

~ ~ ~

Another controversy has arisen since the war concerning the bombing offensive and it relates to questions raised about the efficacy and the effectiveness of the raids on German industry. It has been suggested by some pundits that the effects on production and the war effort of Germany were only minimal. But more recent research does not support that conclusion. Both the USA and Britain's strategic bombing surveys, though critical in some respects, showed that the effects of the bombing on industrial output was quite significant. But perhaps the most telling confirmation of that came from a prominent German source. For example, Albert Speer, Hitler's Chief of Production said:

> *"The bombing of Germany deprived the German forces of seventy-five percent of their heavy anti-tank guns because these 88mm guns had to be used as anti-aircraft guns, scattered all over Germany because we never knew when the bombers would strike next."*

And Field Marshal Milch was forced, because of the raids, to use 900,000 fit soldiers manning those guns. Also, hundreds of thousands of expert tradesmen could not be called up into the army because their skills were needed to repair bomb damage.

Further confirmation of the effectiveness of the bombing was provided by Dr Horst Boog, Chief Historian in the Military History

Office in Freiberg when he commented that, "...*the aluminium in the fuses of the flak shells would have built 40,000 additional fighter aircraft.*"

I would imagine that both on the Russian Front and with the Western Allies advancing through France the troops would have been very appreciative of all that. And more directly so in the case of the latter when the entire Germany garrison at Le Havre – 11,000 men – surrendered after a sustained air offensive. Thirty British troops only were lost.

Field Marshal Rommel expressed the view that unless the bombers could be stopped the war would be lost.

There were many instances of specific actions taken by RAF Bomber Command which helped to shorten the war and to save lives on the Allied side which would otherwise have been lost. It is inestimable, for example, how many more thousands of British lives would have been lost as a result of the V-1 and V-2 rocket attacks, had the RAF not bombed the rocket bases and the rocket laboratory at Peenemunde.

I often wonder, also, why it is that we are constantly reminded about the raid on Dresden, but rarely, if ever, see or hear any mention of *Operation Manna*. As I have said earlier, 103 Squadron, RAF, played a prominent part in that "flight of mercy" and a brief account of it is in the outline history of the Squadron at the front of the book.

It was an unenviable choice for the people of our generation to have to make. A choice between fighting a horrific war or to exist in a world dominated by Nazi Germany and Imperial Japan. Those who were not around at that time will have to make up their minds, in retrospect, about for which of the two evils they would have opted.

And, that was the choice. Let us hope and pray that future generations will never be faced with making such a terrible decision as that; and nor, then, to be compelled to fight fire with fire in order to secure a successful outcome.

In this postscript I have not sought to make a case for the bombing campaign against Germany. My purpose is rather to try to explain - as I perceive it - how and why it happened and whilst I am aware that others may well disagree, I hold the belief that the single biggest factor, the driving force behind the conflict of attrition which the Second World War became was the appalling malevolence and abominable threat posed by Nazi Germany and Imperial Japan.

Additional photographs & illustrations

This sketch of our first Nissen hut on the edges of the sugar beet field was hurriedly drawn over 60 years ago, which puts it on a par with the Dead Sea Scrolls!

Veterans salute the flypast of a Lanc at Elsham Wolds

'The Briefing' a painting signed by members of A Flight including the crew of 'D' Donald and some of the ground crew.

197

The quarry at Elsham, which features in the narrative of this book.

Author and old comrade Bas Lowe standing in front of the main hangar at Elsham Wolds in 2001. The instrument section was on the left of the huge sliding doors.

198

War Games! The redoubtable George Turner and Don Boast.

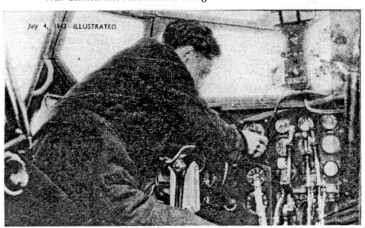

An 'instrument basher' at work on a Lancaster instrument panel.

199

Lancaster instrument panel.

Avro Lancaster displaying symbols of many operations.

Lancaster 'M' Mother coming in to land.

Inn sign of the Fox public house, scene of the author's farewell party when posted overseas in 1943.

The author reclaims his seat inside the Fox when revisiting in 1999.

The Instrument Section soccer team in 1944. Bas Lowe, Frank Wain and Ron Grantham are all in the frame.

Air and ground crews pose with a bomb.

Bas Lowe, Ron Grantham and the author
at the 1991 RAF Elsham Wolds reunion.

The former site of RAF Elsham Wolds as it is today.

Elsham Wolds Sergeants Mess 1957...

...and again in 1970.

Loading food parcels during Operation Manna.

Operation Manna Memorial.